CARRIER WARFARE in the PACIFIC

Smithsonian History of Aviation Series

Von Hardesty, Series Editor

On December 17, 1903, on a windy beach in North Carolina, aviation became a reality. The development of aviation over the course of little more than three-quarters of a century stands as an awe-inspiring accomplishment in both a civilian and a military context. The airplane has brought whole continents closer together: at the same time it has been a lethal instrument of war.

This series of books is intended to contribute to the overall understanding of the history of aviation—its science and technology as well as the social, cultural, and political environment in which it developed and matured. Some publications help fill the many gaps that still exist in the literature of flight; others add new information and interpretation to current knowledge. While the series appeals to a broad audience of general readers and specialists in the field, its hallmark is strong scholarly content.

The series is international in scope and includes works in three major categories:

SMITHSONIAN STUDIES IN AVIATION HISTORY: *works that provide new and original knowledge.*

CLASSICS OF AVIATION HISTORY: *carefully selected out-of-print works that are considered essential scholarship.*

CONTRIBUTIONS TO AVIATION HISTORY: *previously unpublished documents, reports, symposia, and other materials.*

CARRIER WARFARE
in the
PACIFIC

An Oral History Collection

EDITED BY E. T. WOOLDRIDGE

Foreword by John B. Connally

SMITHSONIAN INSTITUTION PRESS

WASHINGTON AND LONDON

This book was copyedited by Bradley Rymph, proofread and indexed by Linda W. O'Doughda,
designed by Kathleen Sims, and typeset by Princeton Editorial Associates.

Library of Congress Cataloging-in-Publication Data
Carrier Warfare in the Pacific: an oral history collection / edited by E. T. Wooldridge.
    p.   cm.—(Smithsonian history of aviation series)
   Includes bibliographical references and index.
   ISBN 1-56098-264-0 (alk. paper)
   1. World War, 1939–1945—Naval operations, American. 2. World War, 1939–1945—
Aerial operations, American. 3. Aircraft carriers—United States—History. 4. World War,
1939–1945—Campaigns—Pacific Ocean. 5. Oral History. I. Wooldridge, E. T. II. Series.
D769.45.C37   1993
940.54′26—dc20   92-43343
                                                                      CIP

The paper used in this publication meets the minimum requirements of the American National
Standard for Permanence of Paper for Printed Library Materials Z39.48-1984.

Printed in the United States of America
10 9 8 7 6 5 4 3 2 1   99 98 97 96 95 94 93

Unless otherwise indicated, all photographs are official U.S. Navy photographs and were ob-
tained from the Library and Photographic Services Division of the U.S. Naval Institute.

Publisher's note: The descriptions of otherwise undocumented personal incidents and recollections of episodes and persons are as they appear in the memories of the individuals so credited.
Every effort has been made to ensure correctness; inaccuracy, if it occurs, is regretted.

To those who lost their lives in service on board aircraft carriers

Contents

Foreword

"Carrier warfare"—a fascinating subject! Carriers, and the men and planes they carried, dictated new strategies and tactics for a Navy at war. This book is a compilation of vignettes by individuals who developed those strategies and tactics that led to victory in the Pacific and left an indelible imprint on a world at war.

This book is not a history of World War II, nor is it a history of the United States Navy. Rather, it is a collection of memories of individuals who experienced defeat and victory, who saw death—face to face—and survived, unlike many of their shipmates who were less fortunate. In these pages are chronicled daring feats of heroism and sacrifice. Although these feats could easily have been told in an emotional outpouring, they are related here in a retrospective manner. Anyone who is at all familiar with the Navy and its leaders will find those valiant men's stories here—Halsey, Spruance, Mitscher, McCain, Burke, and countless others. But this volume does not stop with the recollections of these better-known naval officers. Also included, for example, are a remarkable story by Chief Ship's Clerk C. S. King and the daring exploits of Capt. David McCampbell, the Navy ace of aces with 34 Japanese planes to his credit whose bravery under fire against tremendous odds won him the Congressional Medal of Honor.

I was fighter director officer (FDO) in charge of the Combat Information Center (CIC) on the day McCampbell won the Congressional Medal. His memory as recounted in this book ("Use Your Best Judgment") and mine differ on what happened on that particular day. As I recall that day, we had launched early attacks of fighters and bombers against the Japanese mainland when our task forces came under severe attack from large Japanese raids. We were under such attack that for the first time during the war, so far as I know, I sent out the distress call of "Mayday." This was a prearranged signal to indicate that the base was under severe attack and that all planes should abort their missions and return to base immediately. Then Commander McCampbell had been leading fighter cover for a raid over Japan. He immediately returned to base, where he was quickly rearmed and refueled to take off and hopefully intercept a large raid coming in from the northwest. From the size of the blip on the radar scope, that raid appeared to include 75 or more Japanese planes. Dogfights were occurring all over the sky, guns were firing, and planes were falling. American pilots were ditching, being picked up by destroyers; pandemonium reigned. We launched McCampbell and his wingman and violated all Navy doctrine by sending out seven planes instead of eight. Normally nothing less than two four-plane divisions would be launched, but we could only put together seven aircraft (one four-plane division and one nonstandard three-plane division) in the hopes of intercepting a raid 10 times that size. I was controlling McCampbell on that day.

As soon as we launched the seven planes, they rendezvoused and were given the heading to intercept the oncoming Japanese aircraft. When they finally spotted the huge raid of Japanese torpedo planes and bombers with a high cover of Zero fighters, McCampbell confirmed the size of the raid and asked for reinforcements. I said, "There are none available." He then said, "We are incredibly outnumbered; what shall we do?" After I responded, "Use your own judgment," he and his wingman decided to take the Zero fighter cover by themselves, leaving the other five planes to work on the Japanese bomber and torpedo planes below them. They actually pursued the Japanese planes back to the mainland and were shooting them down almost in the landing pattern. As McCampbell landed back aboard ship and his tailhook caught the restraining wire, his engine died, totally out of gas. He had five rounds of ammunition left in his guns. He had destroyed nine Japanese aircraft, two more probables, and his wingman had got six. An unbelievable day!

Had it not been for the atom bombs that were dropped on Nagasaki and Hiroshima and ended the war, the great story of World War II would have been the development of radar. First developed by the British, enhanced and improved by our own forces, it played an incredible part in the success of the Navy's operations. The U.S. Naval Academy graduates, who were largely in command of the ships, had little or no experience with radar. Rather, those of us who were reserve officers were more familiar with the radar and radios aboard an aircraft carrier. We reserve officers almost universally presided over the Combat Information Centers, which controlled all airborne aircraft and combat air patrols and were responsible for all surface and air contacts. Placing such responsibilities on junior officers was highly unusual.

I was a lieutenant and operated first as a ship's fighter director officer aboard the carrier *Essex.* Later, I was Task Group FDO under Rear Adm. Frederick Sherman and then in the closing months of the war under Rear Adm. Tommy Sprague aboard the *Bennington.* I was transferred there because the *Bennington* came out with a new crew. Admiral Sprague was not wholly confident of the new crew's experience, so he was kind enough to invite me to the admiral's mess aboard ship. I thought this was just wonderful, and it was—until he told me that, when we were operating in a forward area, he wanted me to be in CIC, below deck, 24 hours a day. He told me to get a ship's carpenter to build me a bunk in CIC. Instead, I found a five-foot-long tool box with a padded leather cover, which I used as my bed for weeks on end while we were in the combat areas. I went topside once a day to bathe and change clothes and immediately went back down to CIC. The admiral was kind enough to send my meals down the various hatches on trays, morning, noon, and night. He tarnished this thoughtfulness a bit when we were out of the forward areas and I was permitted to go topside to dine in the admiral's mess—where I was confronted by the admiral saying, "Well, look who's here; we have the mole with us." Still, the *Bennington* turned out to be a happy ship, and, during the last few months of the war, our interception techniques with combat air patrols became so efficient that the ship's guns never once fired on an enemy plane. I must confess that this was also partially due to the depletion of Japanese pilots, particularly experienced ones.

I cannot conclude without mentioning two individuals for whom I have great admiration and enormous respect. While I was aboard the *Essex,* the Combat Information Center was just aft of the flag plot. The executive officer of the *Essex* was then Comdr. David L. McDonald who sat on my right shoulder during every general quarters, sitting around an old-style horizontal plotting table. We did this week in and week out, month in and month out, for a year. He was a superb officer—cool, calm, deliberate, intelligent, fair, and, all and all, as fine a human being and naval officer as I have met.

After a long siege in the second battle of the Philippine Sea, I had been sitting at the plotting board for 52 consecutive hours, living on coffee and sandwiches, while we were almost constantly under attack. My ankles had swollen where I could no longer wear my shoes. Finally, Commander Mc-Donald ordered me to go below to get some sleep. I went to my cabin exhausted, fell in my bunk with the porthole open and remained there unaware that the ship had gone to general quarters and was under attack. The 40-mm and 20-mm guns almost overhead outside my porthole started chattering at incoming Japanese planes, and I was not at my general quarters station.

During this time, Admiral Sherman sent for me, and in my place Commander McDonald went to flag plot to tell him I was not available. The admiral angrily demanded, "Why not?" Commander McDonald told him that he had ordered me below; McDonald explained the circumstances and said that, if the admiral "pleased," he would like to leave me below. Fortunately, the admiral agreed and no trouble ensued, although the task group FDO was not on his station during general quarters, which could have been a serious offense.

Later, in the summer of 1945, I was detached from the *Essex* and sent to the *Bennington*. At about the same time, Commander McDonald was relieved from sea duty after a long extended tour. The next time we met he was Commander of the Sixth Fleet in the Mediterranean and I was Secretary of the Navy. We had a happy reunion aboard his flagship in the Mediterranean. He later became Chief of Naval Operations, which he richly deserved.

The other individual who became a legend in his own time was Adm. Arleigh Burke. I did not serve directly under him during World War II, although he was chief of staff for Adm. Marc Mitscher aboard the *Lexington* and we frequently operated in the same task group. I knew who Burke was, but I never met him until I was appointed Secretary of the Navy and he was Chief of Naval Operations. He and his lovely wife Bobbie invited me to live with them at the Admiral's House (now the Vice President's House) at the Naval Observatory. I did just that for about three weeks, absorbing everything I could from a man who had achieved a remarkable wartime career in the Navy and was then serving his unprecedented third consecutive term as Chief of Naval Operations. He earned his reputation ("Thirty-one knot" Burke) commanding destroyers in the early days of the war in the South Pacific. He was a fighter; a man of fierce determination, with an unquestioned love of the Navy; intelligent, dedicated, indefatigable, and brilliantly eloquent in the defense of the Navy, its mission, and its capacity. He retired several months after I became Secretary of the Navy, and I deeply regret that I did not have the privilege of associating with him longer, although I have been fortunate in seeing him many times since.

In the accounts throughout this volume, a reader will find examples of tragedy, of sorrow, disaster, and death—all told in a rather restrained, unemotional way. The reader's imagination must give full play when stories of the battle of the Coral Sea come into focus. Mighty carriers were sunk, many men died, some were saved. Sadness and joy became a mixed blessing. When you read of the picket lines of destroyers standing as an early warning device for the fleet between Okinawa and Japan, pause long enough over the dry prosaic words to envision these destroyers being hit one after another, time and again, by bombs, by *kamikaze* planes until so many were hit that serious thought was given to withdrawing from the area because of the lack of destroyer support for the aircraft carriers, cruisers, and other ships in the same area.

During this same time, the *Franklin* was hit, with incredible loss of lives—an unbelievable naval disaster. Hear the explosions, envision the fires, the dead, the wounded, the maimed, and hear the demand of Adm. William F. ("Bull") Halsey, "Save the *Franklin* at all costs." Imagine the cruiser *Santa Fe* pulling along side to remove the wounded and the cruiser *Pittsburgh* tying on and towing this wounded giant of an aircraft carrier—both sitting ducks—traveling at four knots, protected by the remaining carriers, battleships, cruisers, and destroyers.

Also during this same period, operating off the Japanese mainland, the *Essex* took her own *kamikaze* hit. The burning Japanese plane plowed into the side of the ship near the number two elevator, burning a hole in the flight deck approximately 20 ft. by 20 ft. The force of the blow was such that it shook this entire 40,000-ton ship to the point where dust settled down over all of us from the radio and radar cables overhead. We felt that we had just experienced a small earthquake, whereupon Commander McDonald arose from his stool and calmly said, "Well, they finally got our cherry."

Every reader who has any knowledge of or interest in the Navy will find herein stories of valor, sacrifice, pathos, glory, tales of incredible luck and mistakes of enormous proportion, both on our part and the part of the Japanese. These memoirs will forever chronicle the determination and the daring feats of courageous people determined to repay with a vengeance the day of infamy at Pearl Harbor, the fall of Corregidor, and the death march of Bataan.

—John B. Connally
(1917-1993)

Acknowledgments

I extend my sincere thanks to Paul Stillwell, Director of Oral History, U.S. Naval Institute (USNI), Annapolis, Maryland, who fully supported this project from its inception and, in an unprecedented display of interagency cooperation, placed the resources of the USNI Oral History Collection at the disposal of the National Air and Space Museum. Joanne Patmore and Linda O'Doughda of the USNI staff were of inestimable help in sorting out the scores of drafts of manuscripts in the collection. Patty Maddocks, director, Library and Photographic Services, USNI, and Linda Cullen and Mary Beth Straight of her staff provided their usual excellent service in the selection of photographs. Dr. John T. Mason, founding father of the USNI Oral History Collection, oversaw the work involved in about 130 volumes of oral history and, with the assistance of Comdr. Etta-Belle Kitchen, USN (Ret.), conducted the bulk of the interviewing.

Many members of the National Air and Space Museum (NASM) staff provided advice, encouragement, and assistance during the project. Special thanks go to Nadya Makovenyi, assistant director for exhibits, and members of her department: David Romanowski, Barbara Brennan, John Clendening, and Diane Pearson. In the Museum Operations Department, Scotty O'Connell assisted in editing portions of the manuscript and, in the process, developed an appreciation of the sacrifices and gallantry of a generation far removed; Annette Newman patiently passed along her considerable skills in the personal computer field to a rank amateur; and Mark Avino and Carolyn Russo of the NASM photo lab provided timely and highly professional support. The invitation of Dr. Von Hardesty, editor, Smithsonian History of Aviation Series, to join that worthy group of aviation historians was much appreciated.

Of most importance, we are eternally grateful to those men who flew and fought from the aircraft carriers and had the foresight to leave their written legacy for our continuing enlightenment and enjoyment.

Introduction

This is a book about United States Navy aircraft carrier operations in the Pacific during World War II, as seen from the unique perspective of men involved in combat operations at sea—pilots and air crewmen of the carrier air group, officers and men of the ship's company, the admirals and their staffs, and the planners in Washington, San Diego, and Pearl Harbor. The glass through which these people viewed the vicissitudes of their occupations was— and always has been—different from the norm. Their perspectives, concerns, and emotional outlooks are not generally understood or appreciated by those who have not experienced or been associated with flight operations at sea. In World War II, the aircrews flew into battle from the decks of ships that would not be in the same location—or possibly even afloat—when they returned hours later at the end of their mission. Their "home" could have been bombed, torpedoed, or hit by *kamikazes;* a hole or two in the flight deck, quickly patched over to permit flight operations, often gave no hint of scenes of incredible carnage, human suffering, and destruction that extended down to the bowels of the ship.

It is impossible to describe aerial combat at sea without becoming involved in scenes and events such as these, as well as the more mundane but *different* aspects of life at sea. Occasionally the reader might wonder if he or she is reading tales of aerial combat or "sea" stories. For example, the distinguished group of 18 officers whose exploits are told here were responsible for the destruction of 69 enemy aircraft in air-to-air combat and the sinking of numerous enemy ships, including battleships and carriers. For these, and other, heroic deeds, they were awarded a Congressional Medal of Honor, 12 Navy Crosses, and scores of lesser awards. Yet 5 of the 12 Navy Crosses, the nation's second-highest award, were awarded for heroism not in the cockpit of an airplane but on the bridge of a ship under attack from enemy aircraft, ships, and submarines, as members of the ship's company or embarked flag staff. Many of these stories are included in this book, and, in these and other instances, the reader must agree that "sea" stories and flying stories are inseparable.

The accounts in this book are based solely on oral histories selected from the collection of the U.S. Naval Institute in Annapolis, Maryland. All of the officer interviewees were aviators with one notable exception—Adm. Arleigh A. Burke. This technicality was rectified in 1981, however, when Admiral Burke was designated an honorary naval aviator in recognition of "decades of vigorous support of naval aviation and decisions which shaped the Navy's air arm as it is known today." Two of the histories are by enlisted men whose accounts of interminable hours at battle stations and life below decks bring a unique perspective and welcome contrast to the views of combat as seen from the cockpit or the bridge. We are reminded that the life of the ship's company is integral to the complete story of aerial combat at sea.

The focus of the book is structured by a number of factors—editorial constraints, availability of relevant manuscripts, and my own judgment and biases as this volume's editor with regard to balance and relative importance. Thus, there are gaps in coverage that will inevitably disappoint some readers.

The oral histories have been edited from a question-and-answer format to a narrative for ease of reading and continuity. Every effort has been made to retain the personal feelings, convictions, and perceptions about a particular event, campaign, or person. Most of the histories were recorded long after the war, when the interviewees were in retirement or engaged in pursuits far removed from their Navy careers. Quite naturally, memories had faded, and recollections of specific dates, sequences of events, and locations were hazy in some instances. Whenever possible, errors such as these were corrected in the editing process. Though the passage of time had dimmed the memories for historical details, the emotions of the moment, when lives had been in peril, were still vivid and are the essence of these accounts. Few histories of the Pacific war have recorded the elation and pride of John S. ("Jimmy") Thach at Midway as he caught a fleeting glimpse of the "beautiful silver waterfall" of Dauntless dive bombers in their dives on the enemy fleet; or P. D. Stroop's fascination as he stood on the flag bridge of the old *Lexington* at Coral Sea, watching the bombs release from Japanese dive bombers and wondering about their accuracy; or the amazement, and occasional stark terror, of Edward L. ("Whitey") Feightner as he was torn from the world he knew, the *Enterprise,* to a world of steaming jungles, snipers, and a fight for survival with the Cactus Air Force on Guadalcanal. These memories make history come alive, and give these valiant men their rightful place in the gallery of history.

—E. T. Wooldridge

1942: Holding the Line in the Pacific

In 1942, the U.S. Pacific Fleet was told "to hold what you've got and hit them when you can." The "hitting" was to be done by U.S. submarines and carriers. By mid-January 1942, the carrier force was comprised of the *Enterprise, Lexington,* and *Yorktown,* with the *Saratoga* out of action for five months because of a torpedo hit. With the aim of diverting Japanese forces and stemming any further expansion, in February and March 1942 U.S. carrier forces conducted hit-and-run raids against Japanese forces and installations in the Gilberts, the Marshalls, Wake and Marcus Islands in the Central Pacific, Lae and Salamaua on New Guinea, and, on 18 April, the famed "Doolittle raid" against Japan. Though these early raids were primarily of psychological value to the United States, they were followed in the next eight months by a series of sea-air battles unprecedented in the history of naval warfare, signaling the beginning of the end of Japanese sea and air power.

The battle of the Coral Sea, 4–8 May 1942, was the first sea battle in history where opposing surface forces never saw or fired on each other. A Japanese plan to take the Allied base at Port Moresby on the southwest coast of

The Southwest Pacific, scene of the six carrier-versus-carrier battles of World War II.

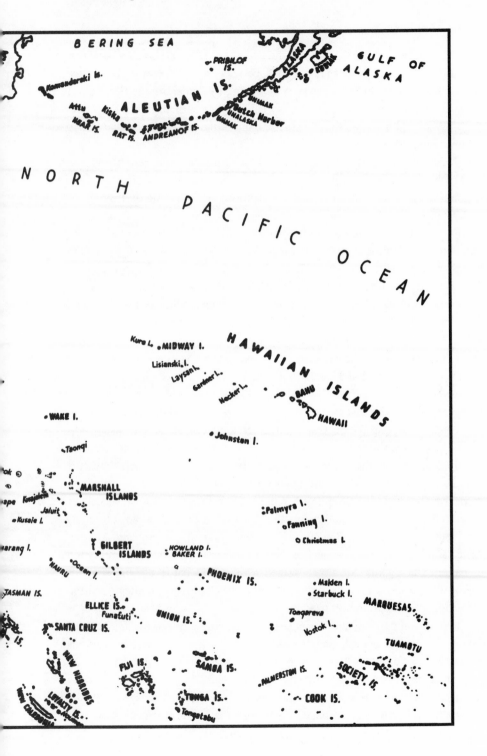

New Guinea was thwarted. Forewarned by American intelligence analysts, who had broken the Japanese naval code, bombers from the carriers *Lexington* and *Yorktown* sank the light carrier *Shoho,* and, by damaging the fleet carrier *Shokaku* and destroying enough enemy carrier planes, managed to keep both the *Shokaku* and her sistership the *Zuikaku* out of the pivotal battle that was to follow a month later—Midway.

The battle of Midway has been called the turning point of the Pacific war. As before, breaking the Japanese code proved to be a decisive factor, as the Combined Fleet, with the objectives of capturing Midway and destroying the U.S. Fleet in a decisive battle, was defeated. A series of skirmishes and battles from 4–7 June were marked by incredible coincidences, miscalculations, indecision, and extraordinary valor on both sides and, in the end, by superb bombing by Navy carrier pilots. Heroes by the hundreds died for their country as the American carrier *Yorktown* went to the bottom and four enemy carriers, all survivors of the attack on Pearl Harbor, were sunk. Midway was the worst naval defeat for Japan in centuries and led to the first limited offensive in the South Pacific—the bloody battles for Guadalcanal.

Following up on the success of Midway, U.S. Marines landed on the islands of Guadalcanal and Tulagi on 7 August 1942 with the immediate goal of seizing control of an unfinished Japanese airfield on Guadalcanal. The landing was to be the first step of an offensive up the Solomon Islands chain to take enemy positions in New Guinea, thus consolidating the Allied base at Port Moresby, and then to advance on the Japanese stronghold of Rabaul on New Britain. For six months desperate air and sea battles raged up and down the Solomons Sea as the Allies struggled for control of Guadalcanal. Although carrier-versus-carrier battles played an important role in the ultimate success of the Allied effort, a key to victory was the "Cactus Air Force," based at Henderson Field on Guadalcanal. Composed of a few hundred outnumbered Marine, Army, and Navy aviators—many of them from carriers put out of commission in battle—the Cactus Air Force waged a desperate battle against superior enemy air and surface forces during the fall of 1942, playing an integral part in the struggle for the Solomon Islands.

Periodic attempts by the Japanese to reinforce their troops on Guadalcanal led to two carrier battles, which resulted in strategic victories, but serious carrier losses, for the Allies. In the battle of the Eastern Solomons, 24–25 August, a day of sharp attacks and counterattacks between the two sides resulted in the light carrier *Ryujo* being sunk by U.S. carrier bombers, while the *Enterprise* was severely damaged. Although that reinforcement effort was delayed, the Japanese continued to exert pressure on the Marines from the land, sea, and air. Japanese submarines took a heavy toll of Allied warships in the Coral Sea, south of Guadalcanal. On 31 August, the *Saratoga* was torpedoed and put out of commission again, this time for three months. On 15 September, the *Wasp* was also torpedoed and ultimately sunk, leaving the *Hornet* as the only operational U.S. carrier in the South Pacific. This was a dubious honor she would share during the struggle for Guadalcanal with the *Enterprise* and *Saratoga,* as each of the ships in turn became the sole survivor, only to sustain disabling combat damage and retire from the scene for repairs.

As the battles for Guadalcanal raged throughout the fall, and the fortunes of each side ebbed and flowed, a final carrier battle occurred, the battle for the Santa Cruz Islands, fought by the *Enterprise* and *Hornet* against the most powerful Japanese carrier/battleship force assembled since the battle of Midway. During one day of intense aerial combat, the *Enterprise* was again damaged and the *Hornet* was sunk after sustaining an unbelievable number of bomb and torpedo hits. Although the United States damaged two enemy carriers and destroyed about 90 to 100 Japanese aircraft, the battle was considered a tactical victory for the enemy. From a strategic standpoint, however, the Japanese failed again to reinforce Guadalcanal to any significant degree, and the loss of seasoned, highly trained combat pilots was a serious blow that would have long-term consequences.

There were no more carrier battles during the Guadalcanal campaign, though the fighting continued unabated until the last Japanese troops were evacuated and the island was secured on 9 February 1943. Eighteen months would pass before the carriers would face each other in battle again.

Lt. Comdr. John S. ("Jimmy") Thach was one of a mere handful of young carrier aviators who not only were outstanding combat pilots but also possessed an unusual grasp of the evolving principles of carrier warfare. Their understanding and insight made them invaluable as tacticians and strategists as the war progressed and the size and offensive power of carrier task forces grew to undreamed of proportions. Before the war, Thach, Butch O'Hare, and other pilots from Fighting Squadron 3 developed the defensive maneuver used by carrier pilots to counter the superior performance of the Japanese Zero fighter.

The "Doolittle raid" on Japan was the most dramatic and morale-boosting of the offensive actions taken by the Allies during the early days of 1942. Army B-25 pilots, led by the renowned pilot Lt. Col. James H. Doolittle, were trained in the fine art of carrier takeoffs by naval aviator Lt. Henry L. Miller, on temporary assignment from his instructor job at Pensacola. His account of the

intensive training period at Eglin Field, Florida, reflects the highly professional, and critical, approach that he brought to the project, plus a genuine
admiration that he developed for Colonel Doolittle and his crew as they trained
for an extremely dangerous, one-way mission.

As the *Hornet*'s intelligence officer, Lt. Stephen Jurika, Jr., viewed the
arrival of the Army fliers aboard his ship from an entirely different perspective.
Although a pilot himself, Jurika was "ship's company"—regulation, proud of
his ship and its crew, and one who approached his job with the precision and
thoroughness of a good intelligence analyst. His job, which picked up where
Lieutenant Miller's left off, was to brief the Army crews on their targets, using
his unusual background as an expert in Far Eastern political-military affairs.

As a flag secretary and jack-of-all-trades for a carrier division commander,
Lt. Comdr. P. D. Stroop's job was to keep the paperwork flowing smoothly,
keep the admiral fully informed, and be aware of all aspects of air and surface
operations as the task force was engaged in combat. At the right hand of the
admiral on the bridge, he watched and listened as the combat action unfolded,
recording decisions, impressions, and facts in the war diary. His is not a
"flying" story, yet it is one of aerial combat as seen from the receiving end—the
bridge of the carrier *Lexington,* under intense air attack by Japanese dive and
torpedo bombers during the battle of the Coral Sea in May 1942. It is a story of
a ship mortally wounded, reluctantly abandoned, and finally destroyed in a
spectacular explosion that sent the ship to the bottom.

At the battle of Midway, Thach finally got his chance to use the "Thach
weave" in combat. During a momentary lull in a running battle with hordes of
Zeros, Thach looked up in the sky, and saw a "beautiful silver waterfall" of
Dauntless dive bombers streaming down in their dives on the enemy carriers.
In his account, Thach eloquently describes the moment that changed the course
of the war in the Pacific. After the battle, he vented his frustration and anger
against his superiors who "violated one of the basic principles of warfare" by
operating U.S. carriers too far apart to afford mutual support and protection.

The battles for Guadalcanal are recounted from two entirely different
perspectives. Lt. Comdr. Francis D. Foley was air operations officer aboard the
Hornet during the fighting in the Solomons until the ship was abandoned
during the battle of the Santa Cruz Islands. He tells of action in "Torpedo
Junction" east of Guadalcanal where enemy submarines sank Allied ships with
frightening regularity. Through all the trials and tribulations, however, the
unique ability of Foley and his shipmates to find the humor in the most dreadful
situations is apparent, as is the sense of leadership and "gung ho" spirit that

prevailed aboard *Hornet* during the brief service life of the ship, the last fleet carrier to be lost in combat.

Lt. Edward L. ("Whitey") Feightner gained an appreciation for the creature comforts of shipboard life when he and many of his fellow pilots from the *Enterprise* air group were temporarily based ashore at Henderson Field on Guadalcanal in late 1942. By day, they flew and fought with pilots from other services and countries of the Cactus Air Force in an early instance of successful "joint" or "combined" air combat operations. At night, a cot in a tent on the fringes of the jungle, with the enemy literally a stone's throw away and shells from Japanese guns offshore whistling overhead, brought the war "up close and personal."

Butch O'Hare and the Thach Weave

Admiral John S. Thach

John Smith ("Jimmy") Thach was born in Pine Bluff, Arkansas, on 19 April 1905. He was appointed to the U.S. Naval Academy in 1923, graduated and was commissioned ensign on 2 June 1927, and was designated a naval aviator on 4 January 1930. He served in a wide variety of carrier-based, patrol, and experimental squadrons and had numerous command tours ashore and afloat as he advanced, eventually receiving the rank of admiral in March 1965. Admiral Thach was Commander in Chief, U.S. Naval Forces, Europe, from 25 March 1965 until his retirement on 1 May 1967.

During World War II, Admiral Thach participated in 12 major engagements or campaigns, operating from seven different aircraft carriers. He was twice awarded the Navy Cross for extraordinary heroism in aerial combat with Japanese forces. He later went to the Fast Carrier Task Force in the Pacific as air operations officer, where he developed the system of blanketing enemy airfields with a continuous patrol of carrier-based fighters and planned and directed the Navy's final offensive blows against the Japanese homeland.

Admiral Thach's decorations include the Navy Cross with two Gold Stars, Distinguished Service Medal, Silver Star, and Legion of Merit with two Gold Stars.

Lt. E. H. ("Butch") O'Hare (left) and Lt. Comdr. John S. ("Jimmy") Thach, Fighting Squadron 3, 1942.

I joined Fighting Squadron 3 in June 1939 and was commanding officer from November 1940 through June 1942. During that time, there were a number of things that we proved time and time again. One of these was that the fighter with initial altitude advantage couldn't be shaken off and should win a dog-fight, assuming that he made no mistakes. I established what we called a "humiliation team." It was composed of myself and three other experienced pilots. We would take newcomers to the squadron, take them up, and give them all the altitude advantage they wanted. Then we'd see if they could come down and get on our tails and stay there long enough to shoot. The experienced ones could give away altitude advantage and still turn the tables on them and lick them every time. It was a good thing to show them that they had a lot of work to do.

This was true with one exception. One person who came to my squadron fresh out of the training command was a young man by the name of Butch O'Hare, and the first time I took him up and gave him altitude advantage, he didn't make any mistakes. I did everything I could to fool him and shake him, and he came right in on me and he could have shot me right out of the air. So I came down and said, "Well, I've had one of these new youngsters up but I want each member of the 'humiliation team' to go up with him and give him a chance." Up they went and, sure enough, Butch did it again. It wasn't long after that before we made him a member of the team, because he had passed the graduation test so quickly.

I think Butch O'Hare, when he learned how to fly an airplane, learned how to fly it real well. He was a good athlete. He had a sense of timing and relative motion that he may have been born with, but also he had that competitive spirit. When he got into any kind of a fight like this, he didn't want to lose; he wanted to win. He really had a dedication to winning, and he probably had worked a lot of this out in his own mind, studied all the documents that we had on aerial combat and just picked it up much faster than anyone else I've ever seen. He got the most out of his airplane. He learned a thing that a lot of youngsters don't learn; when you're in a dogfight with somebody, it isn't how hard you pull back on the stick to make a tight turn to get inside of him that's important. It's how smoothly you fly the plane and whether you pull back with just enough turn to get around in the shortest time.

A good fighter pilot has got to have a competitive spirit. He's got to want to do it more than anything else in the world. This desire to excel has a significant bearing on how people do later in combat, I think. I'm sure that, after a little while flying against a pilot in a fighter, I could tell whether he would be good, mediocre, average, or superb, also whether he would lose his head, was he calm and cool, and would he remember to do the right thing. Would he have the capability to do it, physically, but not do it because he suddenly gets a mental block due to overexcitement, or fear, or something? In the early part of the war, I kept a little black book—I never showed it to anybody—and I listed those people in my squadron whom I thought we might lose first. That's the way it turned out, so I threw the book away.

In the spring of 1941, we received an intelligence report of great significance. This report had come out of China and described a new Japanese fighter, the Mitsubishi A6M2 Zero, that had performance far superior to anything we had, including the F4F Wildcats we were flying at the time. So, when I realized that this airplane, if this intelligence report were correct, had us beat in every category of performance, it was pretty discouraging. I decided we'd better do something about this. I believed we had one advantage, if we could ever get into a position to use it. We had good guns and could shoot and hit even if we had only a fleeting second or two to take aim. We had to do something to entice the opponent into giving us that one all-important opportunity; it was the only chance we had. So every night at home in Coronado, California, I used to work on this problem. I used a box of kitchen matches and put them on the dining room table; each one of them represented an airplane. I decided that the kind of formation we flew—three-plane sections, a leader and two wingmen—was an unwieldy formation, and we ought to just have a two-plane section and a four-plane division, or combat unit. Assuming these two sections were cruising in the same direction, they would have to be separated by a standard distance equal to the diameter of the tightest circle the aircraft can make. Being in that position, we had a lookout doctrine that the two planes on the right watched over the tails of the two planes on the left and vice versa. We wouldn't use any signals; we would have to wait until an enemy plane was almost within lethal firing range of one section, and then the other section would make a sharp turn toward the one being attacked. That was the signal that somebody was within firing range on his tail. So, if the section being attacked is the one on the left, he turns right, throwing the enemy's lead off. If the enemy tries to follow on around, to get back his aim, it brings him right in the sights of the right-hand section of aircraft, which should have a good shot at him—either head-on, if he continues to follow his target, or a good side approach, if he pulls out. Although he has superior performance, we then have a shot at him but he hasn't shot at us accurately. So, this looked like it was, maybe, the only thing to do.

We obviously had to practice this idea a lot to make it work. I told Butch O'Hare to take four aircraft and use full power, to simulate the Zero, and I would take four and never advance the throttle more than half way. That gave him at least superior performance, maybe double, maybe not. We went up and he made all sorts of attacks, and I figured it looked like a pretty good thing to me. Every time that he came in to shoot, we just kept weaving back and forth while these streams of aircraft were attacking. After we landed, he came over to me and said, "Skipper, it really worked. I couldn't make any attack without seeing the nose of one of your airplanes pointed at me. So at least you are getting a shot; even though I might also have got a shot, at least it isn't one-sided. Most of the time that sudden turn, although I knew what you were going to do, always caught me a little bit by surprise because it seemed to be timed just right. When I was committed and about to squeeze the trigger, the target turned and I didn't think he saw me."

Of course, he didn't. That was the beauty of this—you needed no communication. You were flying along watching the other two, and they suddenly made a turn. You knew there was somebody on your tail and you had to really turn in a hurry, and that's all there was to it. You didn't need any radio. So we felt a little better about the situation. We had been proving all of our fighter lives that an airplane with superior performance could knock you out of the air. Now we had something to work on, to keep us from being demoralized. This was something that was worked out before the war, in the summer and fall of 1941, on my kitchen table in Coronado.

After I'd developed this weave business, I recommended that all the squadrons accept this as a standard fighting formation. I got a message back from Commander, Aircraft, Battle Force, that since the two-plane section was such a radical change he wouldn't force all the squadrons to do it, but that I had authority to do it in my squadron. Actually, by this time the idea was catching on anyway, and ComAirBatFor adopted it in July 1941. VF-2 on the *Lexington* was doing it also, and so were some of the others. They were flying two-plane sections, but they had not adopted the weaving tactics. I'm not sure whether the *Hornet* and the *Enterprise* did because I hadn't really seen them. The *Hornet* was rather new in the Pacific, arriving in March 1942, and I hadn't even seen them, but I tried to circulate this around. Jimmy Flatley came along in April 1942 and helped me for a while, and we had many discussions about what was the best thing to do. Neither one of us knew it for sure. Later, in October 1942, he sent a personal message to me saying the four-plane division is the only thing that will work, and "I am calling it the Thach Weave, for your information. Six planes don't work. The two extra ones get lost." He sent another official message describing this and saying that they were convinced that it was the only way for our fighters to fight, especially against superior enemy fighters.

Later on in the Pacific, there were times when we had the advantage and would not have to use the weave, which was more of a defensive tactic. On 20 February 1942, for instance, the *Lexington* was attacked by waves of enemy aircraft, so it was all right to go just hell-bent for election and the airplane that can get there the first, gets there. Butch O'Hare was vectored out after a nine-plane group of Bettys and intercepted them when they were about six minutes away. He went out with his wingman and, as we had a practice of doing, charged all his guns and fired a short burst to be sure that everything was working properly. His wingman apparently had an electrical problem, and he couldn't get any guns to fire. Butch realized this and waved him back over the ship, but he didn't want to go. Butch shook his fist at him and tried to get him to go back, but he came on with Butch and maneuvered around to try to draw some attention to himself while Butch went in and made the attacks on this formation of Betty bombers. Butch made one approach after another—first from one side of the formation and then the other. Inside of six minutes, he had six of them down. He was given credit for only five, at first. They thought antiaircraft had shot down one, but one of them came down and made an approach like he was going to crash into the *Lexington.* We got photographs of that airplane, and one engine had completely fallen out of the wing. Butch had shot that engine out. Apparently the fire had gone out, but that plane was on its way down. Antiaircraft did shoot at it and maybe they did polish it off, but I'm sure that plane never would have gotten home and I'd give Butch credit for shooting down six. He certainly shot it out of the formation. So the net result was that, out of the 20 aircraft we met that day, 19 were shot down. This was using offensive tactics.

Shortly after this incident, Butch O'Hare had finished a combat air patrol and was coming in for a landing. Now, at this time, the *Lexington,* as the other carriers had done, had mounted small-caliber machine guns on the catwalks just to assist against close-in attacks, such as a torpedo plane attack. After this battle with the Japanese Bettys, some of the young machine gunners were a little trigger-happy, and when Butch was coming in for a landing, in the groove with his wheels down, one of the gunners back on the port quarter opened up on him and fired a long burst before anybody could stop him. Butch saw where the fire was coming from, but he came on in and landed. Just to show you the kind of person he was, he got out of his plane and slowly walked back and stood on the flight deck, looking down at this young machine gunner. All he said was "Son, if you don't stop shooting at me when I've got my wheels down, I'm going to have to report you to the gunnery officer." Of course, the young man was horribly embarrassed, in the first place, but somebody asked Butch about it later and he said, "I don't mind him shooting at me when I don't have my wheels down, but it might make me have to take a wave off and I don't like to take wave offs!"

The Doolittle Raid

Rear Admiral Henry L. Miller

Henry Louis Miller was born 18 July 1912 in Fairbanks, Alaska, son of Frank and Mary Miller. He entered the U.S. Naval Academy in July 1930, was graduated and commissioned ensign 31 May 1934, and was designated a naval aviator in June 1938. Subsequent service included extensive squadron, command, and staff duties ashore and afloat, and on 1 July 1960 he advanced to the rank of rear admiral. Rear Admiral Miller was Commander, Naval Air Test Center, from October 1968 until his retirement in August 1971.

In early 1942, then Lieutenant Miller trained Lt. Col. James H. ("Jimmy") Doolittle's "Tokyo Raiders" in carrier takeoffs, then accompanied them to within 700 miles of their destination, on board the USS Hornet *in April 1942. From November 1942 to May 1944, he commanded Air Group 23 on the USS* Princeton *and thereafter had command of Air Group 6 aboard the USS* Hancock. *He was recalled from an air strike on Tokyo when hostilities ceased in August 1945.*

Admiral Miller's decorations include the Legion of Merit with Combat "V"
and one Gold Star, Distinguished Flying Cross with four Gold Stars, Air Medal
with five Gold Stars, Army Commendation Ribbon, Navy Unit Commendation
Ribbon, National Order of Vietnam Fourth Class, and Gallantry Cross with Palm.

Comdr. Henry L. Miller, Commander, Air Group 6, USS Hancock, 1945. (Courtesy
Rear Adm. H. L. Miller, USN [Ret.])

In February 1942, I was an instructor at Pensacola when I received a set of
orders to proceed without delay to Eglin Field, Florida, for temporary duty to
train the Doolittle fliers. I went down on a Sunday, reported to the colonel in
charge of the base, and read him my orders. I explained to him that I was an
instructor at Pensacola, I was a carrier pilot, and I was supposed to come down
and teach the Army Air Forces pilots how to take off from an aircraft carrier. He
still didn't have any idea of why I came down there, so I was just getting up to
say it must have been a mistake, when I asked him if he knew anything about
Lieutenant Colonel Doolittle's detachment there. With that, he closed the doors
and practically asked me to talk in a whisper. Then, the colonel put me in his
car and took me over to the place where I was staying. After I got my gear, he
took me down to a building set aside for Lieutenant Colonel Doolittle's B-25
detachment. Jimmy Doolittle wasn't there; neither was his executive officer,

Maj. Jack Hilger. So I talked to Captains York, Davey Jones, and Ross Green-
ing. I told them who I was and what I was supposed to do—teach them carrier
takeoffs. They said, "Have you ever flown a B-25?" and I said, "No, I've never
even seen one." So we went down the line, climbed into a B-25, and went over
to a field that was set aside for this work. I told them the way to make a carrier
takeoff. First, you held both feet on the brakes; for this plane we would try
one-half flaps. I asked them how much manifold pressure we could hold on for
30 seconds. We would put the stabilizer back about three-fourths, and with
engine full bore, we would release the brakes, start coming back on that yoke,
watch the air speed, and just keep coming on back until the airplane took off. I
hadn't had time to study or even look at the B-25, except I had a feel for it and
they told me they were taking off at 110 miles an hour. So on the first takeoff,
they observed the air speed and it showed 65 to 67 miles an hour. They said it's
impossible; you can't do that. Well, the B-25 that we flew that day was light
loaded. I said, "O.K., come on back and we'll land and try it again."

So the second takeoff, done the same way, indicated an air speed of 70 miles
an hour when we were in the air, and they were convinced that a B-25 could take
off at that slow speed. For the run over Japan, the B-25 was going to be at 31,000
pounds, which was 2,000 pounds over the maximum designed load. To start out
with at this field near Eglin Field, I checked out all the pilots for light loads, then
intermediate loads, then, finally, the maximum load that they would take on the
raid. Everybody did pretty well, including the extra crews. I took data on each one
of the pilots and marked off the field. I used other Doolittle pilots to act as
observers. We got a portable anemometer to find out how much wind they had. We
measured the distance for each plane that got off, and I recorded all that data. In the
cockpit I observed techniques, because you get a feel for who's a good pilot and
who isn't, no matter what his takeoff distance is.

A funny thing happened just before we finished up that first day. I was over
at this room that they gave me, getting my flight jacket because it was chilly,
and I thought, "Gee whiz, here I am a lieutenant in the Navy, and this Army Air
Force gives me a dirty, junky room like this! No carpet on the deck, just cold
concrete, and look at that crumby bed!" So I put on my jacket, and I wondered
who else was staying in this little group of rooms. I went out to see the name of
this place and it said, "VIP Quarters," and I said, "They must be kidding." So I
went up to the next room and looked at the name plate and it was Lieutenant
Colonel Doolittle's name. I went up to the next one, and here was Mr. Kettering
of General Motors. I went over to this other one and I saw Major Johnson. So I
said, "My gosh, this is pretty fast company I'm in; I'd better not complain about

this horrible room that they've put me in, because evidently these guys have the same kind of horrible rooms." But that's the way the Army lived at that time.

I found out where they were going. My only contact as far as the Navy was concerned at that time was Capt. Wu Duncan, who was a special assistant to Adm. Ernie King, CominCh. I took my orders from Lieutenant Colonel Doolittle and Captain Duncan. During this training period at Eglin Field, I was supposed to be there for 15 days, get through with the training, and go back to Pensacola. However, we had some foggy days, and it was going to take longer. But it didn't create any problem because Jimmy Doolittle, on his trips to Washington, would keep Captain Duncan informed, and he would give me permission to stay as long as I wanted down there on this set of orders.

As we went along and everything appeared to be going on schedule, we came to the last day. In the next day or so, all 16 planes were going to shove off for the West Coast. On the last day, I checked out all the crews except one, a pilot by the name of Lieutenant Bates. He finished practice runs, but I wasn't satisfied because he was letting the plane fly him. So I told the observers to get out, and I said, "Bates, you have to try it again. You fly this plane smoothly. You fly the plane; don't let it fly you. Once more around." Well, he took off in a skid; then he pushed into a harder skid. He wasn't at full power, and the plane settled right back down on the runway on its belly and came to an abrupt stop. We were lucky it didn't catch fire, because we had gasoline all over that airplane. All the pilots were there watching it. Fortunately, I had a fire truck there for the first time in days, and it came out alright. The next day, Jimmy Doolittle came back from Washington and he said, "I hear you had an accident." I said, "Yes, sir, but there's nothing wrong with the technique or the airplane. What was wrong was Bates. He just wasn't flying the airplane. The airplane was flying him." So Jimmy Doolittle said, "OK. You know, I'm going to the West Coast today, and we're going to pick up another instructor out there to give us some more of this." I said, "Well, you know, Colonel, it's a matter of professional pride with me. I don't want anybody on the West Coast telling you. Let's start all over again with this technique. If it's possible I'd like to go with you, if we're going to have time to do more of this practice out there." With that, he said, "OK, if it's all right with Washington, you can fly out with me this afternoon." So I called up Pensacola and had some laundry flown down. They picked up my airplane, anemometer, and junk and took it back, and I flew out to Sacramento, California, with Jimmy Doolittle.

We put the planes in the depot at Sacramento to get them all set to go aboard the carrier, and as one plane would come out of that interim overhaul period, I'd take it up with a crew to Willows, to a field there and practice takeoffs. Then, on the last day, Jimmy Doolittle said, "Well, we'll finish up at Willows, then we're going to fly down to Alameda and go aboard. How do you think they're doing?" I said, "Oh, I think it's no strain at all. I think everybody's doing great." He said, "Would you list the crews in order, 1, 2, 3, 4, etc.?" They were going to take 15 airplanes, and we really had, I think, 18 or 19 crews. So I listed the people in order of what I thought was their ability, and Colonel Doolittle and Major Hilger and a couple of others looked over this list. Major Hilger said that he thought Bates should be one of the crews that went and asked why I objected. I explained the accident and said, "After we crashed, they both were going to jump out of the windows, right into those whirling props, and I grabbed both of them, and said, 'Sit down and wait until those props stop, and turn off all your switches.' The switches were still on. I reached back to get my pencil, paper, notebook, came on back, the props had stopped, and they had jumped out. I looked and they had turned off all the switches and turned them all full on again. So I said, 'You know, when you get on over enemy territory and you have some of those Japs chasing you, you've got to really be sharp and you've got to be thinking all the time. If you panic, you're lost.' I wouldn't take Bates." They didn't take Bates, and I guess he is mad at me to this day, but I wouldn't have taken him.

When Jimmy Doolittle had asked me what I thought of the crews, I said, "You know, Colonel, if you want proof, I've had less time in the B-25 than anybody. You can take an extra one along, a 16th airplane, and when we get 100 miles out of San Francisco, I'll take it off, deliver it back to Columbia, South Carolina, to the Army, and go back to Pensacola." He didn't say "yea" or "nay." So I finished the day up at Willows checking out everybody I could, and I got in the last plane going to Alameda. When I landed at Alameda, Jimmy Doolittle came over to me and said he had just been aboard ship, where he saw some old Navy friends—Capt. Marc ("Pete") Mitscher, the skipper of the *Hornet;* Comdr. George Henderson, the executive officer; Comdr. Apollo Soucek, the air officer; and Marcel Gouin, the assistant air officer—and he said, "You know, I talked to them about your idea of taking an extra plane along and they go along with it, so we'll take 16 and launch you 100 miles out." I said, "Gee, that's great."

So 2 April arrived, the day of departure. We sailed just before lunch, and I was up on the flight deck with Jimmy Doolittle. We had parked the airplanes, and we had about 495 feet of takeoff run. Jimmy Doolittle said, "Well, Hank, how does it look to you?" I said, "Oh, this is a breeze." He said, "Let's get up in that airplane and look." So he got in the cockpit, and I was in the copilot's seat. Jimmy Doolittle said, "Gee, this looks like a short distance," and I said, "You see where that tool kit is way up on the deck on that island structure? That's where I used to take off in fighters on the *Saratoga* and the *Lexington*." He said, "Henry, what name do they use in the Navy for bullshit?"

With that, we went down to chow and just before finishing my dessert, they said, "Lieutenant Miller, report to the bridge." I got up on the bridge, and Mitscher said, "Well, Miller, I don't think I'll be able to give you 20 knots of wind over the deck." I said, "Captain, I don't need that, anyway, because we have 495 feet. I taught these guys how to take off from an aircraft carrier with 40 knots of wind and 250 feet. We have lots of room." Captain Mitscher said to me, "Well, Miller, do you have an extra pair of pants with you?" I said, "Oh, yes, sir. I brought all my baggage with me because I'm going to fly nonstop to Columbia, South Carolina." He said, "We'll take that extra plane." I told Pete Mitscher that I was tickled to death, too, because from the very beginning when

Lt. Col. James Doolittle's B-25 bombers, parked nose to tail on the flight deck of the USS Hornet *as it steamed toward Tokyo, April 1942.*

I heard there was going to be a raid on Tokyo I wanted to go to the takeoff spot, so I was delighted with that.

Every day, the pilots aboard the *Hornet* would get an intelligence briefing, check over all the equipment in the airplanes, and get in a sizable amount of poker playing. They roomed with Navy flyers. They were a great bunch of people. Of course, all of them were volunteers for this, and they knew that it was going to be pretty difficult. After they got through bombing Japan, they were supposed to fly down the coast, then cut in at the 38th parallel, and fly to Chuchow, a field that was going to be held by Chinese guerrillas. After landing, they were to take on enough gasoline from hand pumps out of drums to fly on from there to Chungking, then turn the planes over to Chiang Kai-shek and his people, and finally come out of China and back to the States. They were going to take off just before dark. Jimmy Doolittle was going to be off first and carry fire bombs to drop on his targets in the Tokyo area just at dusk. The other planes would be coming in afterwards, and they would be bombing targets in the Tokyo area from the light of the fires that were caused by Doolittle's bombs.

Well, the launch day, 18 April, arrived and everybody was supposed to stay in the ready rooms all day long. Lunch would be served there, because the task force was going to be at general quarters. They had to be on the alert. All planes were spotted for takeoff, tied down. It was a wet, windy, rough, miserable morning, and just at daylight the task force picked up a couple of Jap fishing boats. The cruisers started firing at the fishing boats, and they did a horrible job of hitting them. We had some *Enterprise* planes in the air that were dive-bombing and strafing the fishing boats. They also had a horrible time trying to hit them, and since Admiral Halsey, who was in charge, was afraid that the boats would get off a radio message to Tokyo, he sent a message over to the *Hornet* which said, "Launch Army pilots." When I got up on deck and told Colonel Doolittle, he said, "Would you help get the pilots in the airplanes?" So this I did.

We launched the first one at 8:25 that morning. Jimmy Doolittle was the first one off, and he did a fine job. He's a great aviator; he did it just like the book says. We were about 620 miles off the coast so we knew that the pilots really didn't have a chance of getting to China with those airplanes. It was just too far a trip. Additionally, they were hitting much stronger head winds than were anticipated going in to Tokyo. The position of the *Hornet* at eight o'clock in the morning of the 18th of April was "Imuboesaki Light bears 270 degrees, distance, 642 miles. Surface winds from 300 degrees. Force 26 knots." The planned distance was about 500 miles, and since this put them much farther out than we ever anticipated, we knew it was going to be a tough struggle getting in there.

All the Japanese fishing boats were equipped with radio. This was part of their reconnaissance safety force, you might say, off the coast of Japan. At 2:45 P.M. aboard the *Hornet,* Tokyo radio came on the air and said, "Enemy bombers dropped bombs in the area." They were all excited, and then they went off the air. We knew that the planes were in and the raid was successful.

There is an amusing story about Jimmy Doolittle and Roscoe Turner, two of the best aviators in the United States. After Jimmy had been called back into service by Gen. "Hap" Arnold to help get their war effort going, he ran across Roscoe in Cleveland, and Roscoe said, "Say, Jimmy, I've got an idea. You and I are probably two of the best aviators in the country. Why don't we get some of these kids organized on a bombing raid to bomb Tokyo?" Jimmy said, "Gee, that's a great idea, but I'll see you again, Roscoe. Hap brought me back in the air force, and I haven't had time to do anything, except just work." About a month later, he ran across Roscoe again, and Roscoe said, "Hey, Jimmy, what about that idea of mine?" Jimmy said, "Oh, I'll talk to you again about that." A short time afterwards, big headlines in the papers said, "Doolittle Dooed It," and with that, Roscoe went into a Western Union office and sent a message to Jimmy Doolittle. It said, "Dear Jimmy, you son of a bitch."

When we got back to Pearl Harbor, Captain Mitscher sent me over to see Admiral Halsey and get a set of orders reporting back to Washington to tell Admiral King about the raid, and then for me to report to Pensacola after that. It worked out very nicely that way. I got to Washington, D.C., after a very hectic ride across the Pacific in one of the Pan American clippers. I didn't know at the time when we crashed at Eglin Field that I had hurt my back, but it showed up and took me quite a while to get the soreness out. After I briefed Admiral King, I went back to Pensacola and went to an osteopath who got me fixed up in fifteen minutes' time.

I had started to work in my former job when I received temporary orders to go to Washington. It turned out the purpose of the trip was to help Jimmy Doolittle tell the Secretaries of the Army and the Navy about the raid from the Army and the Navy standpoint. We went over to the Mayflower Hotel, where a dining room was set aside for the Secretaries, the Assistant Secretary, Jimmy Doolittle, and myself. We had some drinks and dinner and lots of conversation on every aspect of the raid. The Secretaries seemed to be very appreciative of getting all the details from Jimmy Doolittle, everything that happened to him in China, and from the Navy side as far as the training of the people was concerned plus life aboard the *Hornet* right to the takeoff point. I enjoyed it; we had lots of conversation and questions. I think we told them just about everything that happened.

They were a great gang, all the Army Air Forces enlisted and officers. They got along beautifully with sailors and officers. We helped them maintain the airplanes. We even took one engine out, took it to pieces, and put it back together. It clicked 100 percent. I was proud of our handiwork, our accomplishment, because they all got off safely. They all did a great job. I think without a doubt every officer and man aboard the *Hornet* would have pinned every medal in the world on those people who went off that deck in those airplanes. They really had what it took, and when you look back at everything that happened subsequent to that, it was a big shot in the arm to the great American public. They saw we could do something. It shocked the Japanese people; it was hard for them to believe that we'd get through like that, and it helped to pull a lot of their forces back to protect Japan. So the raid had a great many things going for it, but at that time the biggest thing was morale for the American people.

≡

Prepare to Launch Aircraft

Captain Stephen Jurika, Jr.

Stephen Jurika, Jr., was born 9 December 1910 in Los Angeles, California, son of Blanche and Stephen Jurika. He was appointed to the U.S. Naval Academy in 1929, graduated and was commissioned ensign on 1 June 1933, and was designated a naval aviator in July 1936. Operational and staff duties included considerable time in the Far East, and his knowledge of that area was of considerable value to the Navy during World War II. Captain Jurika was Commander, Fleet Air Wing 14, and Commanding Officer, Stanford University Naval Reserve Officers Training Corps Unit, before his retirement on 1 July 1962.

In late 1941, Captain Jurika put the Hornet *in commission and served aboard her as intelligence and operations officer during the early battles in the Pacific war, until she was sunk during the battle of Santa Cruz on 26 October 1942. After two months recuperating from wounds, Captain Jurika became gunnery officer on the staff of Rear Adm. Marc Mitscher, Com-*

mander, Fleet Air Nouméa, and then operations officer for Commander, Air, Solomons. From August 1943 until early 1945, he served at the Naval Air Station, Jacksonville, Florida, and then became navigator of the carrier Franklin. *At war's end, he was chief of staff for Commander, Carrier Division 1.*

Captain Jurika's awards include the Navy Cross, Silver Star Medal, Legion of Merit, Commendation Medal, and Presidential Unit Citation Ribbon (two awards).

Capt. Stephen Jurika, Jr., intelligence and operations officer, USS Hornet, *1941–42; navigator, USS* Franklin, *1945.*

Off the east coast of Florida in early 1942, the Secretary of the Navy and Capt. Wu Duncan had come down to visit the *Hornet.* I was the ship's intelligence officer at that time, and, during their visit aboard, both Captain Mitscher and I had been talking to them concerning the possibility of launching a carrier strike or strikes against the Japanese mainland. Ultimately, we discussed the feasibility of Army Air Forces aircraft such as the B-25 or the B-26 twin-engine bombers being loaded aboard at some American port and launched on a one-way trip, bombing Japan en route, and landing either in China or in the Soviet maritime provinces.

At least a week or more before we arrived at Alameda in March 1942, Captain Mitscher told me, and I am sure that he had told Apollo Soucek, the air officer, that we were headed there to pick up B-25 bombers. In view of the conversation we had on the East Coast with Captain Duncan and Secretary of the Navy Frank Knox, we felt that something was up involving Army aircraft and that if a carrier were to be used it would probably be the *Hornet*. We had just completed refresher training with the air group, and the ship was ready to go on out to join the fleet, which sadly needed carriers at that time. When we had orders to go to Alameda instead of to Pearl Harbor, we knew definitely that we were headed for something more than just to join the fleet in the Pacific.

Sixteen B-25s were taxied down alongside the *Hornet* at Alameda Naval Air Station pier, with 70 officers and 130 enlisted men, all volunteers. Every now and then, one hears criticisms, generally from Air Force officers, that we blew the cover on the Tokyo raid by loading the aircraft at the Alameda Air Station on the flight deck and then steaming under the Golden Gate with these Army Air Forces planes visible to people in San Francisco Bay. This was presumably a tip-off that they were going to bomb some target. Of course, that's rather silly because every ship that was headed west and especially to Pearl Harbor or to Midway carried reinforcements. Since these planes obviously couldn't make the 2,190 miles from San Francisco to Honolulu, except under favorable wind conditions, carriers frequently went out with deck loads of aircraft. They'd be loaded to the gunwales and actually, if you weren't an expert, the average American would look at a carrier full of planes and it would make little impression. There were no photographs permitted, of course. Nothing was published in the newspapers. That was covered by the intelligence people. So I don't see really how it could be called a giveaway. You could be ferrying the planes down to San Diego, taking them to Hawaii, taking them to Australia, or any other place. It would have been difficult to put two and two together at that stage of the game and say that these planes were en route to bomb Japan.

We departed Alameda on 2 April and were due on target on 18 April. We bypassed Pearl Harbor. Vice Adm. William Halsey had been designated the task force commander, and his flagship was the *Enterprise*. We didn't rendezvous with him until after we passed Hawaii. We were accompanied by the cruisers *Vincennes* and *Nashville* and some destroyers. The idea was to get within 500 miles of Tokyo and then launch.

I think the initial reaction of most of the officers on the ship was that an all-volunteer crew like this had to be special in their ability to fly and desire to do something as a group. But in looks, in appearance, and in demeanor, I would say that they appeared undisciplined. Typical of this were the open collars and short-sleeved shirts, grommets either crushed or none at all in their caps, worn-out, scuffed-type shoes. They were not in flight clothing. These were people who had a chance to stay in the BOQ and clean up and come aboard the ship.

I would say that our initial impression was pretty well justified by their actions during the time they were on the *Hornet*. We seldom saw Doolittle. He would read, he would study, he would look at maps and charts. He did not come into the wardroom for all of the briefings with his pilots. The others would saunter in. A briefing would be set up for 8:30 in the morning, after breakfast; they would saunter in and the briefing scheduled for 8:30 wouldn't start before 9:00 or 9:15, sometimes as late as 9:30. And their attention span was very short, half an hour at the most. They would be interested up to a point, and yet, from my point of view, their lives were at stake. The success of a raid was at stake. I felt that they took it very, very casually, surprisingly so.

I did not notice a motivation on the part of the Army Air Forces pilots to keep in shape, top physical trim. It was just the contrary. Most of them slept in. Few of them came down to breakfast. Poker games were going, sometimes on a 24-hour basis. I know there were games that went for two or three days. Somebody would go to the wardroom during a meal and bring back enough to keep them from starving. I know that there was also some booze on board.

There were no organized exercises or drills, nobody was jogging around the deck, and there was ample space on the flight deck forward of the stack. It was completely clear. All the B-25s were located on the after section of the deck, from about midway on the island aft. So there was ample deck space.

Captain Mitscher and Lieutenant Colonel Doolittle spoke together quite a number of times, but to my knowledge Doolittle did not address his group during these morning brief sessions or some that were held in the afternoon, except on rare occasions, such as the day before they expected to be launched, when he got them together for sort of a pep and briefing session.

They told me that they would like to cover Japan, not just Tokyo, but Osaka, Nagoya, and Kobe, as well. That meant that, with only 500-pound bombs in each one of these aircraft, they were not going to make a big splash. They were not going to attempt to destroy a major plant like Fuji Steel or Japan Iron and Steel or one of the major petrochemical plants but, rather, were going in for psychological effect, not so much to damage as to have bombs actually drop on Japanese major cities and industrial areas.

Nevertheless, there were these 16 planes. As far as I was concerned, they were to take off with 64 bombs, and those bombs could do a lot more damage where planned than just dropped idly anywhere on marshlands or one of their filled lands. So we did agree on priorities of targets, and then I spent the rest of the time telling them about the locations of antiaircraft defenses and how these would be built up on towers and high buildings, machine guns and small guns, that the Japanese had used in China and up at Nomonhan against the Russians. I briefed the aircrews on the things we knew the Japanese had and the ways they used them.

Then, knowing where all the major buildings in Tokyo were, we would draw a line from that to a target that they wanted. The Diet Building, for example, on one of the highest hills of Tokyo, was something that you could fly over, go a very short distance, and be in Kawasaki, perhaps three or four minutes, no more than that, on a bombing run. The first major point under you would be the Tamagawa River, and just beyond that would be a major petrochemical works. You didn't have to estimate; you didn't have to use a stopwatch. You had these major physical points to look at.

We took out maps of the various cities and would point out these targets, including major buildings that would stick up. If you were down low, they would loom above the horizon. Fly over these and go on an absolute dead reckoning course, you then pass over a river and the next big complex that you see, with chimneys, belching yellow smoke, lay your eggs.

The ship supplied these charts and maps for the targets. They were not hydrographic charts because hydrographic charts all stop at the shore. They had a red dot and a circle, indicating the location of a radio beacon, a radio station, or some mountain, like Fuji.

I drummed into the crews the Chinese phrase *"Lusau hoo metwa fugi,"* which means "I'm American." And then I briefed them on ways to tell a Chinese from a Japanese. Generally speaking, the Japanese wore *tabi,* shoes that separate the big toe from the other four toes, and the Chinese never did. The way to tell whether you were in Japan or China, if you didn't know the landscape or were disoriented, was simply to look at people's feet. The Chinese have all their toes together and the Japanese have the big toe separated from the others because for years they've worn a thong between them.

The group had a major who was designated as the executive officer. Most of the rest of them were young captains and first lieutenants. I knew four or five of them to whom I would speak privately about things. They were the most interested of the group. These few would be interested in the capabilities of Japanese aircraft and life in Japan, and there was time to tell them something of the culture. I expected and told them that, while I couldn't assure them of this, if they were captured dropping bombs on Japan, the chances of their survival would be awfully slim, very, very, slim.

I figured they would be, first of all, paraded through the streets as exhibit A, and then tried by some sort of a kangaroo court and probably publicly beheaded. This seemed to settle them down quite a bit. These four or five that I got to know were much more interested in getting in and getting out, doing a job and getting out in one piece. I would say most of them were really fatalistic. It was a lark. They knew they'd get medals if they got through; they'd probably get promotions. They felt this was a way to "get back at the Japs." They were all light-hearted, except for Doolittle, who was all seriousness. He was the pro, no doubt about it.

These Air Forces people told us, and I knew from looking at their charts, where they were going. Most of them were headed for fields in the interior of China that had been prepared by Chinese with American technological assistance. These fields would be crushed rock and barely suitable to land a plane in, but by that time they would be low on fuel, no bomb load, and the plane would be as light as it could possibly be for a landing.

These fields would be ready; even if it were nighttime when they arrived, there would be no problem lighting the field through lanterns or bonfires or car headlights, and they would be able to sit down and then get out. It didn't happen that way, though. It turned out that there was not only fog shrouding the coast, but some of the fields had not been built. In general, the only part of it that went off without a hitch was their loading on board and their takeoff.

They told me their briefing down at Eglin Field in Florida was in short takeoffs, in effect, carrier takeoffs. Lt. Hank Miller, whom I knew very well and who had put in a lot of time on carriers before this, was certainly extremely well qualified to teach them this. What he really tried to instill in them, and I talked to Hank many a time on this, was confidence. For weeks, it seemed while they were training at Eglin, they were accustomed to simply taking off down the center of a runway and getting to V1, nosewheel up, V2, lift-off. Well, they'd keep that nosewheel on the ground as long as they could and then literally fly the planes off the runway. You just can't do that from a carrier. On the other hand, you seldom have 35 knots of wind over any given land runway, and we predicted in the North Pacific at least 15-knot winds, and we knew that

20 knots was nothing to the Army. We were prepared to have the *Hornet* go, if necessary, to 30 knots during takeoff, if there was a calm. They would have 30 knots of wind, which would mean that with the flight deck we had with the 16 planes set back, and Doolittle's the first aircraft to go off, when he got off, then obviously everybody behind him would feel much better.

When Hank Miller flew out to Alameda with these people, I did see him, and he said, "I've done everything I can for them, and there's nothing they don't know about short takeoffs. It's just when that deck is moving and they're taking off, will they go through with it?"

On 17 April, the day before launch day, when they loaded the bombs on the aircraft, we had one unusual ceremony. A medal that I had received from the Emperor of Japan was pinned onto the tail of a 500-pound bomb in Doolittle's aircraft. I had received this medal when I was Assistant Naval Attaché about 1941, on the occasion of my departure, as a gracious gesture of friendship. It was in commemoration of some special anniversary, not for special services rendered. It was sort of a curious memento. I mentioned that I had it on board with me, and Doolittle thought that it would be a wonderful gesture to photograph this medal being pinned to the tail of a 500-pound bomb and return it with pleasure to Tokyo. Photographs were taken of it by official Navy photographers.

We had to launch early in the morning on launch day, 18 April, because we ran across a line of Japanese picket vessels. The first thing that alerted me was gunfire from the *Nashville*. I do not know whether one of the cruisers picked it up on the radar. On the *Hornet,* we had not picked it up on the radar. I have read all manner of estimates of how far out we were. The Air Force airspeed meters were calibrated in statute miles, and they may have been right when they said 625 statute miles. But we were actually not too far, a half-hour flight, several hours by ship, from our estimated launch point.

We did not change course. We didn't even worry about gunfire, if any, from the small vessels. I stood on the flight deck and then went up to the bridge to get a better view, and I could see the salvos from the *Nashville* against a small Japanese picket vessel on our port, almost abeam. There were heavy swells and the picket boat was bouncing up and down. It would be on top of a swell and then it would be seen, then it would be down, and you couldn't see a thing except perhaps the top of its mast. The shell splashes were all around it, but it was still there.

I was pretty sure that the word had been flashed by radio to Tokyo. I felt certain that these ships were equipped with radio. Why else would they be put out so far? Certainly, there was no reason for them to turn and try to run. In a heavy sea like that, they couldn't possibly make it. If they didn't have radio, if they couldn't communicate at least with the Navy headquarters in Tokyo, certainly they could relay the message through the next ring of picket ships, and from there into Tokyo. These were fishing vessels, real fishing craft, but employed on a picket station.

Captain Mitscher called down and said, "Prepare to launch," and that meant, of course, to rouse all the pilots out of their bunks and get them in for a final briefing. This was early in the morning; there were heavy seas and a wind that I would estimate at least 15 to 20 knots. Visibility was excellent, absolutely excellent. I could see these picket boats I would estimate a mile and a half, maybe two and a half to three miles, off our port side, and there were other picket boats that you could see if you climbed up to the top of the bridge, over to starboard. I estimate that these craft were probably no more than about 10 to 18 miles apart. I was utterly convinced that the word would get in, and therefore there would be Japanese fighter planes in the air to greet our aircraft. The last thing that I could say to them was to come in low, not over 500 feet, on the approach, so they would be undetected. If, by any chance, the Japanese were conducting one of their usual air-defense exercises, they might even be considered part of the drill.

So there we were on the flight deck. Of course, the mechanics were up early. The Air Forces mechanics took good care of their planes. They manned the .50-caliber machine guns that were in the aftermount. The enlisted people were pretty solid citizens, maintaining the engines, revving them up now and then, checking everything about them. The planes were really ready to go, there's no doubt. Those people had worked on the planes. They were working on them all the time.

They started warming up the engines, topped off the tanks after the engines were warm and everything had been checked and tested and ready to go, full fuel, right up to the last bit of it. I understand that some of the people even carried 5-gallon gasoline cans inside the fuselage. Of course, these are awfully heavy, and, with the weight and balance already critical with the load of bombs and with people who had never before made a carrier takeoff from the carrier itself, and in a tossing, heavy sea, I thought that was cutting down the balance in their favor.

In any event, pretty soon the order came, "Prepare to launch aircraft," and we turned into the wind. We were headed toward Japan at the time and going as fast as we could, and spray was coming all over the place. Of course, here was the ultimate in really fine thinking, because of the rise and fall of the bow. You knew how long it would take them to run down that deck, the actual time on deck, and you wanted to start them as the bow started down because it would take them that length of time to get to within about, oh, 50 or 75 feet of the bow, and then, as the deck started to come up, you would actually launch them into the air at least horizontal but on the upswing, in fact, giving them a boost up into the air. You just couldn't take the chance that any of them would be launched with the bow down into the sea. That would have been near fatal, considering the state of training and the lack of practice of this group.

Doolittle's plane was spotted number one. There wasn't any doubt about that. He was the leader, and there was no doubt about who was running that show from the Air Forces point of view. I had a great deal of faith in him. I had met him in Annapolis when he took off in a Curtiss seaplane in an attempt to set a world speed record and couldn't get off the water, running down the Severn. He must have been doing a fantastic speed on the water, on these twin floats, but the plane was so heavy and with insufficient lift he couldn't get off the water. I met him on that occasion, and I had seen him once or twice before. He was all business, when business was necessary, and all fun and games when fun and games were indicated. But when business was to be done, he was one of the few people who not only knew his business but he was confident and he was competent.

From the first takeoff, and that was Doolittle, he was in the air, I would say he was 50 feet in the air within 50 feet of the bow. He went off with the least run and hopped right into the air. That was a great sign, because if he could do it everybody else could do it, too. They had a longer run and, as the planes went down the center of the flight deck, each succeeding plane had a little more room, a few more feet.

The planes were tied down; the wings were tied down and the fuselage, but when you warm up the aircraft the numbers of tie downs were reduced to the point where, ultimately, as the planes were beginning their takeoffs they were free. The pilot was holding the brakes, and there would be chocks on the wheels. The flight deck crew had the wooden chocks, and, when the plane came to rest and before your taxi director would give you a hand signal to move on up, the chocks were put down to prevent any possible slipping on the deck, or necessity for the pilot to hold the brake with his feet.

I don't think that it took an hour to get off 16 planes. I would estimate that they probably got off at intervals of about a minute to a minute and a half. Carrier planes take off at about 12- to 15-second intervals, and it would take about five or six times as long to move one of the B-25s, get them there, give them the signal to rev up, have them move their throttles forward, and then, when they were satisfied, away they were sent.

Only one of them dipped down over the bow to where my heart was in my throat, but he had used every inch of the deck pulling off and, as he went over, I was afraid his tail was going to hit the deck, which was still coming up, and that would have flipped him right into the sea. That, of course, would have been just a screaming mess. But he stayed level, started pulling his nose up, and I guess a quarter of a mile out in front of the bow, he came back into view and pulled up with the rest of them. There was no reason for anybody to have any trouble getting off that deck. If Doolittle could do it with the same fuel load, the same load of bombs and everything else, everyone else could do it very easily.

The captain asked me to go up to flag plot and we tuned to one of the Tokyo AM radio broadcast stations. We figured the time that the groups took off and formed into the groups that were going to the various cities. They did not fly off as one large group. There was no doubt about finding their way in. They'd be there in two, two and a half, hours. So I simply put on the headphones. After the Air Forces planes were off, every man in the maintenance crews, pilots, everybody was busy getting the planes down from the overhead and getting the other *Hornet* aircraft ready for combat air patrol and possible strike if that were necessary. Our planes were lashed to the overhead on the hangar deck; the fighters were lashed to the overhead, and the SBD dive bombers and planes like that had their wings taken off, or their wings were all folded. Many of these had been unbolted to store, stack them as tightly as you could on the hangar deck.

I sat up listening to the Japanese broadcasts from Tokyo. When I knew that the planes should have been in Tokyo and waited another 15 or 20 minutes, there was nothing to indicate from the broadcasts that there was any unusual event taking place. Nothing unusual. We learned that the attack had been successful by intercept from U.S. sources. We did not really know how many of the people survived. I think one plane had landed in Siberia, the others were scattered up and down the China coast.

With respect to the air-raid drill in Tokyo on 18 April, that air-raid drill had been scheduled for about a week beforehand. I heard it on the radio, which was tuned in to Station JOAK, a Tokyo station. It was very, very clear up there on the radio in flag plot. Announcements were being made to calm the people, that there were a few fighters in the air and the fire wardens and air-raid wardens were working during the morning at about the time the planes actually hit, at something like 30 minutes after noon.

I am encouraged to tell a story about Mrs. Jane Smith-Hutton, the wife of Lt. Comdr. Henri H. Smith-Hutton, the Naval Attaché and the Naval Attaché for Air at the time. She was sitting down to lunch when aircraft flew overhead. She could hear them and she knew they were bombers. There were no bombers scheduled to be over Tokyo, and then, she said, she looked up and saw the star and bar of the U.S. insignia. She insists that she said, "Those are American bombers, and I bet you that Lieutenant Jurika is in one of those."

After the war, in private conversations, I talked to some Japanese, including Adm. Mitsumasa Yonai, who was Navy minister during part of the war. He said that the Navy was extremely surprised that we had launched bombers from the carriers. They had not considered that. The planes that they had sent up looking for the *Hornet* or the task force, in fact, expected to make contact with the task force within 300 miles of the Japanese coast. They did not know these were bombers until they were actually over Tokyo and sighted them visually. They didn't know that these had come from carriers. They knew only two things and they ultimately put these two things together: a contact with the No. 23 *Nitto Maru,* which was destroyed by our cruisers; and the other was the appearance of these twin-engine army aircraft over Tokyo, several hours later. It was hard to put these two things together because these aircraft don't come ordinarily from ships.

We were certain of several things. First of all, the Zeros wouldn't come out 500 nautical miles. They'd never get back. Second, if the Japanese sent out bombers they'd have to send some pathfinders out first, and, in the meantime, we'd be making fair speed in the opposite direction. They wouldn't know where these planes came from, so they'd really have to launch about a 180-degree search from the northeast coast of Honshu all the way round to the south. This meant that they wouldn't launch their aircraft for hours, and we'd be so far out of range that even the bombers wouldn't have a chance to get out and back. So I don't think anybody was worried. The crews of our 5-inch guns were manning them. This was standard procedure when a ship was at battle quarters. We didn't run into any other picket ships on retirement.

We returned to Pearl [Harbor], arriving about 25 April 1942. We had been promised, I think, a two-week stay in Pearl because we'd been under way all the way from the East Coast, through the [Panama] Canal, convoying a group to Australia for a couple of days, then turning north into Alameda, all of April, and we'd been at sea for a long time. We were out of fresh food by the time we got back to Pearl; we were eating rice, beans, and potatoes. They had stocked the fantail with cases and cases of potatoes; all of them were sprouting. Everything was sprouting. We'd been out of eggs for some time. Our menu was fairly limited. It was down to staples. I remember we had canned beef, lots of Spam, and all kinds of pressed meats, things like that. That gets pretty tiresome.

But we felt a sense of accomplishment, I think, in getting them off, and getting off a strike at Japan. We felt the psychological impact would, irrespective of any damage they did, be a tremendous accomplishment, and even more, a boost for American morale after our succession of defeats in the Pacific.

Seventy-three out of 80 Army aviators survived that raid, and, as we know, Lieutenant Colonel Doolittle became Lieutenant General Doolittle and went on to greater things. The survivors have held an annual get-together, which is in the nature of a combined Memorial Day, rodeo, drinking contest, and Air Force Association publicity. I've been invited and have had a spot somewhere on the dais along with Rear Adm. Hank Miller and a number of other Navy members of the crew that got them started on their trip. The last few years, as all of us are getting older, the tales get a little bit wilder and it takes just a little bit less in the way of a cocktail to get tongues wagging. They are fantastic achievements and accomplishments. I'm sure they'll get better, as the numbers decline and the time separation between 1942 and whatever year it is enlarges. These annual meetings, convocations, one might call them, have become a hallowed rite. Indeed, the friendships that have developed as a result of people who really did not know each other at the time has been something that it's nice to see.

The *Lexington* and the Coral Sea

Vice Admiral Paul D. Stroop

Paul David Stroop was born in Zanesville, Ohio, on 30 October 1904, son of John H. and Margaret M. (Jacobs) Stroop. He entered the U.S. Naval Academy in June 1922, graduated and was commissioned ensign on 3 June 1926, and was designated a naval aviator in September 1929. He served in torpedo, bombing, scouting, and patrol squadrons in the 1930s, and subsequently served in various command and staff assignments ashore and afloat, advancing to the rank of vice admiral on 30 November 1962. Admiral Stroop was Commander, Naval Air Force, Pacific Fleet, from 30 November 1962 until his retirement, effective 1 November 1965.

During World War II, then Lt. Comdr. Stroop served as flag secretary to Commander, Carrier Division 1, aboard the Lexington *during the battle of the Coral Sea. Assignments on the staffs of Commander, U.S. Naval Air Forces, Pacific Fleet, and Commander, Aircraft, South Pacific, were followed by command of the USS* Mackinac, *a seaplane tender operating in the South and Central Pacific. In February 1944, he was ordered to the Navy Department for duty on the staff of Adm. E. J. King, Commander-in-Chief, U.S. Fleet, as aviation plans officer. Upon completion of this duty, he assumed command of the carrier* Croatan, *operating in the Atlantic.*

Admiral Stroop's decorations include the Legion of Merit with two Gold Stars, and the Commendation Ribbon, each with Combat "V."

Lt. Comdr. P. D. Stroop, Flag Secretary, Commander, Carrier Division 1, 1942. (Courtesy Vice Adm. P. D. Stroop, USN [Ret.])

Early in April 1942, Commander, Carrier Division 1, Rear Adm. Aubrey Fitch was temporarily based ashore at Pearl Harbor. I was assigned to Admiral Fitch's staff as flag secretary, tactical officer, flag navigator, and intelligence officer. I would receive the intelligence dispatches each day and prepare a summary of the situation for the admiral. Admiral Fitch received orders to go aboard the *Lexington* and proceed down into the South Pacific and ultimately into the Coral Sea action. In preparation for the upcoming events, *Lexington* was put in the Navy Yard at Pearl Harbor and a considerable number of 20-mm guns were mounted on her gallery decks around the perimeter of the flight deck. There were some other changes in the ship and we sailed finally from Pearl Harbor on 16 April in company with Rear Adm. Thomas C. Kinkaid's cruiser division and destroyers.

We continued towards the South Pacific, where we were ultimately to rendezvous with Rear Adm. Frank Jack Fletcher, who was flying his flag in *Yorktown*. Also, at the same time, we were to rendezvous with a force of Australian ships under Rear Adm. J. G. Crace, Royal Navy. We didn't realize, of course, that we were going into a carrier action with the Japanese at that time, but intelligence which we received on the way down indicated that there was a great deal of Japanese activity, particularly along the coast of New Guinea. Our mission was to go down and strengthen the U.S. forces in the South Pacific and probably make some raids on Japanese installations ashore.

We rendezvoused with the *Yorktown* group on 1 May 1942 and commenced refueling the task forces. I remember quite distinctly the first communication that we had from our Royal Navy friend, Admiral Crace, had to do with his evaluation of the importance of the Coral Sea area. In his first communication to Admiral Fitch and Admiral Fletcher, he said that he considered this area of the greatest importance and our combined forces should do everything they could to keep the Japanese from coming in to the Coral Sea area. Of course, at this time the Japanese had landed on the north coast of New Guinea and there was strong evidence that they were going to come around the eastern tip of New Guinea and make a landing at Port Moresby, which was an important outpost of the British Empire. The *Yorktown* finished refueling first, on 2 May, and on 4 May launched a series of strikes against Tulagi, with minimum damage to the Japanese. After that raid, that force joined up with the force of which we were a part, and the Australians, on 5 May, and we refueled on a southeasterly course until the night of 6 May. During the night, we changed course to a northerly direction to get us closer to the area where we thought we might find Japanese carriers.

The morning of 7 May, we sent out our scouting planes from the *Lexington* and the *Yorktown* on a regular planned search, which we had laid out the night before. We were searching not only for elements of the striking force, the two Japanese carriers, *Zuikaku* and *Shokaku,* but also we were quite interested in the Port Moresby Invasion Group, which was, according to intelligence, coming around the eastern tip of New Guinea Island. The battle plan was quite standard. It was something that we had used in peacetime maneuvers. We simply drew a limiting circle in the direction of the area of interest and assigned planes to go out on radii so that at the outer end of their search they would be twice visual distance apart. In other words, the objective was to cover the outer limits of your search sector completely. This was visual search, using the scouting planes, which went out about 175 miles. Unfortunately, on 7 May, the

Zuikaku and *Shokaku* had the advantage of weather cover, and they were not discovered by our forces on that day. The *Lexington* and the *Yorktown* also had some weather cover, and we were not discovered by the Japanese until very late in the evening.

We did get a contact report, I think from an Army Air Forces B-17, of the invasion force coming round the coast of New Guinea. So we sent our attack forces to the northwest to hit the Port Moresby Invasion Group. We assumed that the *Zuikaku* and the *Shokaku* were out of range. We didn't really know where they were because we hadn't seen them. We sent our attack force, torpedo planes, and dive bombers up to the eastern end of New Guinea and found the covering group for the Port Moresby Invasion Group, consisting of a number of ships, including a converted carrier, the *Shoho,* and four cruisers. Our forces immediately went in to attack, and it was a very successful attack, except that we had an overkill on the carrier. I think probably we put at least seven torpedoes in the carrier and many bombs, and it was sunk immediately. Looking back on this, it was too bad that the attack hadn't been better co-ordinated and some of the force spread around on other ships. But this being our first battle of that kind, everybody went after the big prize, and they sank this rather soft carrier very quickly.

I remember Lt. Comdr. Bob Dixon was leading one segment of the attack force, and we were out of voice communication with the force during the time of the attack and during part of the return trip, because of the distance. But, as soon as Bob Dixon could get a message through, he called the ship and he sent that message that became rather famous, "Scratch one flattop." We got our attack force back, and it was a very successful day. We hadn't found the main body of the Japanese, and, up until that afternoon, they hadn't found us either. Late in the afternoon, we were under a rather heavy cloud cover when we began getting indications on the radar screen of unidentified aircraft in the vicinity. We put fighters in the air and vectored them out. The *Lexington* fighters were led by Lt. Comdr. Paul H. Ramsey, who was skipper of the fighter squadron. The *Yorktown* fighters were also in the air, led by Lt. Comdr. James H. Flatley. The *Lexington* fighters were vectored in the direction of the uniden-tified aircraft, and Ramsey found a formation of Japanese attack planes which apparently had been sent down in our direction and had not found the *Lex-ington* and the *Yorktown*. He came out of a cloud behind them in perfect position. Immediately he was able to shoot down the last two planes in the formation. I remember Ramsey, during the cruise south, had grown a luxuriant mustache, and he had said that, as soon as he shot down his first Japanese plane, he would shave this mustache off. When he came back to the *Lexington*, he made a quick circle around the ship with his canopy open, and he was stroking his mustache, indicating that he wasn't going to have it much longer. He landed aboard and shaved it off that night.

On the evening of 7 May, we had recovered most of our planes, and we ran a cruising formation at dusk, when we sighted some lights coming over the horizon. On the *Lexington,* we thought that probably these were some of our own planes from the *Yorktown* returning. We were not sure that they had all their planes back. These planes were in very good formation. I remember noticing the port running lights of the formation all in a beautiful echelon, and one of the things that struck me as odd was that the red color of the port running light was different from the shade of running lights that we had on our own planes. They had a sort of a bluish tint, red-blue tint. About the time that we sighted these lights, one of our screen destroyers began firing at the planes. I remember a voice message went out over the TBS to the skipper of the destroyer, telling him to stop, that these were undoubtedly friendly planes coming in. This, of course, was not true; these were Japanese aircraft. The *Lexington* had sent a message out to the task force telling everyone that the airplanes were friendly and not to shoot. The skipper of the destroyer came right back on the radio and said, "I know Japanese planes when I see them." These were Japanese planes which had mistaken the *Yorktown* and the *Lexington* formation for their own ships, and they came in with their lights on, ready to get into the landing formation. There was a lot of confusion, but after they were identified as enemy planes everybody began shooting, and there were a lot of fireworks. The Japanese planes broke up their formation, turned out their lights, and disappeared. There was no night fighting at this point in the war. Night fighting came on later, although we had rather limited experience in night operations; most of the pilots were night-qualified for carrier landing. We felt that we could have limited night operations, but it wasn't a matter of routine at all.

We followed the group on radar and lost them at about 40 miles. I always figured that the Japanese carriers and American carriers after dark had gotten quite close to each other. Radar was not very well developed in that day, and they might have gone over the radar horizon. But another indication was that our intelligence unit tuned in on their airplane landing frequency, and we could hear the Japanese carriers talking to the pilots in the air. As a matter of fact, I even discussed with the admiral the possibility of having a destroyer attack that night, but he felt that the distance was probably too great and it would be too

difficult to locate them. They were talking in Japanese. I remember one conversation that was repeated to me. One of the Japanese pilots couldn't get his
wheels down, and the carrier told him that if he couldn't get his wheels down
he'd have to land in the water. They wouldn't take him aboard, didn't want to
clutter up their flight deck with a crash when they had other planes to bring
aboard. So after he got this order from his air group commander or the captain
of the Japanese carrier, he then requested that the carrier shine a light on the
water so he'd have a spot to land on. This was one little incident, but it
indicated that they were quite close, much closer than we thought they were,
and certainly somewhat surprising.

That ended the action on 7 May, and it was quite obvious to the Japanese
and to us that the carriers were fairly close to each other and that we probably
would have an engagement the next day. The Japanese carriers went north
during the night, and the *Yorktown* and the *Lexington* went west, getting their
air groups prepared for the next day's operations. On the morning of 8 May,
reveille for me was 3:30, and I began analyzing dispatches and getting ready
for launching the search group, which again was led by Lieutenant Commander
Dixon. The chief of staff, Commander Cornwell, and Admiral Fitch read all the
dispatches, and we discussed them together. We started our search groups out
right at daylight, and Lieutenant Commander Dixon took what he thought was
the most likely sector.

It turned out that he was practically right. The first sighting was made
about 8:15 A.M. by one of Dixon's squadron pilots, who sighted the *Zuikaku*
and the *Shokaku* and sent the message back. Dixon himself then moved over
into that sector and sent the young pilot on back. He stayed as long as he could
in the vicinity of the Japanese carriers, giving us location, speed, and direction
of their movement. He did a perfectly classic job of shadowing these carriers,
taking advantage of cloud cover when he could and reporting back to us. I
might add that Bob Dixon, in my opinion, was one of the great heroes of this
two-day operation. He had led the attack on the *Shoho,* which was very
successful, and then he did this tremendously fine job of shadowing *Zuikaku*
and *Shokaku* and surviving, although remaining in the vicinity of enemy
carriers was considered a very dangerous thing to do. Dixon did it and got away
with it. He had been a test pilot at Anacostia and had learned early in the game
how to economize on fuel and get the most out of an engine. This certainly
stood him in good stead that day, because he stayed in the vicinity of the
carriers much longer than anybody thought he could. When all the search
planes came back and Bob Dixon hadn't arrived, we figured that something

had happened to him. About an hour after everybody thought he would be out of fuel, he showed up all by himself over the horizon, came back, and landed aboard. He was a great guy and an outstanding professional naval aviator.

After the initial report came, the decision was made to send off the attack planes from the *Yorktown* and the *Lexington* to make a coordinated attack on the *Zuikaku* and the *Shohaku*. The distance was a little greater than we wanted for all of our air group, particularly the TBDs, the torpedo planes, which were carrying the heavy torpedo loads and would not have too much range. We sent them out at about maximum range, and the *Lexington* and the *Yorktown* then remained in the vicinity on various courses and speeds, waiting for the return of the scout planes, which they took aboard, and then headed north to wait for the attack planes to come back. The *Lexington* and the *Yorktown* were in an area of good visibility, whereas the *Zuikaku* and the *Shokaku* still had the advantage of cloud cover, which, to a considerable degree, affected the action. A good many of our attack planes could not even make contact with the *Zuikaku* and the *Shokaku*. Those that did damaged one carrier, the *Shokaku*, with three bomb hits. However, the Japanese managed to control the damage and to get away.

I recall that the *Lexington* air group commander, Comdr. Bill Ault, arrived over the enemy carriers with, I think, only 4 dive bombers in his division, plus 6 fighters and 11 torpedo bombers. The attack was not a coordinated attack, due to weather and enemy resistance. When he got over the enemy carriers, he went on in and attacked, scoring a direct hit on the *Shokaku* with his bomb. A combination of the weather and uncoordinated attacks, I feel, made us less than successful in attacking the *Zuikaku* and the *Shokaku*. We should have been more effective than we were.

At 10:55 A.M., we began getting radar indications that enemy aircraft were approaching, and I remember making an entry in the war diary at that time, because I thought maybe later on I wouldn't be able to make entries in the log. I was keeping the war diary in longhand in a ledger on the bridge. I made an entry at 11:20 A.M.: "Under attack by enemy aircraft," and that turned out to be exactly right. At 11:20, we began seeing enemy aircraft overhead, and they came down in a very well coordinated attack, with torpedo planes and dive bombers. I can remember standing on the bridge and watching the enemy dive bombers come down. These were fixed-landing-gear dive bombers, and you were convinced that the pilot in the plane had the bridge of your ship right in his sight. Fortunately, they were not strafing, because if they had been, I'm sure that they would have made the topside untenable. The instant he released his bomb, you could see the bomb taking a different trajectory from the aircraft itself, generally falling short because their dive wasn't quite as steep as it should have been.

I watched this a number of times. I was fascinated to watch the bomb leave the airplane and realize that it was probably going to fall short. The torpedo planes came in about the same time—a fine, nicely coordinated attack—and launched their torpedoes at about a thousand yards. They were down to flight deck level when they dropped the torpedoes. First, you saw the plane coming in and drop his torpedo in the water and saw it splash. Then you could see the wake of the torpedo directed toward the ship, and finally, since most of these torpedoes were fired from the port side, and we were on the bridge of the starboard side of the ship, you would lose sight of it, probably 100 yards out before it hit the ship. You didn't know really whether it was going to hit the ship or pass ahead, astern, or go underneath. Then you waited for the explosion. You heard an explosion and you saw some water come up in that general vicinity, so if it hit, there wouldn't be really any doubt in your mind that it had hit. As a matter of fact, if you were in the general vicinity of a hit, you could be hurt; the shock to the deck you were standing on was enough to break people's legs if a torpedo hit in that general vicinity. So there was no doubt about it; as remotely situated as we were up on the 06 level on the bridge of the *Lexington,* we could feel those torpedoes. Of course, there were other things going on at the same time. We were watching enemy airplanes fly by; we were watching dive bombers coming in, so it is a little difficult to be accurate in accounting for all of this. My impression was we sustained two bomb hits and four torpedo hits.

I might add that, in the battle report that was finally sent out later, only two torpedo hits were recorded officially. I personally believe this is wrong. I think the *Lexington* probably took four, all on the port side and pretty well distributed along the length of the ship, because immediately after the attack we took a port list and I watched some of the torpedo planes passing from port to starboard. It was pretty discouraging to see these Japanese launch their torpedoes and then fly very close to the ship to get a look at us. They were curious and sort of thumbed their noses at us; we were shooting at them with our new 20-mm and not hitting them at all. The tracers of the 20-mm were falling astern of the torpedo planes.

At this point, the senior people were completely helpless. They were depending on the training that had been given to the fighter pilots in the air and on the training and practice the gunners had. The commanding officer of the ship, Capt. Fred Sherman, was very busy twisting his ship, trying to avoid torpedoes. I think he was successful in some cases, but he wasn't successful completely. We had fighters overhead, and they were credited with knocking down some Japanese planes. As a matter of fact, we saw one or two come tumbling down. We had also taken some of our dive bombers and put them on close-in stations as defense against the torpedo planes, figuring that they could overtake them possibly and disrupt the torpedo plane attack. They were not successful, and the torpedo planes pretty much got through.

One of the most spectacular of our bomb hits was on the port gun gallery. A bomb exploded and immediately killed or burned gun crews in that area. I walked down there when the attack was over, and here were the Marine gunners burned right at their stations on the guns. That particular bomb started a fire down in the officers' country the next deck below; the admiral's living quarters were set on fire, and a couple of stewards who were down in the pantry in that area were killed. I considered going down later to get into the stateroom to take some gear out of the safe, and it couldn't be done. We had another bomb in the after part of the island, or stack, and a near miss pretty well aft damaged the boat pocket where the captain's gig was stored.

All these bombs started fires, which we figured we could control and put out. We learned a lot from this action—that ships of that kind were tinder, with too much inflammable stuff aboard. The furniture in the admiral's cabin, for example, was wood and fabric that burned. Paint all over the ship had an oil base, and, wherever we got a fire, the paint on the bulkhead burned. That was something that had to be corrected. We learned that our fire-fighting equipment was not adequate, that we needed to redesign our hoses and hose nozzles so as to have fog instead of solid water. These were lessons that came out of the war and which were quickly used to improve situations on other ships.

Even though we took two bombs and four torpedoes, we were still able to make 24 knots, and we had the ship under control. An hour after the attack, we had the ship back on an even keel by counter flooding. The damage control officer came up to the bridge, and I saw him discussing things with the captain after he had gotten the ship on an even keel. His station was down in central station, where he took charge of the damage control parties and counter flooding. After the attack, we were able to steam into the wind and land some aircraft aboard, including Bob Dixon who had been out there scouting. The *Yorktown* was also suffering the same kind of attack. She took one bomb that I recall went down about four decks and exploded, killing over 30 people, but she was in much better shape than the *Lexington* and was able to have her damage repaired and go on to the battle of Midway.

We kept under way making about 24 knots, and, after we got our planes back aboard, the decision was made to head for Australia. The other ships formed up—the cruisers and destroyers and the *Yorktown*—and we were headed for Brisbane. At 12:47 in the afternoon, we heard a rather loud submerged explosion; my first reaction was that a Japanese submarine had sighted us and fired a torpedo which probably had an influence fuse and had gone off under the hull. It seemed like that kind of an explosion, right under the ship, deep down. However, when this explosion occurred, we found out later it was not an enemy torpedo at all; it was gasoline fumes. Leaking fuel caused by the bomb hits had collected in the compartments surrounding the IC Motor Generator room, and some spark had set off the fumes. The immediate effects were quite disastrous. As soon as this explosion occurred, communication between the bridge and central station was lost, and later testimony showed that Pop Healy, the damage control officer, and most of his crew down in central station were wiped out at that time.

More explosions occurred at 2:42 and 3:25 P.M., and finally word came engineering spaces were untenable and had to be abandoned, so the engineering crews on watch shut down the main engines. So, by 4:00 P.M., the ship was dead in the water, and, worst of all, there was no fire-fighting capability for the ship. All power was lost. From then on, the case was hopeless. We actually had a destroyer alongside to try to get hoses over, but to no avail. The fires began increasing in size, and at 4:52 P.M. the decision was made to get the wounded and the air group personnel off the ship. These people were not needed in the fighting of fires, and they could be useful if the ship were lost, which we began to feel would happen. They brought destroyers alongside to get these people off.

Some of our planes had landed on the *Yorktown,* but the majority were still on the *Lexington,* and they were lost with the ship. All we hoped to do was save personnel, without belongings. We continued trying to fight the fires, but it became increasingly evident that the ship not only couldn't be saved but that it was very dangerous to stay aboard much longer. Fires had gotten increasingly violent on the hangar deck, and we were beginning to get explosions. On the hangar deck, you could hear an explosion, towards the fantail on the hangar deck, that sounded like a freight train rumbling up the hangar deck. Actually, it was a rushing wall of flame which would erupt around the perimeter of the elevator. These flames would shoot up two or three feet, and these were occurring with increasing frequency. Finally, Admiral Fitch, in order to ease the captain into making the proper decision, said, "Well, Fred, it's about time to get the men off." This was around 5 o'clock in the afternoon.

So the order was given to abandon ship; everybody sensed this was the proper thing to do, and they ought to do it in a hurry. We had lines over the side, the sea was calm, the water was warm, and it was still daylight, so it was a pretty good situation. There were destroyers and cruisers in the vicinity of the ship, so that we had places to go. The men started going down over the side on lines and being picked up by boats from the other ships. We didn't have any of our own boats in the water. We had a destroyer alongside almost continuously, taking off the wounded first, and then the air group, and later on they were taking off other people when this order was finally given.

We had a total of about 2,735 people on board. Strangely enough, loss of life was rather minor. About 216 people were lost in this total action, many of whom were killed in the initial attacks, and then from the internal explosion down deep in the ship, where it wiped out most of the crew of the central station. I'm sure others were lost throughout the ship due to smoke and fighting fires, and there may have been a few lost in abandoning ship. This we don't know. I remained on the bridge with Admiral Fitch and other members of his staff. We were probably the last to abandon ship, except for the captain.

We all left the bridge area about the same time. By this time, it was quite noticeable that everybody else had gone. Captain Sherman went down on the flight deck and made a trip aft and inspected the ship to see that everybody was off. He intended to carry out the tradition to be the last man off the ship. The admiral and the few of us on the staff who were left selected port side, forward, as the place where we would go over the side. I remember going across the flight deck and realizing it was pretty hot and pretty soon the whole thing was going to be in flames. Port side, forward, we had what little breeze there was that made that the coolest part of the ship. We got up to the port side of the flight deck, and there were these lines all hanging over the side, large mooring lines that made it very easy to haul yourself down into the water. Boats from the other ships were close aboard, ready to pick up survivors.

Actually, we had plenty of time, about half an hour. I remember, as we crossed the flight deck, one rather interesting incident. The admiral's Marine orderly was still with Admiral Fitch, and the orderly walked across the flight deck in absolutely correct position, one step to the left and one to the rear, carrying the admiral's coat over his arm. The admiral was the only officer who arrived on the rescue ship with a jacket, just because the Marine orderly had taken it with him. The Marine orderly also had kept all of the dispatches that were handed the admiral during the action. This was to be important later on. My job as flag secretary had been to keep the war diary, which I was keeping in longhand on the bridge. Just before I left the bridge, I tore all the pertinent pages out, folded them up in a square, and stuffed them in my pocket. This too was useful in writing a battle report later.

We arrived up at the forward port edge of the flight deck just as it was getting dark. The sun was going down, and the boats that had been in the water picking up survivors were all heavily loaded and headed back to their ships. There was no boat immediately available for the admiral and the rest of us, so I silhouetted myself against the edge of the flight deck and began trying to attract attention from the nearest cruiser. Pretty soon, I got an acknowledgment by searchlight, and they saw that I was trying to semaphore to them. This was 1942, and I hadn't semaphored a message in 15 years, but it all came back. I sent a message in wigwag semaphore, "Send a boat for admiral." They got the message, and right away a motor launch came round from the bow of the cruiser and headed right for our spot. When the boat was quite close, we started getting ready to go down the lines and get into the boat. The admiral's orderly tried to insist that the admiral go first. He was still very proper, and finally the admiral got a little annoyed and ordered the orderly to go down. The admiral, of course, wanted to be the last one to leave the flight deck.

The communications officer, Lieutenant Bowen, and I had selected the same line to go down, and we didn't argue over protocol. I got on the line first and started lowering away. I had been a rope climber at the Naval Academy, and I never felt stronger in my life. So I started down the line, and I got down to the water, but I didn't want to get wet. The boat wasn't quite there yet. I'd timed my descent so that I'd get there about the time the boat came. So I stopped with my feet just short of the water, and I felt Lieutenant Bowen's feet on my shoulders. He was much heavier and longer and didn't have the arm strength. He couldn't hang on any longer, and he said, "Pardon me, sir, while I pass you." So, he went clear down, dropped off the line and went in the water. The admiral and the orderly were still arguing about who should go down first, I think. The boat got under their line and picked the admiral and his orderly up dry shod, so they got off the ship dry. The orderly still had the admiral's coat and the dispatches. I hung on the line until the boat came over and picked me up.

Then we cruised down along the side of the ship, picking up a few individuals that had come down and were still in the water. The rescue craft did a very fine job, picking everybody up. As far as I know, they searched up and down the side of the ship and nobody was lost from not being able to be found in the water. Captain Sherman was rescued by another boat and put aboard the

Hammann. We were taken over to Admiral Kinkaid's flagship, and, as soon as we got aboard, we went right up to the bridge. It was getting quite dark and just about the time we got to the bridge of the cruiser, there was a tremendous explosion on the *Lexington,* and the no. 2 elevator, right abeam of the island, lifted out of the ship. There was a sheet or solid mass of flame just the size of that elevator that came up and went as high as the mast of the ship, and the whole mass of the bridge area broke out in flames. It was quite spectacular, silhouetted against the night sky. If the decision hadn't been made when it was to get the men off, there would have been a lot of people lost because anybody who was in that bridge area would have been enveloped in that flame.

It seemed to be an awfully difficult decision to make, to abandon ship at that time. Here was a very valuable ship; she had a very brave and stubborn captain, and he just didn't want to make the decision to leave the ship. As a matter of fact, I think finally the admiral recognized this and encouraged that decision by making it himself. We on the staff had been advising the admiral for about half an hour or an hour that this was the thing to do. The ship was dead in the water, there was no power, the fires and the explosions were increasing throughout the ship, and to remain aboard made no sense at all. The only thing that I could fault was that the decision wasn't made earlier. It could have been made an hour earlier and would have left even more time. Whether or not we lost anybody due to confusion of the last half hour, I don't know. The process might have been a little more orderly, though it wasn't bad. There was no panic, no confusion. Everybody did what he was supposed to do, and it was done, I think, in a quite creditable manner.

After our rescue, we proceeded to the bridge and, of course, all eyes were turned on the *Lexington.* They had heard this tremendous explosion which I spoke of earlier, and following that the whole top side of the ship was in flames. We had over 30 aircraft parked, tied down in the launching area of the flight deck, and many of these aircraft were loaded with ammunition in their fixed guns and with fuel in their tanks, and they made a most spectacular fire. As the aircraft began to burn, the ammunition cooked off and the night sky was filled with tracers coming up off the afterdeck of the *Lexington,* as well as this fire which was still engulfing, outlining the entire bridge area clear up to the top of the mast. It was a spectacular sight.

The task force then was ordered to steam away, and one destroyer, the *Phelps,* was left behind with orders to sink the *Lexington.* We felt very sorry about the whole business and wondered what could have been done to have prevented it. I guess the ship I was on was about 10 miles away when the

Phelps fired her torpedoes. I was down in one of the officer's state rooms getting cleaned up, and we felt the effect of a tremendous underwater explosion. I sensed at the time that this must have occurred after the *Lexington* had gone down, and to this day I don't know really what caused that explosion, but I read later that the *Phelps,* which was closest to the ship, felt the same thing. As a matter of fact, the captain of the *Phelps* reported that he thought he had been torpedoed. He himself had launched eight torpedoes against the *Lexington*—four had exploded. This had occurred earlier, and the ship sank from the effect of those torpedoes. But what caused this tremendous underwater explosion when the *Lexington* might have been down several hundred feet below the surface, I don't know.

Eventually, Admiral Fitch's staff reassembled in the *Yorktown,* in Tongatabu in the Friendly Islands, and it was here that I organized the carrier part of the battle report for the Coral Sea action. I forgot to mention earlier that on day of the battle, the morning of 8 May, Admiral Fitch received a message from Admiral Fletcher, who was senior and who was in command, directing Admiral Fitch to take tactical control of the fleet. This was another admission, or recognition, that an admiral with aviation experience and a staff with aviation competence and background should be in charge of these kinds of combat operations. So, for the rest of the day until after the action, Admiral Fitch was in tactical command. I believe that Admiral Fletcher, who was still in the *Yorktown,* directed Admiral Kinkaid to take charge of the rescue operations. Of course, when the *Lexington* sank, Admiral Fitch and his staff were off the ship, and they had no official responsibilities. We were survivors.

We were aware at the time that the battle had an effect on the Japanese advance in the Pacific. This discouraged the Japanese, who canceled the invasion of Port Moresby and turned round and went back to land on the north coast of New Guinea. We didn't realize how long this was going to stay that way, we didn't realize that it was a major turning point of the war, and we didn't know what was going to happen next. Actually, the Japanese then came down and landed on Guadalcanal, after that. I remember quite distinctly a day or two before the battle, I was on the bridge of the *Lexington* with one of our very capable intelligence people, who was a Japanese language officer, and we were looking over charts. He pointed to Guadalcanal and said, "This is going to be important in the immediate future."

≡

A Beautiful Silver Waterfall

Admiral John S. Thach

The *Yorktown* left Pearl Harbor on 30 May 1942 after a quick repair of her damage in the South Pacific at the battle of the Coral Sea. The *Yorktown* was about 50 or 100 miles off Pearl Harbor when the air group landed aboard. VF-3, my squadron, had been augmented with airplanes from VF-42 to bring our complement to 25 operational airplanes. The *Yorktown* was to join the *Enterprise* and *Hornet* and form two task groups. Capt. Elliott Buckmaster was commanding the *Yorktown* and Rear Adm. Frank Jack Fletcher and his staff were aboard as Commander, Task Force 17. Adm. William F. Halsey was in the hospital with a very severe infection of the skin, so Rear Adm. Raymond A. Spruance was sent to take his place. Admiral Spruance, Commander, Task Force 16, had most of Admiral Halsey's staff with him. But Admiral Fletcher, an aviator, was the senior officer, although he had a more or less nonaviation staff; in other words, it was not a staff designed to operate aircraft carriers.

Before I left Pearl Harbor, I was given very brief indications of the fact that we expected an attack and there was obviously a big battle coming up in the middle of the Pacific. That's about all I was told before I landed aboard the

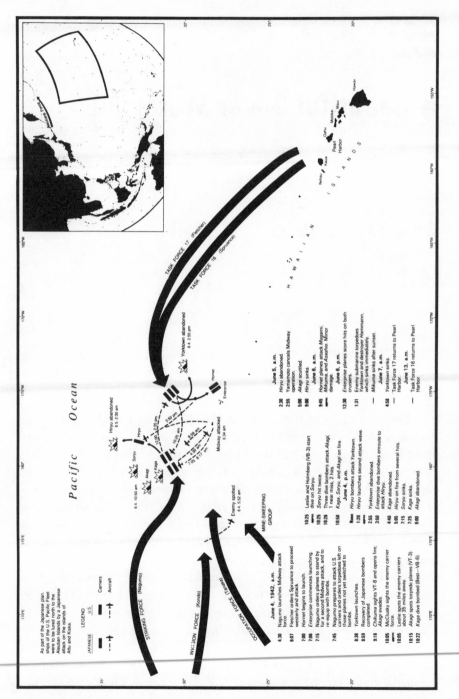

Battle of Midway, showing carrier actions, 4–5 June 1942. (Courtesy NASM)

Yorktown. That night, after we were all aboard and everything was buttoned up, all of the squadron pilots were brought into the wardroom and Comdr. Murr Arnold, the air officer of the *Yorktown,* gave us a complete briefing on everything they knew about the opposing Japanese forces and their probable intentions. So we had a day or so before we arrived in position, and before the Japanese arrived, to think about it. There was no doubt in my mind of the vital importance of the impending action because of the indications that there was a large Japanese force coming. They didn't tell us at the time that the Japanese code had been broken and they were getting most of their information that way, but very soon, of course, Navy patrol planes did pick up a large force, and so that was all verified then. The Japanese obviously had the intention of coming in towards one of the Hawaiian Islands, and the objective must be Midway first. They had more than enough to take Midway, so after doing that they probably would consider charging on down the Hawaiian Island chain, Midway being about 1,000 miles from Honolulu.

After getting this briefing, it was obvious that a very serious and crucial engagement was coming up and we were all mightily impressed. It meant that if we could win this one, we might be able to stop the Japanese advance. So the time that we had before we finally launched our strikes we utilized in getting all the ammunition ready, carefully checking and rechecking each airplane. I remember the night before we had been having trouble with an engine on one of my squadron's F4Fs, and I wanted every one of our 25 planes in commission. I went down to the hangar deck and talked to my engineering chief and he said all the planes were going to be up, and I knew they would be. There wasn't any question about it. This man knew what he was doing, and he had a good crew working for him.

I got word that Maxwell Leslie, the commanding officer of the dive bomber squadron, VB-3, was going to lead it, along with part of VS-5, the scouting squadron. Lem Massey would lead the torpedo squadron, VT-3. We decided that we should have a conference. I'd talked a little bit to Lem Massey before and told him I thought that the fighter escort should go with him instead of at high altitude with the dive bombers. He said, "I think you ought to get up with the dive bombers because that's where the Zeros are going to be. That's where they were in the Coral Sea battle." So we had our conference, and we were trying to decide whether the fighter escort should go with the dive bombers or the torpedo planes; we knew we weren't going to have enough to split them and send a few with each. I had a plan, and I thought it was approved to take eight fighters because I wanted two divisions, that was the basic tactical breakdown that we had developed. I couldn't believe that anybody would try to break this up, because if you're going to send any number of airplanes, it's got to be divisible by four, otherwise you've left two planes without wingmen. So we planned to take eight. Max Leslie said he thought that I should go with the torpedo planes, and I said, "How about letting me decide it?" Because they were playing Alphonse and Gaston, trying to give the fighters to the other squadron, I decided that, since in the Coral Sea battle the torpedo planes had gotten in pretty much unopposed and done the work in sinking ships, the Japanese would be more concerned about the torpedo planes. The way to sink ships is to put a hole in the side of the ship below the waterline; that's the best way to do it. That's what a torpedo's designed for; the Japanese know this, and they're going to be very concerned about any torpedo attack and try to knock it out before it gets there. So they all finally agreed that I would go with Lem Massey and VT-3.

During the night of 3 June, I thought a lot about whether the torpedo planes could get in or not, and I knew that, if the Japanese were together in one formation and had a fighter combat air patrol of defending fighters from all the carriers, we would very likely be outnumbered. We were also quite concerned with the fact that the Zero fighter could outperform us in every way. We felt we had one advantage in that we thought we could shoot better and we had better guns. But, if you don't get a chance to shoot, better guns matter little. I was thinking about all of this and also which pilots I would take with me. I picked out the ones I thought would do a good job. I didn't sleep much that night, but we were all pretty optimistic because we felt that we were going to get tactical surprise. We didn't think the Japanese knew that we were anywhere near there, and this was a great morale builder, when you think you're going to have one of the basic principles of warfare on your side—surprise.

I suppose we could have taken eight planes with the bombers and eight with the torpedo planes, but that decision was not mine, and I have to agree with it, under the circumstances. Buckmaster, or Fletcher, I guess, made the decision that next morning before we launched that we would have only six fighters to go, and I didn't have time to work my way up to him to talk to him about it, but I did go to Murr Arnold. I said I was appalled that the *Yorktown* was in one task group separated from the *Enterprise* and the *Hornet,* but I wasn't too worried at the time because I thought they would stick close enough for mutual defensive support. But the next morning we were separated by at least 20 or 30 miles, and Captain Buckmaster, I suppose, made the decision—I never found out who made it—that I could have only six fighters to go. He

TBD Devastators of Torpedo Squadron 6 prepare to launch from the USS Enterprise, *4 June 1942. Each of the three U.S. torpedo squadrons was decimated by Japanese fighters during attacks on the enemy carrier force.*

wanted to keep as many as possible back to defend the *Yorktown* because if you send a strike against an enemy carrier force, usually you can expect attacks on your own carriers. So I had to quickly revise the formation that we were going to fly over the torpedo planes.

We did have a last-minute briefing before we took off, although I had spent so much time trying to get my six-plane escort changed back to eight that only a few minutes remained before takeoff time. I told the people that were going with me that I wanted that formation to stick together, that nobody was going to be a lone wolf, because lone wolves don't live very long under the circumstances we were going into. They just had to stick together no matter what happened because I was convinced, and I thought they were, too, that was the best way to survive and protect the torpedo planes. I said our primary job was to protect the torpedo planes and keep the enemy fighters engaged as much as we possibly could, all the way in and all the way out. It was a pretty serious thing because we had gotten the information now on really how big they were.

Then word came for escort pilots to man their planes. I still had some misgiving about my inability to get eight airplanes instead of six. I was mad, but I realized that it wasn't primarily the fault of the man who made the decision; if he's going to be out alone with only one carrier, he's got to have enough fighters to have a strong combat air patrol. Six isn't divisible by four, so I had Ram Dibb as my wingman with Macomber as my other section leader, and his wingman was Ed Bassett. That left two, Tom Cheek and Sheedy. So I decided that we would put them just astern of the torpedo planes, more or less under my four, down at a slightly lower altitude than I would fly. I would fly 1,000 or 1,500 feet above the torpedo plane formation, and down sometimes below them, and on the same level during the battle. The torpedo plane formation was in the shape of a triangle, sort of a V of Vs; that's the way they would fly up to the target until they had to split and spread out to make the torpedo attack. We had to do S-turns to slow down so we wouldn't run away from them because they were so slow. We didn't want to be stalling along with no ability to maneuver in case something hit us before we anticipated it.

It was a beautiful day. There were little puffy clouds up around 1,000 feet to 1,500 feet that sometimes would get a little thicker and other times they'd open up and be very scattered. It was that way all the way into the enemy formation. We took off later than the *Enterprise* and *Hornet*. They started taking off at 7:00 A.M., and we didn't start taking off until around 8:40. By 9:00 A.M., I was in the air and departed *Yorktown*. A strange thing happened on the way. We were flying along, and, all of a sudden, ahead of us and out a little bit to the side, there were two big explosions in the water that threw the water way up high. I hadn't the slightest idea what they were. There didn't seem to be anybody around, but I sort of wondered if someone hadn't inadvertently dropped a couple of bombs, and that's exactly the way it turned out. In arming the bombs—the arming device worked in a way that released the bomb as well as arming it—a couple of the planes in Max Leslie's squadron had inadvertently jettisoned their bombs.

So we went on. All of us were, of course, highly excited and admittedly nervous. I think most other people did pretty much what I did—kept going over my checkoff list, and as soon as we got in the air I had each section test their guns so they'd be all ready, and all the switches on and not on safety. This seemed to work all right, so on we went. Lem Massey made a small change of course to the right. We took off on a heading of about southwest, and I wondered why he did that. I wondered if he'd gotten some more information, but about that time, looking ahead, I could see ships through the breaks in the

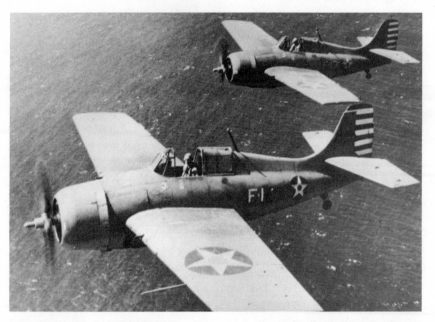

Jimmy Thach (F-1) and Butch O'Hare (F-2), flying obsolete F4F Wildcats, developed the Thach Weave as a defensive maneuver to counter the superior performance of the Japanese A6M Zero fighter.

little puffy clouds, and I figured that was it. We had just begun to approach about 10 miles from the outer screen of this large force; it looked like it was spread over the ocean, and several colored antiaircraft bursts appeared out in our direction— one red one and another orange—and then no more. I wondered why they'd be shooting at us because we weren't even nearly in range. The bursts were obviously fired from the nearest ship, which was quite a distance from the main body of carriers and battleships, but we soon found out what that was. We'd been sighted from the surface screen, and they were alerting the combat air patrol. A very short time after those bursts occurred, before we got anywhere near antiaircraft range, Zero fighters came down on us. I tried to count them, and I figured there were 20.

The first thing that happened was that Bassett's plane was burning. He pulled out, and I didn't see him anymore. He was shot down right away. I didn't see the Zero that got to him, but I realized later that they were coming in a stream on us from astern. I was surprised that they put so many Zeros on my six fighters. I had expected they would go for the torpedo planes first. They must have known we didn't have the quick acceleration to catch them the way they were coming in at high speed in rapid succession and zipping on away. But then I saw they had a second large group that were now streaming in right past us and into the poor torpedo planes.

Macomber's position was too close to me to permit an effective weave, and I was not getting very good shots at the Zeros. I called him on the radio and said, "Open out more—about double your present distance—and weave." No acknowledgment. His radio must have been dead. (He has since stated it was.) How ironical this situation had become! I had spent almost a year of effort developing what I was convinced was the only way to survive against the Zero, and now we couldn't seem to do it. I kept wondering why Macomber was so close instead of being out in a position to weave. Of course! He had never practiced the weave. He was one of the VF-42 pilots based aboard *Yorktown* during the Coral Sea battle, and he had tangled with some Zeros then. But, like the other former VF-42 pilots, he had reported to VF-3 just before we flew out to land aboard *Yorktown* en route to Midway. I had assumed that my exec, Don Lovelace, had briefed them or required them to read the squadron tactical doctrine. I suddenly realized Don didn't have much time to brief anyone before he had died in a landing accident. Then I remembered telling my flight during the last minute briefing to "stick together." Macomber must have thought I meant for him to fly a closed-up formation. What I actually meant was I wanted no "lone wolf" tactics.

Too late to correct that misunderstanding now. I couldn't see Cheek and Sheedy so I called Ram Dibb, my wingman, and said, "Pretend you are a section leader, and move out far enough to weave." Several Zeros came in on a head-on attack on the torpedo planes and burned Lem Massey's plane right away. It just exploded in flames, and, beautifully timed, another group came in on the side against the torpedo planes. In the meantime, a number of them were coming down in a string on our fighters; the air was just like a beehive, and I wasn't sure at that moment that anything would work. It didn't look like my weave was working, but then it began to work. I got a good shot at two of them and burned them, and one of them had made a pass at my wingman, pulled out to the right, and then came back. We were weaving continuously, and I got a head-on shot at him, and just about the time I saw this guy coming, Ram had said, "There's a Zero on my tail." He didn't have to look back because the Zero wasn't directly astern, he was about like 45 degrees, beginning to follow him around, which gave me the head-on approach. I was really angry then. I was mad because, here, this poor little wingman who'd never been in combat before, had had very little gunnery training, the first time aboard a carrier, and a Zero was about to chew him to pieces. I probably should have decided to duck under this Zero, but I lost my temper a little bit and I decided I'm going to keep my fire going into him and he's going to pull out, which he did, and he just missed me by a few feet; I saw flames coming out of the bottom of his airplane. This is like playing "chicken" with two automobiles on the highway headed for each other except we were both shooting as well. That was a little foolhardy, but I think because I hit him—the first reaction on being hit is to jerk back—it pulled his stick back and his nose went up. I didn't try that any more.

They kept coming in and, by this time, we were over the screen, and more torpedo planes were falling, but so were some Zeros, and we thought, well, at least we're keeping a lot of them engaged. The torpedo planes had to split so that planes would come in against a carrier from various points around at least 180 degrees of the compass; if the ship turns to the right, he's left a broadside shot for several torpedoes. If he turns to the left, then the ones on the other side get the same advantage. We used to call it the "anvil attack."

We could see the carriers. They were steaming at very high speed and launching airplanes that looked like fighters. I couldn't tell. I just got a glimpse, and they were beginning to maneuver. We thought we were doing pretty well until the torpedo planes split. Then, of course, they were extremely vulnerable, just all alone with no mutual protection. The Zeros were coming in on us, one after the other and sometimes simultaneously from above and to the side; we couldn't stay with the torpedo planes, except for one or two that happened to be under us. I kept counting the number of airplanes that I knew I'd hit going down in flames; you couldn't bother to wait for them to splash, but you could tell if they were flaming real good when you saw something besides smoke; if it was real red flames, why, you knew he'd had it. I had this little kneepad, and I would mark down every time I shot one that I knew was gone. Then I realized that this was sort of foolish. Why was I marking marks on my kneepad when the kneepad wasn't coming back? I was utterly convinced then that we weren't any of us coming back because there were still so many of these Zeros and they'd already gotten one, and looking around, I couldn't see Cheek or Sheedy anymore, so there were just two others that I could see of my own—Macomber over there on my left and Ram Dibb and me. Pure logic would convince anyone that, with their superior performance and the number of Zeros they were throwing into the fight, we could not possibly survive. So I said, "This counting is a foolish thing. It takes a second or two to look down to your kneepad and make this mark—a waste of time. Well (still talking to myself), we're going to take a lot of them with us if they're going to get us all." We kept on working this weave, and it seemed to work better and better. How much space of time this took, I don't know; ever since then, I haven't the slightest idea how many Zeros I shot down. I just can't remember, and I don't suppose it makes too much difference. It only shows that I was absolutely convinced that nobody could get out of there, that we weren't coming back, and neither were any of the torpedo planes.

Then it seemed that the attacks began to slack off a little bit. Whether they were spreading out and working more on the torpedo planes that were unprotected, I don't know. The torpedo planes went on in, and I saw three or four of them that got in and made an attack, and I believe that at least one torpedo hit was made. Now, all the records, and the Japanese, said that no torpedoes hit. I'm not sure that the people aboard a ship that is hit repeatedly about the same time by dive bombers really know whether they got hit by a torpedo or one of the bombs. I was aboard the *Saratoga* when she was torpedoed and the *Yorktown* when she was bombed, and I couldn't tell the difference. I think I saw at least one hit, but it occurred either during or very shortly before the dive bombers came in. Naturally, being pretty busy, I couldn't do any more than every now and then get a glance.

Then I saw this glint in the sun, and it just looked like a beautiful silver waterfall, these dive bombers coming down. I could see them very well, because that's the direction the Zeros were, too. They were above me but closer than the dive bombers. They weren't anywhere near the altitude that the dive bombers were. I'd never seen such superb dive bombing. It looked to me like almost every bomb hit. Of course, there were some very near misses. There weren't any wild ones. Explosions were occurring in the carriers, and about that time the Zeros slacked off more. We stayed around. We brought out two torpedo planes, one after the other, and tried to get them out clear and then we could go back and pick up another one that we saw, stay right with him and over him, hoping that the Zeros wouldn't have him all to themselves. Of course, they may have been badly hit and some of them were in the water, and we didn't see them after the torpedo attack. I know more than two attacked. We came in a little earlier than the dive bombers by a matter of just minutes, and drew most, if not all, of the enemy combat air patrol. They were ready and waiting for us as we came in a full 30 minutes after the VT-8 and VT-6 attacks.

I was just terribly depressed at the time, feeling it had been a wasted effort. I felt that way while it was going on. I couldn't understand why the Japanese were throwing everything at us, but apparently they saw us first; we were the only fighters they saw, they were anxious to wipe us out, and that was it. They didn't see the dive bombers, and they didn't have anybody up at high altitude. Jim Gray had the VF-6 fighter escort from the *Enterprise*. He had 10, and he was at high altitude. He had an agreement with the torpedo planes that if they needed him they would call him and tell him. Well, of course, everything happened so suddenly and the torpedo planes were getting shot up so badly that he didn't hear anything from them. He may have seen VT-3 instead of VT-6, if he saw torpedo planes down there. Being at high altitude, you can't tell. If there are any fights going on below, you don't see them, with the water right underneath, so he saw no enemy aircraft.

So those torpedo planes never got any protection; VT-8 from *Hornet* and VT-6 from *Enterprise* had no fighter escort. The dive bombers from the *Enterprise,* led by Wade McCluskey, took off early and didn't find the enemy force at the place where it had been estimated that it would be. He turned and went back northwest and saw a destroyer high-tailing it, leaving a terrific wake, and he thought that destroyer must be catching up with the carriers. So he followed it and, pretty soon, he saw the carriers, which made him arrive almost simultaneously with Max Leslie and his dive bombers. So that was a coincidence, the arrival of those two at the same time, but it was no coincidence that the torpedo planes and the dive bombers from the carrier *Yorktown* attacked in coordinated fashion. That is doctrine and its plan had been practiced for many years, and it worked. It was a beautifully classic attack; although the torpedo planes were almost annihilated, it still went like it was supposed to go.

Our decision to cover the torpedo planes was the right one. These torpedo pilots were all my very close friends, Lem Massey especially, and he was lost. I felt pretty bad about this, just sort of hopeless. I felt like we hadn't done enough, that if they didn't get any hits this whole business of torpedo planes going in at all was a mistake. But, of course, you couldn't fail to send them, and in thinking about it since then I realize that these people hadn't given their lives in vain. They'd done a magnificent job of attracting all the enemy combat air patrol, all the protection that the Japanese carriers had was engaged and held down, so we did do something, and maybe far more than we thought at the time. We engaged the enemy that might have gotten into the dive bombers and prevented them from getting many hits.

After the dive bomber attack was over, I still stayed over there, between the screen and the carriers. A single Zero appeared flying slowly below and to one side of us. I looked up toward the sun and sure enough there were his teammates poised like hawks waiting for one of us to take the bait! We didn't. I could only see three carriers, never a fourth one. One of them, probably either the *Soryu* or the *Kaga,* was burning with bright pink, and sometimes blue, flames. I remember looking at the height of the flames from the ship and noticing that it was the same as the length of the ship—just solid flame going up, and, of course, there was a lot of smoke on top of that. I saw three carriers burning pretty furiously before I left there, then came back and picked up one torpedo plane and headed back to the *Yorktown*. I had been over the Japanese fleet a full 20 minutes.

As I found out later, the squadrons from the *Hornet* had taken off about the same time as the *Enterprise* attack group and searched in the direction of the estimated position and found nothing. The dive bombers and the fighters continued to search beyond their combat radius and, having found nothing, half of the dive bombers headed for Midway and the rest back to the *Hornet*. The 10 fighters couldn't even make it to Midway, so finally they ran out of gas and landed in the ocean. They got their life rafts going and were later picked up. That's the reason that only VT-8 of the *Hornet*'s squadrons was able to engage, and also the reason that the *Hornet* fighters were not present when the attack was going on. So it turned out that my squadron, VF-3, was the only one that saw aerial combat, both over the enemy force and, later, over the American force.

In my flight of six, Bassett was the only one who was killed. Cheek and Sheedy were surrounded and chased by Zeros and got badly shot up but finally got back, and Sheedy was wounded and bleeding pretty badly. His cockpit was riddled with bullets, and he came aboard the first carrier he could see, which was the *Hornet*. They gave him a cut, and, when he came in, his guns went off and killed five people. Later, we found that his master switch, which he had turned off, was just welded across the wires by bullet holes so that you couldn't turn it "off"; the circuit was complete, and, when he hit the arresting gear wire, he jolted forward. He hit the deck pretty hard. He was not in very good physical condition, and his hand was on the stick; that's where the trigger is, and he fired a burst into the island superstructure.

On the way back, when we were going along with this torpedo plane, I felt my shoes were a little squashy. I reached down and I felt this slippery liquid all over my leg, and I thought it was blood. It felt like blood, but I didn't want to look at it, so I just didn't look at it for a while. I wiggled my legs, and they felt all right, except I remember a little place on my shin that didn't feel too good, and I thought I bumped it getting in the airplane. Then I picked up my glove and looked at it, and it was oil. I was never so glad to see oil on my hands in my life. So when I got aboard, I didn't have any oil in the engine. The oil pressure had dropped to zero by then.

After we'd landed aboard, we were getting ready to go on a combat air patrol, having the planes rearmed, refueled, and checked over, and taking stock of what we'd lost and what we had left. We had a combat air patrol of 12 fighters in the air. I was in the ready room with the remainder of the fighters when suddenly they picked up on the radar, about 30 miles out, an attack coming in that was reported as being about 40 aircraft. Actually, it was 18 dive bombers supported by 6 fighters, and they came on in. The combat air patrol did a terrific job and shot down most of them, but seven got through, and they were very accurate because they got three hits on the *Yorktown*. One of them exploded in the smoke stack, in the uptakes, and it created quite a problem because the soot, being on fire, was being spread around quite a bit. This stopped the ship. It blasted out all but one boiler. Then, within maybe an hour and a half at the most, we heard that the engineers had run auxiliary flexible steam lines, and we got under way. We received word in the ready room that they thought they could make 16 knots; could we take off? I said we can take off if you're making less than that. We could start way back at the stern; there weren't many planes left aboard. Very soon after I got aboard, here came the attack of the enemy dive bombers, so Max Leslie and his dive bombers didn't have time to get aboard. So he was still in the air.

We took stock of all the planes we had. When this attack came in, they had to shut down refueling the airplanes and purge the lines with CO_2 gas. They were still fighting fires in some places when they got under way. There was a fire caused by one of the bombs down near the main gasoline tank in a store room, so we couldn't get more gasoline. I said, "Let's take off all the airplanes that have as much as 30 gallons of gas and any ammunition that you can get." So we got together about 8 planes, and the ship got under way slowly and finally built up. I think they were at 19 knots when I took off, because I just got over the bow and dipped a little bit. Just as we were rolling down the deck, another attack came in. These were torpedo planes from the one carrier that was not found, the fourth carrier, and they were also escorted by six fighters. We didn't have too many combat air patrol in the air at this time. I think there were about four or six, including Scott McCuskey. As we were rolling down the deck, the antiaircraft fire had to open up. The torpedo planes were that close. I got my wheels up; it took about 36 hard turns with a crank. I was looking out to see the firing on the starboard and started over there. By that time, Ens. Milton Tootle had taken off. He turned toward the torpedo planes, right into our own antiaircraft fire, shot down a Japanese torpedo plane, and a Zero promptly shot him down. He was in the air less than 60 seconds. This is probably the shortest combat flight on record, where a fighter shot down anything. He said a Zero was shooting at him, but he was also, like the rest of us, in the middle of our own antiaircraft fire, so who knows who brought him down, but I think the Zero probably did. He bailed out and was picked out of the water.

I saw a torpedo plane. They split, just like we do, so they were coming in from different points of the compass. This torpedo plane was real low on the water; I could see a bright red-colored insignia shaped like feathers on his tail that no other Japanese aircraft had, and I made a good side approach on him, and got him on fire. The whole left wing was burning, and I could see the ribs showing through the flames, and that devil still stayed in the air until he got close enough and dropped his torpedo, and that one almost hit the *Yorktown*. He was a dedicated Japanese torpedo plane pilot. Even though he was already shot down, he went ahead and dropped his torpedo. By that time, the whole airplane looked like it was on fire, the top surface of both wings was burned away, everything but the ribs. He must have had some wing surface underneath to hold him up, but he was obviously sinking all the time and he fell in the water right after he dropped his torpedo. They were excellent in their tactics and in their determination. In fact, as far as determination was concerned, you could hardly tell any difference between the Japanese carrier-based pilots and the American carrier-based pilots. Nothing would stop them, if they had anything to say about it.

The *Yorktown* had taken two torpedo hits, but again most of the torpedo planes were shot down before they got in, and yet they got hits. So that stopped the ship, really. Since we never did join up, we weren't even in a formation, we just turned individually off the bow of the ship into the torpedo planes, so I didn't have a wingman. In fact, I didn't see anybody else. I saw a Zero, and I went at him. He apparently had been fighting with some of our combat air patrol, and he was going to catch up with what he thought was left of his torpedo planes. I was hoping he wouldn't see me, but he saw me soon after I started for him, and he just pulled up very neatly and came right round over the top of my head and right on my tail. Fortunately there was a little cloud I was heading for, and I went right into it, did a split-S, pulled out and didn't see him any more. He almost had me.

The *Yorktown* never took any more airplanes aboard. It was a very sad thing to see the ship listing more and more. I thought she was going to roll over and capsize. Apparently so did the skipper because it wasn't long before he ordered "abandon ship." We were directed to land aboard the *Enterprise*. At this time, I was mad all over again. I was angry—here were the *Enterprise* and *Hornet* sitting about 50 miles away with combat air patrol, plenty of it, over them and too far away to help the *Yorktown*. There was something wrong with this, and I was unhappy about it. If we'd just had one or two more airplanes in the air to fight this attack, the *Yorktown* would never have been sunk. I'm sure of it. It was too far, too late. Of course, they couldn't afford to denude themselves. There they were, too far away for mutual support. I'm sure that the people who made the decisions to have two task groups, separate, expected that they would remain close enough for mutual support, but it didn't work out that way. When Buckmaster realized that he was farther away than he wanted to be, that's when he or Admiral Fletcher cut me down to six fighters. Neither Fletcher nor Spruance were naval aviators—they had not grown up in carrier-based squadrons or had command of an aircraft carrier, where all the experience and knowledge is absorbed which would qualify one to command a carrier task force.

Admiral Fletcher had directed Admiral Spruance, Task Force 16, to proceed toward the enemy and launch a strike, saying he would follow with Task Force 17 as soon as *Yorktown* recovered her scouts. So Frank Jack Fletcher caused the initial separation. Did he realize he was violating one of the basic principles of warfare? That they should be in two task groups was obviously Admiral Nimitz's decision. The failure to keep them together is obviously the man in charge, the admiral and his staff. You can say Fletcher or Spruance, but, of course, Fletcher didn't have an aviation staff, and they had no real background of experience in operating carriers. Spruance had Halsey's staff, but they were ordered to proceed southwest and launch a strike. Spruance was junior to Fletcher. The *Yorktown* had sent out scouts, and she had to land them aboard, but I know the wind was such that we could have kept them closer together and could have kept the same speed of advance if they had paid more attention to it and realized how important it was. You can do it, if you insist on it being done, and if you look ahead a few hours, you can do it.

I was very bitter about this for a long time. I was bitter at Admiral Nimitz, Admiral Fletcher, Admiral Spruance, and Captain Buckmaster. I was a young lieutenant commander then, and, since then having grown up and gotten to be a four-star admiral in charge of naval forces in Europe, I haven't changed my mind one damned bit! I think one of the basic principles of warfare was violated, not intentionally, I presume. It wasn't just an edict or bible, because the basic principles of warfare weren't invented, they were discovered. They exist as a law of nature, and the law of strategy and tactics, and people who violate any one of them are at a disadvantage, and people who exploit one of the principles, such as concentration of force, usually do better than the other fellow, if he doesn't. The element of surprise we had and utilized. This was the main reason for our success. Otherwise, we might have had all three carriers sunk, if we hadn't had that surprise.

There's no question that our training and the fact that the people in our squadron did follow the doctrine was what brought them all home, but one. I was very proud of the fact that my squadron claimed 31 enemy aircraft destroyed. This is the total including the VF-3 combat air patrol against enemy dive bombers and enemy torpedo planes and enemy fighters. There was the Japanese attack on the *Yorktown* and our attack on them—the total. It's also interesting that those six fighters from VF-3 were the only fighters of all our three carriers that got any combat over the Japanese fleet.

I flew over and landed on the *Enterprise*. Immediately, they said Admiral Spruance wanted to see me on the flag bridge. I went up, and he said, "Well, how do you think we're doing?" I said, "Admiral, we're winning this battle. We've already won it, because I saw with my own eyes three big carriers burning so furiously they'll never launch another airplane. Of course, that fourth one is a dangerous thing. We certainly ought to be able to get him. I think we ought to chase them, because we've got the advantage now." He said, "Well," and he kind of smiled, "you know we don't have any battleships. All we have are cruisers, and if we start chasing them, it's going to get dark pretty soon, and if we suddenly catch up with them, they may be able to chew us up before we can get within gun range at night, and we don't have much of a night attack capability." I said, "I think they're on the run, and I think we ought to chase them," and I left him with that thought.

Returning to Pearl Harbor on 13 June was another bitter blow. We came back in, and people were showing us all these headlines, "B-17s Win Battle of Midway," and people would say, "Where was the Navy? Didn't you all go out there? Didn't you take part in it?" This is true. This is what people were asking. They didn't know, because the Navy was very careful and deliberate about making press releases, and, of course, it was several days before we got back ashore, and there just wasn't much press concerning the Navy's participation in the battle of Midway. But the B-17 pilots flying from ashore could talk to newsmen, which they did, and told them what they thought they'd done. The fact is that they didn't get a single hit on anything in the battle of Midway. They may not have realized it at that time, but I suspected it, because I saw all the carriers in very good shape, steaming at 30 knots into the wind and not any smoke coming from them, not even from the smoke stacks.

Not long after that I was detached. Butch O'Hare came back from the United States, having received from the President the Medal of Honor. I had recommended that when and if I were relieved, he should be the one to take the squadron because he had been promoted to lieutenant commander and was well qualified to command the squadron. It was on 24 June 1942 that he relieved me and I returned to the United States for duty.

The *Hornet* and the Santa Cruz Islands

Rear Admiral Francis D. Foley

Francis Drake Foley was born 4 July 1910 at Dorchester, Massachusetts, son of Capt. Paul Foley, USN (Ret.), and Josephine Drake Foley. He graduated from the U.S. Naval Academy and was commissioned ensign on 2 June 1932 and was designated a naval aviator on 1 February 1936. Subsequent service included extensive command and staff duties ashore and afloat, and he advanced in rank, eventually to that of rear admiral effective 24 July 1958. In July 1971, Rear Admiral Foley became senior member of the United Nations Armistice Commission, Seoul, Korea, and in March 1972 he was assigned to the Office of the Chief of Naval Operations, pending his retirement, effective 1 July 1972.

In the summer of 1942, he joined the USS Hornet *as air operations officer. After the* Hornet *was lost in the battle of Santa Cruz Islands, he was ordered to duty as assistant operations officer on the staff of Commander, Task Force 65. He later served at Guadalcanal as assistant operations officer on the staff of*

Commander, Air, Solomons, and then on the staff of Commander, Fleet Air, South Pacific. Between 1943 and 1945, he was head of the Officer Flying Section, Office of the Chief of Naval Operations.

Admiral Foley's awards include the Legion of Merit, Bronze Star with combat "V," Navy Commendation Medal with combat "V," Joint Services Commendation Medal, and the Chou Su Cross of South Korea.

Rear Adm. Francis D. Foley, air operations officer, USS Hornet, *1942.*

I arrived at Pearl Harbor on a pitch dark night in June 1942 and immediately reported aboard the *Hornet,* a black mass of ship at Ford Island. I couldn't see anything. As a matter of fact, in the next four months, I saw my ship only twice after that; once when I went flying from her in a Grumman amphibian utility plane and a second time abandoning ship. She was back in Pearl and she was feeling pretty damn good about herself, except for Torpedo Squadron 8, which was lost with almost all hands. There was one survivor.

Capt. Marc Mitscher was just being relieved as skipper. The new captain, Charlie Mason, had brought me out with him from Jacksonville to be part of his team. I was assigned as the air operations officer, and I was delighted with that. Since I wouldn't be in a squadron, this job placed me about as close to the air group as I could possibly get. In early carriers, such as the *Hornet,* air plot was up in the island structure just aft of the charthouse—the bridge, the charthouse, and air plot, in that order. The CIC and air control business, including the fighter directors, were also in the island structure. They were directly beneath me. I had an open scuttle and could look right down and see what their status board showed and what their radars were picking up. But, of course, it was a very vulnerable place to be, as we found out. I was feeding everything from air plot to the squadron ready rooms by teletype, and they were firing things back to me.

We departed Pearl on 17 August 1942 as flagship of Task Force 17, commanded by Rear Adm. George Murray. We had two cruisers, six destroyers, and an oiler. About an hour or so after our departure, our attention became riveted upon a member of the crew who had climbed the mast and crawled out along the starboard yardarm with the obvious intention of committing suicide. Signalmen had seen him start up the mast, but they thought he was a radar technician or something and didn't stop him. So there he was, clinging tightly to the yardarm, and trying to get up nerve enough to let go and drop the 120 feet or so into the sea below. The task force was then making about 18 knots, the best the oiler could do. The poor fellow became scared as hell but was apparently determined to go through with it. Everyone started yelling at him until Captain Mason quieted them down. The chief master-at-arms went aloft and climbed out on the yardarm too, pleading quietly with the man to calm him. Then the chaplain, Eddie Harp, and one of the ship's doctors went up the mast to add their pleas.

Meanwhile, flight deck personnel rigged a cargo net between two tow bars to try to catch him if he let go. The man was finally persuaded that suicide was not the answer and was helped back to safety. At the first opportunity, he was sent back to the States for psychiatric evaluation and treatment. Ironically, he was returned to the *Hornet* later, just before the ship was lost, thus having to face up to the same situation he had tried to escape!

Our air group consisted of close to 80 airplanes, counting our spares, plus an additional 21 fighters that were stowed, with wings folded back, up in the overhead of the hangar deck. In carriers of those days, the gallery deck did not extend all the way across the ship under the flight deck. It wasn't a continuous deck, so there were bays up there between the girders that were big enough to accommodate a fighter or, in fact, a spare dive bomber or two. We had 21 F4F Wildcats up in the overhead, one of which was an F4F-7, a photographic reconnaissance plane with a fantastic range over 3,500 miles. The other 20 were pure fighters. We took these aircraft aboard before leaving Pearl, preserved the engines and many fittings in Cosmoline, taking special care with their guns. We hoisted them up into the overhead not knowing whether we or someone else would be the ones to use them. Fate decided that in short order, as we were en route to support the struggle for Guadalcanal, where the Marines had made their landing on 7 August.

The Marines had a big air battle over Guadalcanal in which they lost a lot of airplanes. So we went down near Espíritu Santo, in the New Hebrides, flew our torpedo squadron into the beach, and ferried back a bunch of Marine pilots. Many had not had time to become carrier qualified with a war going on, but it's not very difficult to fly off a carrier. It's a little more difficult to land on board!

We had rotated our own fighters for combat air patrol over the task force to and from Espíritu for refueling. In the meantime, we had broken out all the replacement aircraft except the F4F-7. We had the Wildcats lined up all the way down the hangar deck, just like in an aircraft factory. And boy, they were getting those engines cleaned and run up, guns depreserved and bore-sighted, ammo loaded and ready to go, and topped off with fuel. For run-up, they had to stick the tails out the open bays of the hangar deck because of the heavy smoke from the Cosmoline. On 13 September 1942, the Marine pilots flew the fighters back to Guadalcanal while a huge air battle was going on. A couple of those fighters were shot down before they ever even landed. However, several of them shot down Jap planes, too—a standoff. It was fantastic.

In two months of operations in the South Pacific, we were in port, Nouméa, New Caledonia, for five days. We spent quite a bit of time up in "Torpedo Junction," which is east of Guadalcanal and north of Espíritu Santo. We were present on 15 September when the *Wasp* was sunk and other ships were hit in the battle of the Eastern Solomons. The *North Carolina,* part of our task force and close aboard at the time, was hit by a torpedo forward. The *O'Brien,* one of our destroyers, lost her bow. I remember that she was right there on our port beam. She took a torpedo that was meant for us, and so did the *North Carolina,* as a matter of fact. When the torpedo hit the *O'Brien,* the pillar of smoke resulting went right straight up in the air and engulfed the ship in a vertical plume that settled back over her. You couldn't see the ship. I had the watch in primary flight control, and my talker sang out, "Scratch one small boy," and he scratched the *O'Brien* off our board. Then, out of all the smoke and everything, came the *O'Brien*—with a clipper bow! She sent a signal over saying "Torpedo hit forward x CPO quarters destroyed." She mentioned the number of casualties, then added, "Speed reduced to 15 knots x request permission to remain in company." The task force commander sent word to her, "Negative," peeled off another destroyer as an escort, and ordered them out of the area.

The *North Carolina* took a torpedo hit abreast number two turret, but instead of the smoke rising vertically, it ran horizontally along the hull of the ship to port. The hit was down low, close to a magazine, but didn't penetrate that far. She sent a signal to Admiral Murray, saying that her speed had been reduced to 25 knots. Torpedo Junction was aptly named! We thought we had run into a whole submarine wolf pack and were astounded to later learn that one Japanese submarine did this whole thing. She got in the middle of that concentration and let go with bow and stern tubes, and hit everything in sight. It was amazing.

By September 1942, things were pretty grim. As a matter of fact, the general public had no idea what dire straits the Navy was in. We were really hurting in the South Pacific, carrier wise. The *Lexington* had been lost in the battle of the Coral Sea, the *Yorktown* at Midway, a torpedo hurt the *Saratoga,* and damage to the *Enterprise* in late August had sent her back to Pearl Harbor for repairs. Now the *Wasp* had been sunk, leaving the *Hornet* our only carrier remaining in the area. When we learned that the enemy had proclaimed her destruction as the primary objective of the Imperial Fleet, the announcement evoked a resounding defiant cheer from the entire ship's company which could be heard on the bridge!

Our pilots were all gung ho. The squadron commanders would come up, or someone who had done something particularly noteworthy; they'd send for him to come up to the bridge and talk to the captain. Every time anybody ever came up, they did so with enthusiasm—like Gus Widhelm when he was shot down in his airplane. He was riding in his rubber boat with his rear-seat man from his SBD, actually thumbing his nose at the Japanese destroyer that was going by at 35 knots, and the Japanese were about to shoot him with an automatic rifle, but put the rifle away and laughed at him. He was thumbing his nose. All he could think about, he said later, was that he had won $1,200 in a crap game the night before and put it in his safe, and he wondered whether the safe was still going to be there when he got back. Well, he never got back; the ship and his money were gone.

I attribute the spirit to the leadership, which started with Marc Mitscher, and then it was carried on under Charlie Mason and Apollo Soucek. Those people could apparently do no wrong. But it was all down the line. Another outstanding person was Marcel Gouin, the air officer. He carried a little black notebook in his hip pocket, and he knew everything about every airplane that ever left that ship. He knew what its number was, who the pilot was, what the mission was. How he got it all in that little book, I don't know, but he did. He could whip out that little black notebook and tell you nearly anything. He had the word, and the same way when the planes came back, he checked them off, and he had the landing intervals and everything. It was all in his little black notebook.

Following a brief respite in Nouméa, TF 17 resumed support of the Solomons area with strikes at Tonolei, Kieta, and Faisi-Shortland, served as a covering force during the fateful night battle of Cape Esperance, and worked over targets in Rekata Bay and Santa Isabel. A day-long pounding, close aboard, of numerous targets in the Tassafaronga area of Guadalcanal near Henderson Field topped our effort. We carried out shuttle strikes, even allowing our CAP fighters to participate in strafing targets of opportunity. We had a virtual field day.

However, by late October the enemy had marshalled major forces at Truk and New Guinea to regain control of Guadalcanal. Their composition, not fully known to us at the time, consisted of 5 battleships, 4 carriers, 8 heavy and 4 light cruisers, 27 destroyers, 12 submarines, backed up by 220 land-based aircraft at Rabaul. Their mission was obvious.

On the night of 25 October 1942, Rear Admiral Kinkaid's TF 16 and Rear Admiral Murray's TF 17, operating together, were conducting a counterclockwise sweep north of the Santa Cruz Islands, some 200 miles east of Guadalcanal, to stem the threat from the major portion of the Truk force. TF 16 consisted of the *Enterprise,* recently returned from Pearl Harbor, the battleship *South Dakota,* 2 heavy cruisers, and 8 destroyers. TF 17 was comprised of the *Hornet,* 2 heavy and 2 light cruisers, plus 6 destroyers. Closer to Guadalcanal in a supporting role was TF 64 under Rear Admiral Lee in the battleship *Washington* with 3 heavy cruisers and 6 destroyers. At that time, we had about 60 combat aircraft at Henderson Field plus a mixed bag of some 111 F4Fs, B-17s, PVs, PBYs, and OS2Us at Espíritu Santo about 400 miles to the southeast.

Two enemy forces were initially located about 300 miles to our northwest by PBYs. However, contact reports were garbled and delayed, so we refrained from launching the moonlight night strike we had planned. Early on 26 October, the *Enterprise* armed scouts located the enemy when the range had closed to under 200 miles, and the disabled carrier *Zuiho* as an added dividend.

However, an enemy float plane pinpointed TF 17 before we were aware of the location of his third carrier force. At 7:10 A.M., the Japanese launched a strike group. About 20 minutes later, the *Hornet* followed suit, and by 8:15, the Americans had 73 planes airborne and proceeding towards the enemy force. Stacked overhead were 38 CAP fighters. Opposing strikes passed in the air with some attrition action between them but mainly continued on their respective primary missions.

The *Enterprise* and *Hornet* were operating about 10 miles apart, with the *Enterprise* shrouded by a rain shower. Consequently, the enemy concentrated his initial attack on the *Hornet*. Our speed was 29 knots, and we were maneuvering radically, as the enemy attacked from the port side. Despite very effective antiaircraft fire, a heavy bomb hit the flight deck aft, causing severe damage and numerous casualties; two near misses shook us up. The leader of a flight of dive bombers, his plane on fire, bore on in, hitting us with three bombs; one detonated on the flight deck abreast the island, another at the forward part of the stack, and the third was a dud which penetrated to the gallery deck. The fuselage shattered the signal bridge, causing 12 casualties and a stubborn gasoline fire, all just over my head.

Meanwhile, a dozen Kate torpedo bombers, in line abreast about 100 feet apart, bore in from the starboard side so low that they had to hop over our screening ships to avoid hitting their masts. Two torpedoes hit us amidships, adjacent to the forward engine room, which began flooding. A third, less-violent shudder occurred when a torpedo apparently detonated upon hitting the wake during a hard right turn, jamming our rudders full right. A torpedo bomber, damaged by antiaircraft fire, raced the length of the ship, made a hard turn of 270 degrees, and plowed into us, lodging under the number one elevator and causing a stubborn fire. Its unexpended ammunition detonated slowly. We found a chart of Costa Rica and Panama in the cockpit!

We had no power whatsoever afterwards. The engine rooms were getting flooded by this torpedo damage. The ship was beginning to list. We were being attacked by successive waves of Japanese planes coming in. The ship was dead in the water and she was listing, and there was no power. We had 11 fires in the ship. None of them were very big, but they were troublesome. They were just damn hard to put out with buckets and P-500 portable pumps.

Two destroyers came alongside to port in turn and gave us steam, but we couldn't do very much with it. We were trying to get some electric power in the ship, for some of the damage was to the auxiliary generators, the diesel generators. We couldn't get them going. The *Northampton,* one of the cruisers, tried to tow the ship, and we roused out anchor chain and hooked it up to her towing wire. She started towing, but as soon as the line was tight, the *Hornet* started shearing out to the right because her rudders were jammed. So then they'd just drag her around to more or less of a straight course again. The minute there was any slack in the towline, out she would shear again. Then an attack would come in, and the cruiser would have to cast off because she was a sitting duck. That happened three times. Finally, the anchor chains were both hanging straight up and down; we had no power, no way to raise them.

Then we got our own towline from back on the fantail and ran it the entire length of the hangar deck by hand, men just pulling. I guess there must have been 500 people working on the thing, hauling that heavy wire lengthwise up the deck. With a 15-degree list then on the ship, this was pretty difficult. There was foam all over the hangar deck, so it was slippery as hell. They hauled the wire out through the forward hangar bay and outboard up to the forecastle as a replacement towing line. In the meantime, our instructions to the pilots were to go to the *Enterprise*. The *Enterprise* was madly refueling her own airplanes and trying to make room by flying airplanes ashore to Guadalcanal and Espíritu Santo.

My job in air plot was about over. But I had this long tape from my teletype machine which had information such as our position, course, and speed, the wind, and the enemy's position and composition of his forces. It was a copy of all of the intelligence material sent down to the ready rooms, reams and reams of it. I must have had 50 feet of it all on a roll, all lying out on the deck in air plot. I said, "Whoa, wait a minute, we better save that." So I got my teletype operator to roll it up again. We rolled it up into a tight bundle, put waterproof tape around the thing, and had this package like a cartridge for a player piano, about two inches in diameter and about 10 inches long, which I stuck in my shirt. I thought, boy, this is the story of our action.

Then I went out and down to help with the fire-fighting parties on the flight deck. We were all using buckets fighting these damn fires. Comdr. Apollo Soucek, the exec, came down, and he said, "Francis, come with me. Let's you and I make an inspection of the ship." So we did as much as we could. We were mainly concerned about what was going on up on the forecastle. We had to climb down on the port side. The ladder had been damaged by the second plane that had flown into the ship, but we wormed our way down.

Apollo Soucek and I managed to get down from the flight deck to the forecastle deck, and there the first thing we saw was a large unexploded bomb sitting on the deck, fused of course. It apparently had been knocked off the Jap plane in the elevator well. Fortunately, the shear of the ship was such that we could see water directly below us. We managed to roll that bomb over the side and then jumped back. I want to tell you, we were glad that thing didn't go off when it hit the water!

Then we went up on the forecastle, where the exec had been in charge most of the morning, and observed what was going on under the first lieutenant. We tried to encourage people and let them know that the exec was there. A whole bunch of boatswain's mates and at least 300 crewmen were up there doing everything humanly possible to hook up tow lines. We encouraged them and mentioned the possible use of our own towing cable on the fantail. We then made a tour of the whole hangar deck and went back to the fantail where all the badly wounded were. A destroyer had her bow close aboard and was receiving them by highline. We lost 111 men in the *Hornet,* and a lot of them were being buried over the fantail in sacks. Two chaplains were saying prayers and anointing the dead. The senior medic and an honor guard squad were there. The mortally wounded had morphine tags on them to so indicate. It was grim.

A damage control party opened some watertight hatches and doors for us to inspect the steering engine room, and we confirmed that block and tackle would be necessary to move the jammed rudders. Later, the rudders were returned amidships—how, I don't know.

Soucek and I didn't go down below into the engineering spaces because the damage control people were doing all that could be done to get those engine rooms back in commission and restore power. Although we did eventually have three boilers back on the line, successive dive-bombing attacks and a third torpedo hit sealed our fate. The horizontal bombers which came last added insult to injury.

We went on back up to the bridge and conferred with Captain Mason and to tell him what we had found and what people were doing. About mid-afternoon, we were ordered to abandon ship. The orders were to abandon the *Hornet* and sink her.

My abandon-ship station was on the fantail. I got back there and found that I was the senior line officer present. We had several dozen life rafts stacked up under the ramp area. The wind was almost zero, maybe three or four knots at the most, and the ocean was like a mill pond. We started dropping the life rafts, big jobs that would hold 12 men each and support a lot more. The trouble was that they started drifting away. Even with little wind, there was enough to take them away. So that meant that the one closest to the ship was the one that everybody started going for; and some were jumping over the side, but most were going down lines we had rigged. With the life rafts floating away, they started fighting over the one that was closest. That had to be stopped somehow, which I did. The next to the last one to go down was the ship's doctor, Dr. Emil Stelter. He got on a line but wouldn't go down, even though he was wearing a life jacket. I pleaded with him, so he went. He didn't drop, he just eased on down after I persuaded him a little bit. He thanked me later.

Then when I got in the water, I had a gun, a .45-caliber, and a whistle, of all things. The role of teletype paper was still tucked in my blouse. I had my Abercrombie and Fitch watch, too. I got in the water, and I could see that I was virtually helpless. What the hell to do with all this fighting over the life rafts? So I just started blowing my whistle. I just blew that damn whistle and yelled, "Follow me!" Then I started swimming away from the ship, and people started following me. The rest of the task force was circling around the *Hornet* like Indians around a wagon train. One destroyer would peel off at a time and come in and pick up survivors and then get back out. When she was full, another one would come in.

While we were in the water, I saw more Japanese bombers. There was a layer of fleecy clouds about 5,000 feet, and they were just above it. Boy, I remember hearing those things. I thought, "My God, how in the hell did they get way down here?" and then those bombs came through the clouds. We could see them. Wow, I thought, if we get away with this, we're really going to be lucky. But the bombs, of course, were aimed at the ship, not the people in the water. Some did hit the ship, too. I remember one blew a 5-inch gun maybe 30 feet in the air, a whole gun mount. When the bombs hit the water, I want to tell you, you really felt like you had been hit by a blockbuster.

I swam on out away from the ship with these people behind me, and the destroyer *Barton* came in. There was a chief petty officer up on the bow with a line-throwing gun. He'd see somebody out there having trouble, and he'd say, "Hey, sailor! Sailor!" He had a megaphone. "Hey, sailor! Heads up!" And he'd take this line gun—"boom!"—he'd put the projectile right over the guy's head, in the water. Here's this little line and he said, "Just hold on. Wrap it around your waist and hold on." So they'd gradually pull him into the ship. Then he'd pick out another one. He did that with 20 people—I didn't count them, but that's what they told me later—until he ran out of line.

I got to the destroyer which had cargo nets over the side, and I climbed aboard. Two hundred and thirty-five people from the *Hornet* joined me aboard that destroyer. The skipper of the *Barton* was a fellow named Douglas H. Fox, who later went down with his ship during Guadalcanal action on the night of

13–14 November 1942. There were a half a dozen officers in our group, and we went up and took saltwater showers with saltwater soap, getting ourselves cleaned up as best we could. Outside the shower room, there was a shell hoist for the forward 5-inch gun on the bow. The gun started going off to repel an air attack, and the shells were rattling up the hoist. We decided, "To hell with it. Let's just stay in the shower and get clean." Where else were you going to go?

After they got all the people off the *Hornet,* the task force retired to the southeast at high speed. They'd left two destroyers there to sink the *Hornet,* and Captain Mason had the unenviable job of watching his own ship being sunk. You can imagine what a traumatic experience that would be. I understand that our destroyers fired 16 torpedoes at the *Hornet,* but only nine detonated, placing the ship back on an even keel! She was very low in the water—helpless, but not sinking. She had taken so much of a beating, you couldn't believe it. After the torpedoes, the destroyers started with 5-inch ammunition. The figure that sticks in my mind is 350 rounds, before they finally ruptured the gasoline system. They managed to set the ship on fire. I understand the Japs moved in later and administered the *coup de grâce,* using several more torpedoes to speed her demise. The reason we sank her was because we couldn't tow her away. If the Japanese had taken her and towed her away, if they had succeeded in doing that, our name would have been mud, really mud.

There's one thing in particular that I would like to add about the battle of Santa Cruz, and that is about the fighter direction of the two task forces, Task Force 16, under Admiral Kinkaid, and Task Force 17, under Admiral Murray in the *Hornet.* The *Enterprise* was the flagship for Kinkaid. When the Japanese airplanes were approaching the two ships, the two task forces were quite close together. All of the fighters from both ships were airborne, the combat air patrol, all taken over by the fighter director from the *Enterprise,* who was fairly new at the job. We had what we considered the finest fighter director in the Navy, a fellow named Al Fleming. We thought Al knew more about it, even in those primitive days. Radar was just in its infancy, but Al Fleming seemed to have a better hand on the fighter business than anyone. We had a very large fighter contingent in the *Hornet* under Mike Sanchez, very aggressive and very good. But all our fighter combat air patrol from the *Hornet* were taken over by the *Enterprise* and they were all being vectored by the fighter director from the *Enterprise.*

He was new at the job, in addition. The result was that they splashed a lot of planes attacking the *Enterprise,* but I think very few attacking the *Hornet,* although this is debatable. And it was very unfortunate that this happened.

Later in the day when it was too late to do anything, our planes not shot down landed on board the *Enterprise,* refueled, and flew off again to Guadalcanal. It was too late to do anything else. Al Fleming, our fighter director, had closed down air control; our radar was out. Al Fleming was out on deck and was very, very badly injured in his face. Half of his face seemed to be gone. I didn't think Al would ever recover, but he did. The plastic surgeons aboard ship and in Nouméa and aboard the *Lurline* going home all did a wonderful job on him. He gradually made it back, and he's a fine-looking man today.

I saw a spirit of enthusiasm in everybody in the *Hornet.* Everybody seemed to be a professional. That included the pilots, hangar deck people, technicians, engineers—both crew and air group. Everything people did was gung ho, right now, don't wait for anything. I think it was really very, very unfortunate that the ship lasted only a year. She had a lot to give, and she was a tough baby to sink.

Despite loss of the *Hornet,* it so happens that the enemy never did initiate another major carrier strike against the Solomons to follow up. Damage to his carrier strike forces had been heavy and loss of trained carrier pilots severe. The battle of Santa Cruz marked a turning point in the area, although night air raids by land-based aircraft and heavy bombardments by the "Tokyo Express" continued for several months. The *Hornet* was our last major carrier lost in World War II, or since then. She did not die in vain.

The *Enterprise* and Guadalcanal

Rear Admiral Edward L. Feightner

Edward Lewis Feightner was born in Lima, Ohio, on 14 October 1919, son of Amos Evan and Mary Story (Roths) Feightner. After graduation from Findlay College, Findlay, Ohio, he enlisted in the U.S. Naval Reserve on 16 June 1941 and was designated a naval aviator and commissioned ensign on 3 April 1942. After distinguished war service, Admiral Feightner served in a wide variety of aviation assignments ashore and afloat, including tours as a test pilot at the Naval Air Test Center, Patuxent River, Maryland, and as a member of the Flight Exhibition Team "Blue Angels." He progressed in rank to that of rear admiral, effective 1 February 1971. Admiral Feightner was Deputy Commander, Naval Air Systems Command, from 1972 until his retirement on 1 July 1974.

During World War II, he initially flew fighters with VF-10 aboard the USS Enterprise *in the Solomons Islands area, participating in the battle of the Santa Cruz Islands, and flying with the First Marine Division, Reinforced, at Guadalcanal. He later served with VF-8 based aboard the USS* Bunker Hill *and participated in combat operations in the drive through the Central Pacific. Admiral Feightner's record in aerial combat included nine enemy aircraft destroyed.*

Admiral Feightner's decorations include the Legion of Merit, Distinguished Flying Cross with three Gold Stars, Air Medal with 11 Gold Stars, Navy Commendation Medal, and three awards of the Presidential Unit Citation.

Lt. Edward L. Feightner, ca. 1944. (Courtesy Rear Adm. E. L. Feightner, USN [Ret.])

In October 1942, while assigned to VF-3, Butch O'Hare's squadron, I received unexpected orders to join VF-10 on the *Enterprise* at Pearl Harbor. The commanding officer of VF-10 was Lt. Comdr. Jimmy Flatley, who was one of the most amazing people I had ever encountered. Talk about a true leader. Jimmy Flatley just sort of epitomized what you think of as a squadron commander. He got along well with everybody in the squadron, was a good pilot, and had the respect of all the aviators in the squadron. He was a very religious and patriotic man, and felt very deeply that anything we did as a squadron should be done with an eye toward helping not only the squadron and the ship, but also the country. He was concerned about such things as safety to the point that he invented the shoulder harness, although it was really a chest harness. We actually modified all our airplanes; we had a strap around the chest, which we religiously put on, at his insistence, of course.

He was a great person for sitting down with people in a small group to talk tactics. He would talk about the philosophy that he thought the Japanese lived by, what we should expect from them. He was great for writing letters to the squadron. It worried him when we lost somebody. I can remember distinctly the first day in combat we had with the squadron. Ten days out of Pearl Harbor, we thought we had lost 11 people on the first day of combat. It turned out we hadn't really lost that many; some of them were sitting on other ships out there in the task force, but we thought we'd lost them. That really hurt him, the fact that we had lost that many people.

He was extremely innovative. For instance, the day the *Chicago* was sunk, 30 January 1943, we were on combat air patrol. There were 12 Bettys that came after the *Enterprise,* and we managed to turn them away and they then headed for the *Chicago.* We shot down some of them before they got there, but the rest of them bunched up together and since they could outrun us in a dive, they were out of gun range when they reached the *Chicago.* They dropped four torpedoes into the *Chicago,* which was under tow, and they sank it. But, once they were out of the dive and down on the deck, we were able to slowly overtake them. I was flying wing on Jimmy Flatley, and we were very slowly overhauling one which was out of range in front of us. Jimmy Flatley pulled his nose up, fired, and put tracers in front of the Betty, which panicked him. He turned right and headed for a cloud layer at about 2,500 feet. Being a dumb ensign, I went after him in the cloud. Apparently he turned upon entering the cloud layer, and the next thing I saw, in the cloud, was this big shape directly in front of me. I fired and managed to avoid him somehow and broke out on top of the cloud layer, but he didn't come out on top. I immediately went back down below, joined up on Jimmy Flatley, who gave me a thumbs up and said, "You got him." That's the kind of man he was. When we got back aboard, he would take no credit for that airplane at all; he gave me full credit for it. He said, "No, all I did was turn him. You shot him down."

Shortly after I reported to VF-10, we left Pearl Harbor, and 10 days later the *Enterprise* and the *Hornet* were in the battle of Santa Cruz, in October 1942. I'll never forget, on the day before the battle actually started, 25 October, we had reports that the *Zuikaku* and the *Shokaku* were up north of us and coming our way, so we organized a search-and-attack group. The group commander, Comdr. Dick Gaines, was flying a TBF, and we had about five TBFs with torpedoes. I think there were 6 SBDs, all carrying 1,000-pound bombs, and we had 8 fighters. This was late afternoon, along about 3:30, when we launched. We got out to 175 miles, and it was absolutely one of these days you could see for 100 miles. We still didn't have a task force in sight, so we flew another 75 miles northeast of there. When we got to that point, according to our original mission, we should have been landing aboard ship. I was completely confused. I thought I was a navigator, but by this time we'd made those two unscheduled turns and we fighters were continuously weaving over the bombers. There was no radio transmission at all; we were under complete radio silence, so nobody touched his radio. By now I didn't have any idea what was going on. If somebody had said, "Go home," I would have had a hard time finding my way back to the ship.

We finally headed back for the carrier. About 20 minutes out on that leg, headed back toward the ship, Lt. F. D. Miller, one of the lieutenants in "Killer" Kane's division, dropped back, and I turned to look at him because I was tail-end Charlie in the other group. This pilot bailed out of the airplane. I saw his chute open, and he went drifting back. I didn't know what to do, but everybody kept going, so I kept going with them. He obviously had run out of fuel. We were all down to about 42 gallons, and we were still a long ways from home at this point. Right after that, it got dark. All at once the group commander started to circle; this was where the carrier should have been. It was now dark, and there was nothing visible down there. Still no radio transmission. We had the YE in those days, but I don't think the ship had it on. There was a concern that it might be a beacon for the Japanese and bring them in. We knew they had the code, and they also had some captured equipment they could home in with. It had been decided that we wouldn't break radio silence because we knew the Japanese task force was somewhere around, but we didn't know where. The ship wasn't there because some submarines had fired torpedoes at the force, and so they headed off out of the rendezvous area. We were expendable, I guess.

We started to spiral down through a ceiling of broken clouds with bases at 600 to 800 feet. The moon wasn't up yet; it was really black. The next thing I know, I saw clouds going by me and we're down under this cloud deck. We've got 25 or so airplanes all milling around under the cloud layer. No carrier was visible, and about this time, unbeknownst to us, the bomber leader decided to drop the bombs that they had been carrying around all this time. When they dropped them, there was the biggest flash you've ever seen. One of those bombs didn't safe, and when it hit the water it blew. When I saw that flash, I thought one of our people had inadvertently flown in the water, but it was actually one of the bombs going off. About that time, I noticed I could see my wing lights reflecting off the water. I was flying stepped down on Swede

Vejtasa. He had let down, and, boy, I immediately pulled up above him. He was down low, making small turns, and all of a sudden he just straightened out and headed off. He later said he had found an oil slick from the task force with his wing lights, down on the water. We were literally only 10 or 15 feet off the water at this point, and everybody else was following us. Forty-five miles away, we found the task force. Swede did it by just following that leak. We wouldn't be here today if it hadn't been for somebody as innovative as Swede.

I'll tell you, talk about a really competent aviator—now, there's one. Swede Vejtasa was about as cool and laid back as anyone you'd ever want to meet. Early in the war, he and his rear-seat man shot down several airplanes in the SBD. He switched over and became a fighter pilot, and I'll tell you, he was just superb as a fighter pilot. He never wanted to be anything else. I remember the day he shot down seven airplanes in one flight. He got in the midst of this group of torpedo planes and just stayed there picking them off one by one, from the back to the front. Swede Vejtasa was single-minded; he was an airplane driver whose mission was to find and kill the enemy.

We found the task force, and they decided that, since the fighters were the lowest on fuel, we should get aboard first. Swede went around, and I was right behind him. That was my first night carrier landing, and it didn't bother me in the least. I'd done it on the field before, but I'd never landed aboard the ship at night. That's how short we were on training in those days. We got aboard and the group commander was still circling in his TBF, but the other TBFs started dropping in the water. In fact, the executive officer of the squadron came around and was in the groove when he ran out of fuel, and went under the fantail. Most of them made good water landings, and they survived. Then the group commander came around and landed last. He had not been carrying a torpedo. We got all the fighters aboard except for Miller, who had bailed out on the return flight. This was the night before the big battle, so, of course, we were minus a few airplanes.

The next morning, 26 October, was the day of the battle of Santa Cruz. We put together a strike group, and we launched about 8 A.M. I was a "spare" or "standby" for this mission, but I ended up going anyway. I remember I was flying with Flatley that morning, in the second section. We were about 20 miles from the carrier and had just formed up and were headed out, when Flatley signaled us to check our guns. Everybody was checking to make sure that their guns were charged. We looked up, somebody yelled, and Zeros were all over us. They had gotten up about two hours before we did, I guess, and they were already that close to the task force. They took out three fighters on the other

During the battle of the Santa Cruz Islands, the Enterprise *bore the brunt of co-ordinated attacks by Japanese bombers, sustaining multiple bomb hits. With the loss of the* Hornet *during the night of 26 October 1942, the* Enterprise *remained the only operational U. S. carrier in the Pacific.*

side of the formation, plus several other planes out of the attack group. Those early Japanese pilots were good. Flatley didn't let us turn away a bit. He just said, "Keep going." The Zeros made that one pass and went on to our task force, and we headed off on to their task force. Apparently, unbeknownst to us, there were about three waves of attackers that actually hit the *Hornet* and the *Enterprise* while we were gone. We found the enemy task force and made an attack. We headed back home, and I'll never forget the sight. I looked up on the horizon, and the first thing I saw was our happy home, listing and smoking heavily. We got there, and it turned out to be the *Hornet,* not the *Enterprise;* the *Enterprise* was about another 30 miles beyond the *Hornet* group.

We got back to the *Enterprise* really low on fuel, got in the traffic pattern, looked down, and saw torpedo wakes. The ship was zigzagging, S-turning like mad, but continued taking us aboard. I landed aboard, and there were airplanes stacked up clear back across the barricade; there weren't any barricades up at all. The landing signal officer was standing out there giving us the cut. The ship was in a terrific right turn when I came aboard. Here I am in a left-hand pattern, and they're making a right turn. I came around and got to the stern, he gave me a cut, and I landed. I'll never forget the shock; they taxied me forward, and I got out of the airplane and there was no no. 2 elevator; it was stuck in the down position. I got down to the hangar deck and was wading around in water halfway up to my knees, fuel, and dead bodies. Something had burned on the ship; you could smell this all over the place. They had taken bomb hits forward and amidships. In the meantime, not only are these torpedoes going by, but there's a dive-bombing attack going on at the same time.

At some time during these attacks, Robin Lindsey, the landing signal officer, got in the backseat of an SBD on the flight deck and started shooting those twin .30-calibers at an airplane coming across the fantail of the ship. Robin Lindsey was almost legendary among LSOs. Here was a person that everybody respected as much as a pilot as they did as an LSO.

Things were pretty hectic. It turned out, when we got organized, that we had a bunch of airplanes airborne with no room to land them. What was left of the *Hornet*'s air group was now aboard the *Enterprise,* or else was still airborne. We had so many airplanes that we had to send 13 planes to Espíritu Santo. By 30 October, the ship was in Nouméa, New Caledonia, where they were going to do major repairs, while the air group camped ashore at the grass field of Tontouta.

We were based ashore in Nouméa until 11 November, when they pulled the ship out long enough to take us up close, and launch us for Guadalcanal. The whole concept was that we were to search and find a bunch of enemy transports coming down to reinforce Guadalcanal, and that's about all the information that we had. Red Carmody, flying search in an SBD, ran across the ships on 14 November. That afternoon 8 SBDs with 1,000-pound bombs and 12 F4Fs led by Jimmy Flatley launched to attack the transports. We were cruising at about 25,000 feet, when we saw the Japanese task force, about 25 miles away. All of a sudden, we looked up and about 40 Zeros were coming right at us, maybe 5,000 feet above us. I've never heard anybody so calm in my life. Jimmy Flatley got on the radio and said, "Don't anybody flash any wings or canopy. Just sit still. Our mission is to attack the ships down there." With these airplanes going overhead, he assigned every bomber a separate target. Fortunately, the Zeros didn't see us, and we pressed right on in. There were still 7 of the original 11 transports coming down the slot; the rest had been taken care of by repeated strikes by planes from Henderson Field. We went in and strafed, and there were people all over those decks. I have vivid recollections of seeing people leaping over the sides of the ships. Eight airplanes strafing down the deck of a transport, with people all over the topside, must have been devastating. By the time we had finished strafing we had Zeros all over us, but we managed to get the bomber group together, and we covered them all the way back in to Guadalcanal. That attack was pretty successful, but there were still five transports heading for Guadalcanal. By nightfall, after further attacks from the *Enterprise* and Henderson Field, there remained only four damaged transports still headed down the Slot.

We flew to Guadalcanal to land. They put the bombers on the bomber strip and sent the fighters to another field called a fighter strip. This was a grass field with some Marston matting along the sides of it, where they were parking the airplanes. I landed and off to my left a big geyser of dirt went up. I thought the place was being bombed. It turned out the Japanese had some howitzers up on the side of the hill, and they were shelling the airfield. I looked around, and there was a Marine standing over there, beckoning me to come over under the trees, so I taxied over there. They grabbed the tail and pulled it around underneath the trees. I jumped out of the airplane and had the shock of my life. There was a hole about two-and-a-half feet across, in a big winding spiral down into the ground. I was told that it was a 14-inch shell hole, where the battleships had been shelling the place. I almost fell in that thing.

They put me in a Jeep, went around collecting pilots, and took us over to a tent area back under the trees, while these guns are still shelling the field. Right in the middle of this, a Marine with a campaign hat on and smoking a big cigar comes strolling across the middle of the strip. It was Joe Foss; he's strolling along across to the area, saying "Hello" to all these people as if nothing was happening, and he welcomed us to Guadalcanal. At the time we landed, the Marines had three fighter airplanes that were operational, and that night, that guy up in the hill managed to bag a couple more airplanes; both of them were ones that we had brought in. I guess we ended up with about 20 fighters left out of that whole melee.

The next morning, when it got to be daylight, we were about to get up, and a Marine came by and said, "Stay in your tent." The next thing, we hear all this automatic fire, and the Marines are out there machine-gunning the tops of the trees. The Japs had infiltrated during the night, and were sitting around up in the tops of the coconut trees, waiting for us to come out. The Marines got several of them out of those trees, and then we were allowed to come out.

I remember, in the tent at night, we were all lying there, and it was muggy and hot. Until they'd start shelling from the ships out in Savo Bay, we'd try to get a little bit of sleep. One night we could hear the Japanese walking around outside and trying to climb up into the trees. Of course, every bird sounded like a Japanese, so people were really on edge. There were maybe 20 of us in this tent when all of a sudden one of them let out a blood-curdling scream, and I heard a .45-caliber being cocked. Somebody in that tent said, "I'm going to shoot the first guy who moves." Well, I didn't even breathe. A little bit later, some guy said, "I'm all right." He had been lying there barechested, and a lizard had crawled across his chest. He thought it was a Japanese that was after him.

While we were there in November, we were part of the First Marine Division, Reinforced. Anybody who was available flew together. We had such a tenuous hold on that place, and it was just touch and go whether we were going to survive and stay there. The P-39s were flying coffins in those days; in air-to-air combat, they didn't have a chance against the Zero. They were hanging bombs on them, and when the Japanese would set up these guns up in the hills, they would go up and dive bomb them from low altitude; practically skip bombing them is what they were doing, and they were pretty effective. Some P-38s moved in while we were there. The pilots had very little time in the airplanes at all. I talked to one pilot who had never fired the guns in it; somebody stuck him in a P-38 and said, "Go."

Those days on Guadalcanal I wouldn't care to repeat. Thank goodness, on 17 November, we left to begin the return trip to Nouméa. We turned all our airplanes over to the Marines and got a new set of airplanes that came out on a "jeep" carrier. We came back later in February 1943 for a short stay. I tell you, you can have my share of being a ground soldier. I want no part of that.

1943: The Carrier Buildup

The first year of the war in the Pacific was one of decisive carrier battles resulting in severe attrition in ships, aircraft, and people on both sides. There followed a lull in carrier warfare in 1943, although U.S. carriers continued to provide support for the Allied offensive up the Solomons archipelago. A new Allied strategy evolved, and a U.S. fleet reorganization took place. In the Pacific, the Fifth Fleet (officially the Central Pacific Fleet until early 1944), commanded by Vice Adm. Raymond A. Spruance and spearheaded by the Fast Carrier Task Force, would drive westward through the Central Pacific to bring the war into Japanese waters; the Third Fleet under Adm. William F. Halsey would constitute the South Pacific Force; and the Seventh Fleet, eventually under Vice Adm. Thomas C. Kinkaid, would be part of Gen. Douglas Mac-Arthur's Southwest Pacific Forces, which would coordinate with Halsey's South Pacific Force in a drive toward the Japanese stronghold of Rabaul on New Britain.

By the end of November 1943, the South Pacific Force had advanced to Bougainville and constructed airstrips there. Carrier planes had struck Rabaul twice in November, substantially reducing enemy opposition to the Bougainville landings and destroying Japanese carrier planes and pilots based at Rabaul. By the end of the year, MacArthur's Southwest Pacific Forces were making good progress up the northeast coast of New Guinea and the Marines had landed near Cape Gloucester on New Britain. Following a decision to neutralize Rabaul at the north tip of New Britain, rather than take it by force, an intensive land-based air campaign followed, and by February 1944 the Allies were in control of the surrounding air and sea areas.

The Central Pacific drive, the centerpiece of the new Allied strategy, began in the fall of 1943 with carrier strikes on Marcus, Wake, and the Gilbert Islands, all a prelude to an invasion of the Gilberts. On 20 November, Makin and Tarawa were assaulted, and, although Tarawa was secured by 23 November, it was a bloody battle with unexpectedly high casualties. Lessons learned, though extremely costly, were invaluable in preparing for the forthcoming assault on the Marshall Islands, in February 1944.

The offensive initiatives of 1943 and later would not have been conceivable without a tremendous influx of new weapons for the war at sea—ships, aircraft, and small craft for the amphibious landings—and trained officers and men to man them. The first of the *Essex*-class carriers arrived in the Pacific in the spring, followed by *Independence*-class light carriers. The smaller escort, or "jeep," carriers, so essential for aircraft resupply and support of amphibious landings, began to arrive in significant numbers. The F6F Hellcat and F4U Corsair fighters entered combat service and proved to be more than a match for the Japanese Zero. Because of carrier suitability problems, Corsairs were shore-based in the South Pacific with Marine and Navy squadrons until cleared for carrier operations in April 1944. The SB2C Helldiver, supposedly a replacement for the venerable SBD Dauntless dive bomber of Midway fame, arrived on the scene, but was not immediately accepted by hardline SBD pilots.

In the fall of 1943, the Fifth Fleet had 6 heavy carriers, 5 light carriers, and 8 escort carriers. Scores of new battleships, cruisers, destroyers, and other combatant ships were at its disposal. Supported by a growing logistics train that would eventually stretch across the entire Pacific, the Fifth Fleet was finally in a position to project military power across the Pacific to the Philippines by the fall of 1944.

Prewar carrier pilots were well aware of the many shortcomings of the 1927-vintage *Lexington* and *Saratoga* and the newer carriers of the 1930s.

Catapults, arresting gear, maintenance and storage facilities, damage control capabilities, and creature comforts were primitive and would prove to be liabilities in combat. It was the Navy's good fortune that Lt. Comdr. James S. Russell applied his considerable engineering expertise, operational experience, and powers of persuasion to the design of the *Essex* during a two-year tour of duty in the Bureau of Aeronautics just before the war in the Pacific began. The result was a survivable carrier "optimized for its primary mission of flying and servicing airplanes." The ability of the *Essex*-class carrier to absorb incredible damage and continue to fight was due in no small part to the great vision and ability of Jim Russell.

Lt. Comdr. Herbert D. Riley sandwiched a 14-month tour at the Bureau of Aeronautics between two combat tours in the Pacific. As a planner in Programs and Allocations, he was heavily involved in the Navy's efforts to expand to 27,500 airplanes, train the required pilots, and match the air groups with Jim Russell's *Essex*-class carriers as they began to join the fleet in 1943. His story is a different view of the Pacific war, seen from the end of the logistics trail that began in wartime Washington, D.C. He provides a rare, and somewhat offbeat, insight into the vagaries and politics of dealing with aircraft companies as he coped with aircraft design problems, production delays, and less than patriotic motives of defense contractors.

Commissioning a new class of ship has always been fraught with unforeseen problems, frustrations, and occasional mishaps. Comdr. Fitzhugh Lee experienced all of these, and more, as the first air officer of the *Essex*. The ship sailed to the Pacific in company with the new *Yorktown,* nicknamed *The Fighting Lady.* The *Essex* participated in the first Rabaul strikes in November 1943, and the crew discovered new and wonderful things about their new ship. For the first time, many experienced the stress, strains, and fears of combat, and Fitzhugh Lee is particularly adept at relating his personal experiences working with young men in the close confines of the Combat Information Center (CIC), watching and waiting as the "blips" of enemy torpedo bombers moved across their radar scopes at night.

The arrival of new carriers and their aircraft in 1943 brought many new challenges to the planners and operators back at Pearl Harbor. Capt. Truman J. Hedding worked on a special board of experienced carrier aviators to work out new tactical instructions for carriers. It was obvious to everyone that, as aviators, they knew a lot about airplanes and they had learned a lot about tactics in the battles of 1942; but maneuvering 12 to 16 carriers and support ships in formation at sea in a combat situation posed challenges of totally new dimensions. War at sea would never be the same again.

Since the days of Lord Nelson, life for an enlisted man at sea has never been a comfortable one, and Roger Bond's sea stories of life on the old *Saratoga* are reminiscent of a Navy of another era. Bathing and washing clothes from buckets of water warmed by a steam jet, sleeping in hammocks strung from the overhead of the mess decks, making booze from torpedo alcohol—Roger explores another dimension of carrier life in the Pacific.

Design for Combat

Admiral James S. Russell

James Sargent Russell was born in Tacoma, Washington, on 22 March 1903, son of Ambrose James Russell and Loella Janet Sargent Russell. After graduation from high school and a tour as a seaman in the Merchant Marine, he entered the U.S. Naval Academy in 1922 and was designated a naval aviator in 1929. There followed normal tours of aviation duty both afloat and ashore, including two years in the Bureau of Aeronautics, during which he was closely associated with the design of the Essex-class carrier. His service included extensive command and staff tours of duty as he advanced in rank to that of admiral, effective 21 July 1958. Admiral Russell became Commander in Chief, Allied Forces, Southern Europe, on 2 January 1962, and served as such until his retirement, effective 1 April 1965. Since retirement, Admiral Russell has twice been recalled to active duty. In 1967, he conducted a major investigation of two carrier fires in the Gulf of Tonkin, which resulted in extensive changes to existing carrier operational procedures during the Vietnam War.

At the beginning of World War II, then Lieutenant Commander Russell was in command of Patrol Squadron 42, which he led in action against Japanese forces in the Aleutian Islands campaign. After duty in the Office of the Chief of Naval Operations and the Bureau of Aeronautics, Captain Russell returned to the Pacific area as chief of staff to Commander, Carrier Division 2, Rear Adm. Ralph Davison, operating as a task group with famed Task Forces 38 and 58 in action against the Japanese.

During his illustrious career, Admiral Russell was awarded the Distinguished Service Medal with one Gold Star, Legion of Merit with two Gold Stars, Distinguished Flying Cross, Air Medal, Navy Unit Commendation Ribbon, numerous campaign and service medals, and several foreign decorations.

Adm. James S. Russell, air department, USS Yorktown, *1937–39; carrier desk officer, Bureau of Aeronautics, Navy Department, 1939–41.*

In 1937, I had been in a wonderful dive bomber squadron, Bombing Squadron 5-B, a little over a year when I was ordered to a strange assignment. I was ordered to the fitting out of a new carrier, the USS *Yorktown.* My wife, first child, and I lived in an apartment in Newport News, Virginia, and I went daily to watch the construction of this ship. Having flown from the old *Ranger,* I was very much impressed with that ship's inadequacies, so I had a lot of ideas. The *Ranger* was a fairly small ship. She had two airplane elevators that went through the centerline of the flight deck, and each arrived at the hangar deck level encased in an elevator well open in only one direction, so there was only one way to get an airplane off or on an elevator from the hangar. Not only that but the elevators were placed on the center line of the ship at the extreme ends of the hangar so there was no dead space, no quiet space, in the hangar. If you were at flight quarters, there was always traffic between the two elevators and the flight deck.

The *Langley,* our first carrier, had been a makeshift affair. It was a flight deck superimposed over the length of a collier, a coal ship, with electric drive propulsion and a maximum speed of 12 knots. I remember in a big maneuver off San Francisco, when I was in an observation squadron, we just couldn't fly from the *Langley* because the ship couldn't generate enough wind on her own to let us get airborne. Twelve knots plus the speed your aircraft could get in the half length of the deck, or whatever was allowed for the takeoff, wasn't enough.

In most of the older carriers, the ready rooms for the pilots waiting to man their airplanes were atrocious. On the *Lexington* and *Saratoga,* we used a chart room and usually stood up around a big chart table. We'd stand there in the chart room with our parachutes on, each carrying a little plotting board of our own which we took out and put into the airplane to work our navigation. Carrying a parachute through a bunch of whirling propellers to get into your airplane is rather a ticklish business, because if the parachute gets loose and caught in a propeller, you're gone. The ready rooms on the *Ranger* were very simple things. There was a wooden bench in our ready room on which we sat facing portholes so the light was in our eyes. Not only that, but, to add insult to injury, there was a head forward, and therefore upwind of us, and in the early morning when it was being used there was a "perfume" that came back into the ready room. All these things combined to make me a fanatic in trying to figure out the optimum arrangement of an aircraft carrier.

So, while I was in Newport News fitting out the *Yorktown,* we fought for a lot of things. We put reclining chairs in the ready rooms, all facing in one direction, with a blackboard, and a teletype information system that could be operated from a central point, air plot. Underneath the seat of the chair, we had a little locker with a three-combination lock, so that one could lock a confidential code book under the chair. Not only that, if you were on a long alert, waiting for your flight, you could recline and get some rest. Air conditioning came in, too, and if you were sitting for long hours in a flight suit you would appreciate that very much, particularly in the tropics. So we did a lot of these things in the *Yorktown,* and then later in her sister ship the *Enterprise.*

The senior officers in the *Yorktown* were willing to listen to new ideas and be helpful. We had an understanding air officer, Comdr. Clifton A. F. ("Ziggy") Sprague. I remember one unsolved problem. We used to have 24-volt electrical circuits with storage batteries in the airplane, and, if you had a pilot who was a little inexperienced with the engine, he would overprime or underprime, and eventually run his battery down so we couldn't start him. I had the idea of running a direct current loop of about 28 volts all the way around the flight deck, so that, if you had a fellow who was a dud due to his running his battery down, you could run a jumper cable out as you do with an automobile and put it on the terminals of the battery in his airplane and get him started, in spite of himself. Then you wouldn't have to cut him out of the pack and go through all the pain of finding a place to park him while the other planes took off past him. So I got permission from Ziggy Sprague, and then the captain, to fly on up to Anacostia [in Washington, D.C.] and go on over to the Bureau of Steam Engineering, I think it was called then, to see if I could get such an installation authorized for our ship. After many referrals, I wound up in the electrical division officer's office. This division office was manned by a chap with the name of Lieutenant Rickover. You would have thought that every inch of copper wire in the United States Navy belonged personally to that guy. When I explained what I wanted, he said, "Do you know how much copper that would take?" I said, "Yes. I've made a rough calculation." I had put four motor generators around the deck to reduce the voltage drop. He said, "We don't have that much copper wire in the United States Navy!" I went away saying if I ever meet that guy in a black alley I'm really going to let him have it! I was very much unimpressed. I met this gentleman later on many times, and I learned to respect him for what he'd done, but that was my first exposure to the Rickover type of treatment. I flew back down to Norfolk with my tail between my legs and admitted to the air officer I had failed in my mission.

Newport News had made such profit on the *Ranger* that they thought they would take a little more risk on the next carrier. They decided to cut the reduction gears in their own facility there at Newport News. To do so, they set up the gear-cutting machinery in a room with very carefully controlled temperature so that there would be no temperature distortion in the cutting of the teeth. But apparently what they forgot was that they were on tideland, and every freight train that went by left its phonographic impression on the face of the gear teeth. So when we went to sea in our trials, the noise from the gears was just fantastic; it was 120 decibels on the engine room floor plates. This, of course, was not acceptable, and they put us in the Norfolk Navy Yard after our shakedown cruise and cut great holes in the deck to lift the four main reduction gears right out of the ship and replace them with gears that were made by a professional gear-cutting outfit.

In 1939, after two years in the *Yorktown,* I went to my first shore duty in Washington, as the carrier desk officer, Ship Installation Division, in the Bureau of Aeronautics. There was a very interesting ship, just a few pencil lines on vellum, over in preliminary design in the Bureau of Ships. It was the *Essex*-class carrier, which was eventually completed in 1942. We in Aeronautics fought to get that ship optimized for its primary mission, namely flying and servicing airplanes. We did all sorts of innovative things to her. We were to have three airplane elevators between the flight deck and the hangar. We asked to have them placed at the quarter lengths of the ship and displaced to the side as far as possible. The forward, or no. 1, elevator had to be left on the centerline of the ship because of the narrowness of the hull at that location. The midships, or no. 2, elevator platform was put entirely over the side, a position which is used today and is preferred because it obviates the need to cut through the main (hangar) deck for a well into which the elevator platform fits when it is at the hangar level. The after, no. 3, elevator was displaced to starboard as far as practicable to give width of deck on which to move airplanes. Open hangar space was left abaft no. 3 elevator in the hangar where airplanes under repair might be parked free of the traffic between elevators. Around, and outboard, of this space were located the aviation repair shops. Thus, an airplane under repair could be lashed down and left undisturbed during flight operations and, further, be in close proximity to repair shops. Although two catapults were provided, World War II propeller-driven airplanes could take off under their own power in half the length of the flight deck and be arrested in landing, also in half the length of the flight deck. Thus, with airplane elevators at the quarter lengths of the flight deck, one always, and two sometimes, were available to bring up airplanes from the hangar to the flight deck during launching. Likewise during landing, two elevators were available to take airplanes below to the hangar.

In planning the design of the *Essex,* I dealt primarily with Commander Kniskern, the preliminary design officer in the Bureau of Ships, and I had lots of support from the Ship Installations Division of the Bureau of Aeronautics. Any or all suggestions were considered, and we had many good suggestions.

By mid-June 1943, nine fast carriers were commissioned, including four of the Essex-*class (shown here) and five converted light cruisers of the* Independence-*class.*

We had experts in arresting gear, experts in catapults, and, of course, we had an aeronautical engineer as the head of the division. He was very amenable to argument; he supported me in everything we did, and Kniskern was delightfully broad-minded in his approach, but I came against considerable resistance when I asked for rectangular outlines of the flight deck. They wished to narrow the deck as it went forward because the lines of the ship were that way. I said, "Well, we don't want that; we want to carry the width of the flight deck right up to the bow, because when you're taking off the point of maximum error is right at the bow, and if you narrow the flight deck there you're giving the aviator less chance to make a successful takeoff." Kniskern said, "Well, okay, we can do this, but it's going to be difficult, and we won't be able to support properly, from the standpoint of the structure, those two forward corners of the flight deck. If you get in very heavy weather, they'll fail." The load on the overhang was so great they would fail. I said, "Well, until we get the ship into very heavy weather, we've had a proper flying field. How about it?" He said, "Okay." Now you may remember that Halsey eventually got the *Essex*-class carriers in a typhoon out west, and sure enough some of the forward corners of *Essex*-class flight decks bent down under the weight of the seas. But think of the hours and hours and hours of flight that had occurred before those failures happened.

The ready rooms were another particular consideration. We tried to put the squadron ready rooms with ready access to where the airplanes of that squadron would normally be parked. The torpedo planes were usually way aft, bombers were farther up, fighters up forward, and so forth. In the ready rooms, we put reclining chairs all facing in one direction where you had a blackboard and a teletype from air plot that could display the information you needed for navigation.

On the carriers, one of the most vulnerable commodities was the high-test aviation gasoline which we carried. Gasoline was carried in saddle tanks, so-called. A saddle tank was constructed with a central, more or less cylindrical tank, and then a saddle around that, and again a saddle around the saddle. In no case were there air and gasoline in the same tank together. The gasoline was displaced by saltwater, which was pumped in and provided the pressure to force the gasoline up to the refueling stations on hangar and flight decks. The amount of gasoline was computed for rather intensive operations and it was a balance between the amount of ammunition you had, the gasoline for flying, your own ship's fuel, and so forth. The aviation gasoline was displaced by salt water, and displacement occurred first in the outer saddle, so that as you drained down your gasoline, you wound up with a saltwater blanket around the interior tank. And then the inboard saddle tank was next to be exhausted of fuel, and, finally, you got down to the core. You never got below about 5 percent of fuel, because you began to get a mixture of gasoline and water, if you got too low. But the gasoline was very carefully filtered at the outlet to prevent water from getting into the aircraft fuel tanks. It was very necessary, of course, to have a pure supply of fuel for the aircraft.

So that was one protection; but the whole vertical trunk, where the pumps and piping were, was protected with armor. Electric motors drove pumps through stuffing boxes in a bulkhead, so that there would be no electric motors to make sparks in the trunk. Also the whole trunk, which contained the aviation fuel system, could be flooded with CO_2 gas. There were big storage cylinders of the gas, and, if you pulled the right ripcord, you would just flood the whole trunk, and fill it with the inert gas, CO_2. Also, when we fueled aircraft, the moment we finished refueling, the gasoline which was up to the hoses was put back into the system. By pumping water out, you sucked the gasoline down all the risers back into the tanks, so there was no gasoline above the storage space. Flight deck and hangar crews were also very careful; if there was any gasoline spilled on the deck, it had to be swabbed up immediately.

Then, as far as fire fighting was concerned, there were foam, fog, and regular salt water through fire hoses on the flight deck. Overhead in the hangar there were sprinklers that gave a regular tropical rainstorm in the hangar if they were cut loose, and then later we had hangar doors to divide the hangar into spaces. In the hangar, there were conflagration stations, sealed-in cubicles with thick glass ports, from which all the fire-fighting devices in the hangar could be controlled. Of course, there were foam, fog, and water in the hangar, too, which could be applied manually. Each bay of the hangar had its conflagration control station. The men stationed there could see what was going on in the hangar and by remote control could turn on the valves which would do the sprinkling. Magazines were floodable; they could be sprinkled or flooded.

Damage-control training was heavily stressed. We had damage-control schools ashore. We had fire fighting where students actually set fire to various structures. We had gasoline and oil fires, and the men were drilled on how to put fires out. There were damage-control specialists, but the entire crew was also trained. At sea, damage control was one of the standard drills. Fire on the flight deck, and you'd run everything out and test everything, make sure you had fog and foam. You would put the foam over the side to keep the ship clean, and you'd be timed as to how quickly the foam arrived at the scene.

In the combat zone, if a carrier was on fire, we counselled our skippers to put the carrier into a tight turn to starboard. A carrier of the *Essex*-class lists outboard in her turn, and putting her in a tight turn to starboard would slope the decks to port away from ship control on the island, the conflagration control stations in the hangar, the repair lockers on the flight deck, and the main intake for air to the machinery spaces, which was below the island on the starboard side. Listing a ship in that way would carry any flaming gasoline over the side of the ship away from the part that was more useful.

We had two cruisers paired off for each carrier, depending upon their position in the task group formation, one to go to the aid of the carrier to assist as possible with fire hoses and repair parties from alongside, the other cruiser to take the cripple in tow, if she had lost propulsive power. In those days, we had a circular screen of about 24 destroyers, which served as an antisubmarine screen, as well as an outer screen against aircraft, but primarily against submarines detected by underwater sonar. Four destroyers, assigned according to whatever position they occupied in formation, had the duty of screening the cripple.

By the end of World War II, we had 17 *Essex*-class carriers. Of those 17, all but 3 got into very hot action in the Pacific. There were none lost, yet none that got in action came through without some sort of battle injury. Design and training really paid off.

Filling the Pipeline

Vice Admiral Herbert D. Riley

Herbert Douglas Riley was born on 24 December 1904, son of Sarah M. Riley and Marion H. Riley. In 1923, he was appointed to the U.S. Naval Academy, was graduated and commissioned ensign on 2 June 1927, and was designated a naval aviator on 1 July 1930. He subsequently served in various command and staff assignments ashore and afloat, including all types of naval aviation squadrons. He advanced in rank to that of vice admiral, effective February 1958. Admiral Riley was Director of the Joint Staff, Joint Chiefs of Staff, from February 1962 until February 1964 and soon thereafter was transferred to the retired list, effective 1 April 1964.

At the beginning of World War II, he had duty as operations officer on the staff of Commander, Fleet Air, West Coast. Later, he participated in air operations at Guadalcanal in January 1943. He then served as aviation planner on the staff of the Deputy Chief of Naval Operations (Air), Navy Department, Washington, D.C. In October 1944, he was ordered as commanding officer of the USS Makassar Strait, *which participated in the Iwo Jima and Okinawa operations. Detached from command of the* Makassar Strait *in June 1945, he became operations officer on the staff of Commander, First Carrier Task Force, and as such saw the end of the war in Tokyo Bay.*

Admiral Riley's decorations include the Distinguished Service Medal, Distinguished Flying Cross, Bronze Star Medal with Combat "V," Army Commendation Ribbon with Oak Leaf Cluster, Commander, Distinguished Order of the British Empire, and the Peruvian Air Cross (First Class).

Comdr. Herbert D. Riley, ca. 1945. (Courtesy Lynne L. Riley)

In October 1942, Vice Adm. John S. McCain returned from the South Pacific to Washington to become Chief of the Bureau of Aeronautics, relieving Vice Adm. John H. Towers, who moved on to become Commander, Air Force, Pacific Fleet. I reported to Programs and Allocations in the bureau with a determination that I was going to get out of there as soon as I could and get back in the Pacific. I went up to see Admiral McCain the day I reported, renewed acquaintance, reported in to him, and so forth. I said, "Admiral, I'd like to get you to make me a promise that you'll get me out of here just as soon as possible, so I can get back in the Pacific." He said, "I'll make a deal with you. The day that I get my orders, I'll see that they cut orders for you." I couldn't ask for more than that, and I knuckled down to my new job.

I spent about 14 months back in Washington in the middle period of the war. It was the first time that naval aviation had ever been able to build up to really significant proportions, both in numbers of planes (27,500) and training the tremendous number of pilots needed. The training organization to make such a program possible was built by the foresight of Admiral Towers, who had been a very long-range thinker and a great planner. He surrounded himself with very capable people, including Capt. George Anderson in Programs and Allocations. Capt. Arthur Radford, who much later was to become Chairman of the Joint Chiefs of Staff, was put in charge of the aviation pilot training setup, to establish the huge training plant that blossomed from Pensacola to Corpus Christi and Jacksonville. Comdr. Luis de Florez was there, and he was the fellow who really brought training devices into being. He was the one that developed practically every training device used by both the Navy and the Army Air Forces during the war. The bag of tricks he had in his establishment was absolutely uncanny for that day and age. You could get in one of his simulators and do everything you could do in an airplane, including instrument flying, landings, everything else—with movies for background. You would feel that you were right in the air flying the airplane, and it was monitored from outside all the time. There would be tapes of what you had done right, or wrong. This simplified the training operation, and cut down the cost and time tremendously. Luis de Florez single-handedly was responsible for the whole program.

The 27,500-plane program was formulated by George Anderson. We did, during my time, push it up to 31,000, 32,500, and so on, but the real push was to get to that 27,500-plane goal, with the pilots to match it, and then to match air groups with the *Essex*-class carriers. They came out like sausages there for a while, and we had to have an air group ready and trained to go aboard. It was nip and tuck, particularly in shifting over from the old SBD to the SB2C. The SB2C was a wartime plane, which was full of bugs and all sorts of difficulties. It was a very complex plane, a very difficult plane to maintain, but there was the capability of "cranking them out." That's what we had to have, building capacity. It was never a question of money; we could always get the money in those days. It was a question of the capacity of American industry to produce airplanes.

I had direct relationship with the manufacturers and with their key officials, particularly production managers, to try to gear their production up to the maximum we could get. For instance, building up to 500 F6Fs a month at Grumman was quite an accomplishment. That happened during my time in programming. Although Grumman was the best manufacturer we had, there were limitations to what could be done with his plant. Of course, they kept building additional plants, but it still took time to get production up. Further, all manufacturers wanted the credit for the number of airplanes they produced, but the airplanes they produced weren't worth a damn if you didn't get the concurrent spare parts to keep the planes flying that you already had. This was our greatest battle at Grumman; the only battle really that we had with Grumman was the business of getting them to deliver the spare parts. When planes were grounded for lack of spare parts, we didn't want people to get in the habit of drawing a new airplane just because a tire had blown on the old one. So I had to take the very drastic step at one time, in which I was backed by Admiral McCain, of shutting down the Grumman production line. In other words, we refused to take delivery of any more new airplanes until we got the spare parts we needed, and for which we had contracted. Grumman was way behind in spares delivery. He had only a small field at his plant, and the planes would come out of the factory and be parked on that field. Ferry pilots would take them away right away. But it didn't take long to choke up the field if we refused to fly them out. That is what I did to force a shutdown of the production line in order to force him to build the spares that we needed. Oh, it broke his heart. But there was nothing he could do about it. He had to do it. He had no place to put new airplanes. He had to stop his production line and get out the spares. Well, we got the spares, and we never had similar trouble again. It worked.

As for other airplanes, like the SB2C, there were tremendous shortcomings in design and bad workmanship. We had different plants making them, plants that had never built airplanes. For instance, Goodyear was building SB2Cs just from the Curtiss blueprints, without ever having built an airplane before. In the automotive area of production, the people weren't trained for the close tolerances that must prevail in airplane production. If the parts don't fit in automobile production, the worker pulls them together, puts a bolt through them, and that's good enough. That will work for an automobile; it won't work for an airplane. An airplane built that way would vibrate itself apart. We had to take all sorts of drastic steps to get workmanship improved and then to try to time the SB2Cs into the carriers. Everybody knew that the SBD was outdated terribly, too slow, low performance, et cetera, but it was a very fine flying airplane. Most any plane that Douglas built was a fine flying airplane. The SBD was among them. Then the SB2C was so tricky to fly, compared to the SBD, and so hard to maintain that the skippers of the new carriers preferred to have the old SBDs to the SB2Cs. We had quite a battle forcing the SB2Cs down their respective throats. But, finally, they got them.

The same thing happened with the introduction of the F4U Corsair. Eventually, it got to be a very fine plane after the bugs were out of it. A lot of its ultimate success was due to Lt. Comdr. Joseph C. Clifton, who was commanding officer of VF-12, the first Navy F4U squadron, when it was formed at Naval Air Station North Island in October 1942. A relatively simple change took the biggest bug out of it. The greatest trouble with it was poor visibility for the pilot. The engine loomed in front of him in his narrow cockpit, and he just had to hang his head out of the sides of the plane to see where he was going. This was particularly true in a nose-high attitude, as in coming in to land on a carrier. The pilot couldn't see the deck, the LSO's signals, or anything important. Joe Clifton liked the Corsair; he thought it was a good airplane, basically, although it had a lot of faults, such as poor visibility, to be ironed out. Eventually, somebody was smart enough to say, "Why don't we just raise that seat about six inches?" What they did actually was to build up the canopy a little bit and raise the seat so that the bottom adjustment on the seat was six inches above where it had been before. Then when the plane came in to land, the seat could be raised to get the pilot's head up high enough for him to be able to see enough to bring the plane aboard the carrier. Once they got the seat raised, the Corsair was fine.

This was the kind of program we had to cope with back in the Programs and Allocations Division. We also had a production capacity problem with the PBYs. We wanted to get all the PBYs built that we could get, and Consolidated was limited in the number they could turn out in the facilities that they had. So we contracted with Canadair, the outfit in Canada which turned out the Hurricanes for Britain. There were two Canadian facilities that we were able to sign up to produce PBYs. Neither had ever produced anything larger than a fighter before that. The Canadian Car and Foundry Company was the other company. Both were given Consolidated's blueprints for PBYs and proceeded to turn them out. At that time, we were having great trouble with production workmanship, due to the great expansion in size of Consolidated. We decided that we would work up some sort of competition, with unmarked airplanes to be built at each of the three facilities. Then we had a group of production experts go over each plane for workmanship. It turned out that the two Canadian facilities came out one and two, and the original producer of the airplane came out number three, on their own airplane. Needless to say, we had no further workmanship trouble after that.

I mentioned once before that I had made a deal with Vice Admiral McCain, when he took over first as Chief of the Bureau of Aeronautics, and then as Deputy Chief of Naval Operations for Air. It was that he would spring me for duty in the Pacific again on the day that he got his orders. Those were his terms, and I told him that, of course, I had no choice but to accede to those terms! He acquiesced. Finally, in August 1944, Admiral McCain was relieved by Vice Adm. Aubrey W. Fitch, commonly known as Jakie Fitch, and I had my opportunity to become commanding officer of the carrier *Makassar Strait*.

First Cruise of the *Essex*

Vice Admiral Fitzhugh Lee

Fitzhugh Lee, son of Colonel George Mason Lee, U.S. Army, and Kathro Larrabee Burton Lee, was born in Batangas, Philippine Islands, on 19 August 1905. He was appointed to the U.S. Naval Academy in 1922, graduated and was commissioned ensign on 3 June 1926, and was designated a naval aviator 16 September 1929. Subsequent service included extensive squadron, staff, and command tours ashore and afloat, and he advanced in rank to that of vice admiral, effective 31 December 1959. On 31 July 1964, he became Commandant of the National War College, Washington, D.C., and served as such until relieved of active duty pending his retirement, effective 1 August 1967.

During World War II, he assisted in fitting out the USS Essex *and served as air officer and then as executive officer from December 1942 until April 1944, participating in some of the greatest naval air victories of the war. In 1944, as commanding officer of the escort carrier* Manila Bay, *he was involved in the invasions of Leyte, Mindoro, and Lingayen Gulf and was twice awarded*

the Navy Cross for extraordinary heroism in the battle of Samar Island and in
operations in support of landings in the Philippines.

   Admiral Lee's decorations include the Navy Cross with one Gold Star,
Distinguished Service Medal with one Gold Star, and the Legion of Merit.

*Capt. Fitzhugh Lee (left) and
Rear Adm. Calvin T. Durgin,
commander of the escort car-
riers in the Lingayen Gulf in-
vasion, confer aboard the
USS Manila Bay, 1944.
(Courtesy Vice Adm.
Fitzhugh Lee, USN [Ret.])*

In late 1942, I was initially ordered to command of Air Group 9, which was
forming for the carrier *Essex,* then being built. But, before the orders could be
written, they decided they had to go up another notch in rank and job. So, since
I was about to become a commander, I was made air officer of the *Essex*
instead. I went back to Newport News where she was being built and to get her
ready for commissioning.

   We were in competition with the carrier *Yorktown,* which was supposed to
be commissioned three weeks after the *Essex.* The *Essex* had as a skipper Capt.
Donald B. ("Wu") Duncan, and the skipper of the *Yorktown* was Capt. J. J.
("Jocko") Clark. Jocko Clark was a great driver, and he was determined that the
Yorktown would get finished and commissioned, and get out there and be
fighting before the *Essex* did. The contest was on. The rivalry was great. We
thought that a lot of dishonest things were done to get things provided for the
Yorktown which should have come to the *Essex* just so we wouldn't get finished
in time, but we never were able to prove anything. We did get out first by a

week. We sailed out to the Pacific together actually, but we were commissioned a week before they were. As a sidelight, I had visited many of the ships in Pearl Harbor that came back with battle damage, talked to the people and crew, seen the dedication of everybody in the war zone. At the Newport News Shipbuilding plant, I was air officer due to take charge of everything that the Air Department would use on the ship—the arresting gear, the catapults, all the gear that goes into aviation supply, et cetera—and I was extremely upset by the attitude of the shipbuilding workers. They were on union hours. They knew they weren't going to be drafted. They were swiping materials and selling them to a big scrap organization in town—all kinds of things that shouldn't have been declared scrap. But, in the pressure of war, things are done—get it done quickly; don't ask questions. I was so upset by the fact that I would go around in the ship while it was being finished and the people who were supposed to be working were sitting there having a cup of coffee and a talkfest, or napping, especially at night when you had the night shifts. I would talk to some of them once in awhile and say, "Why are you sitting here doing this when people are dying?" I'd get emotional about it. Well, it never did any good. I can remember writing a long letter to the Superintendent of Shipbuilding attached to the Newport News Shipbuilding and Dry Dock Company to make a public complaint, but I never sent it. It was a sour note to me that these men, many men in their thirties, should have been doing better. In many cases, probably they were not working because they were waiting for some part to come or there was another good reason, but when asked about it their attitude was, "Who the deuce are you to ask? You don't like it; go lump it. We're doing our part, and you do yours." Kind of a Billy-be-damned attitude, which just killed me. Nothing ever came of it, and we got the ship in commission. I'm sure it was only a minority of them that did it. It left a bad taste in my mouth. Others who had been in the war zone felt as I did. It was one of the sidelights on human beings as human beings.

The *Essex* was commissioned on 31 December 1942 so we would be commissioned in that calendar year. An amusing but tragic episode occurred just before the commissioning. I had the watch on board ship, and we had a very green crew who had just moved aboard. We had a very elaborate apparatus for flooding the hangar deck of the ship in case of fires and bomb damage. The hangar was divided into compartments, and there were massive spray systems for making curtains of salt water to screen off a fire and tons of water to douse the location of the fire. This was all controlled from a booth that looked down from the top of the inside of the hangar deck. It was called the conflagration station. On the midwatch, we had a big sailor up in the conflagration station. He was sitting in front of a big battery of long valve handles, which controlled all the water. The telephone at one end of the booth rang, and he had to go along this line of valve handles to answer it. He lurched along, and his fanny swung against about eight of these valves. It was about two o'clock of a December morning, very, very cold, and with all of the ship's company sound asleep. Thousands of tons of water were let loose in the hangar deck, and went on down into the living spaces below. Well, the confusion was out of this world. It was a blow and damaged a lot of equipment, and was bad from every point of view. As a public relations effort, it was one of the world's worst. Actually, the ship took on so much water that before we could get everything stopped, the ship took a perceptible list. Since the ship was still in the hands of the shipbuilders, it wasn't technically my responsibility, but I certainly shared the blame. If we'd had a small skinny man on watch, it might never have happened.

The *Essex* went to the Pacific in company with the *Yorktown*. Many of the scenes which were taken in the movie called *The Fighting Lady,* a famous film about the war episodes of the carriers, were taken on the carrier *Essex* by a small photographic team that was going to go out to make such a film. I think they came first to the *Yorktown,* but they spent a lot of time on the *Essex,* and many of the scenes of *The Fighting Lady* (which became the nickname of the *Yorktown)* were actually taken on board the *Essex.* This irritated the *Essex* sailors because the film became known as the story of the *Yorktown.* Many scenes showed aviators in the wardroom and in the pilots' ready rooms. The fellows who were doing the photographing were very good. They selected a number of people to portray distinctive personalities. One young officer pilot in one of the *Essex* squadrons was a good-looking young fellow. By happenstance, he became sort of a featured face in the film, and people remembered him as a principal character in it.

At the time the *Essex* and the *Yorktown* got out to the Pacific, which was mid-1943, we were the first big carriers to get out there of the 17 *Essex*-class carriers that were commissioned during World War II. We had not been able to hit back at the Japs in any significant way until these two carriers arrived. As a sort of a warm-up for us, we elected to make a strike at Marcus Island, which was pretty far west in the Pacific but very isolated, very small, and of no very great significance other than the fact the Japanese had a radio station and a weather station there which were valuable to them. The value of the strike was mostly psychological and training for us, to make sure that we were operating pretty well. The *Yorktown* and the *Essex* both struck it on 31 August 1943. We got practically no opposition, but there were antiaircraft batteries on it. One of our planes that was shot down at Marcus was the young officer who had been in *The Fighting Lady* film. We thought he had been killed because another pilot said that they saw flames and explosions when his plane hit the ground. We didn't know until we saw him on the *Missouri* during the surrender ceremony in 1945 that he had survived and had been a prisoner of war.

We were pretty exuberant that everything had worked well. The ships were showing themselves to be very fine ships. The technical design of the *Essex*-class carriers was in the hands of one man who said what characteristics should be in the ships to make them good aircraft carriers—the aircraft handling arrangements, the aircraft bombing and rearmament arrangements, fueling arrangements, catapulting, arresting gear—all the things that had to do with making them work well in their principal job as the operators of aircraft. This man was in the Bureau of Aeronautics, and his name was then Comdr. J. S. Russell. He went on to become a four-star officer. He was a man of great vision and ability; he had been on carriers; he knew them; he insisted on getting things done that he felt were necessary, and getting them done in the face of opposition from other people who wanted other things done which would have impaired their efficiency as a carrier. The fact is that we built 24 of those ships. They all functioned beautifully, not one of them was sunk. It's a wonderful tribute to him. I wonder if he has been accorded the place he should have in naval history. He deserves a good share for that job, and for many other jobs that he had. He was a man of great ability and foresight, and he applied it in making those ships very workable as aircraft carriers. They were superb ships. We found out that these things that he had been fighting for worked really well at Marcus—comparatively few bugs, and with assets that we never knew were there.

In November 1943, the *Essex* participated in strikes against Rabaul, one of the principal bases of the Japanese. We worked from an anchorage at Espíritu Santo in the New Hebrides. The *Essex* sortied from there to make the carrier strikes with four other carriers against the shipping concentrated in Rabaul. Our intelligence wasn't too awfully good in some respects because I don't think we were aware of the fact that most of the Japanese naval air group survivors of the carriers they had lost earlier in the battle of the Coral Sea were then land-based near Rabaul. They had a whole bunch of naval aircraft down there available to oppose our strikes. Some strikes had been made before the *Essex* had arrived, but the *Essex* made two strikes on 11 November which were very successful. However, the Japanese made a major attack on the *Essex*. This was our first real taste of battle for the crew of the ship, because the whole air battle was fought very close to the shore and almost over our ship.

The *Essex* was the first ship to arrive out there with any reasonable kind of CIC with radar in it, and the Rabaul strike was the first real test of radar in control of aircraft. By that time, I had become executive officer of the *Essex,* and my battle station was in the CIC, as the CIC officer. Capt. Ralph Ofstie was now the skipper of the ship. This was one of the earliest uses of an effective CIC in air defense. We were trying to use our new radar, which worked well at long range in the early stages of the battle, but it soon became too much of a melee in which we didn't know whether we were shooting at our own planes or the Japanese planes. We saw planes trying to dive on us and hurt us, but nobody actually damaged the ship at all. On the other hand, quite a number of Japanese planes were shot down in sight of us, and some of our own people were shot down. We were very keyed up as you always are in combat. A couple of them that we fired at we found out later were our own people. Some of them landed in the water and went floating by the ship in little rubber boats, and we fired at them from the deck of the ship. They were picked up later and saved, but it was just one of the exigencies of war.

This battle gave the ship a great deal of confidence. The actual exchange of aircraft, those lost by the Japanese and those lost by us, was very greatly in our favor, and there was a great deal of damage done by our planes in Rabaul. The whole thing was a good maneuver for us.

In later operations, Japanese land-based bombers came out and attacked us, usually at night. They were uncomfortable for us because you could see them coming on the radar. Our means of shooting them down at night with radar-directed guns was not efficient because the planes came in low over the water. We couldn't see the airplanes; all we could see was the radar blip at long range. We were not sufficiently advanced technically to shoot these planes down at night before they could drop their torpedoes. I can remember spending many unhappy hours in CIC watching these blips coming at us, knowing what they were doing, and hoping that our guns would shoot them down, seeing them turn around on the radar screen, and then knowing that the torpedoes were in the water and on their way to you. Those minutes seemed like years, when you are sitting there waiting to see whether you're going to get hit.

CIC was not a happy place to be. It was interesting psychologically to me, even then at the time. It was my first experience of real fear—being in the face of what you thought might be death at any moment, and I was interested in seeing how other people took it. Here you sat around these radar screens and watched these things happen with young seamen who were 18 or 19 years old, just off the farm or out of the shoe store, or what have you, and their reactions were for the most part wonderful. Every once in awhile you'd find one that couldn't take it. You could usually see this coming, and I found that I could spot when somebody was getting a little hysterical or was about to be hysterical. There were not many cases. You could see that some poor kid was getting too emotional. If he got very emotional, it would spread so you had to think of something quick—sending him out to do something right away and get him out. I found that I benefited myself. I was the senior officer in the place, and, by looking around carefully to find any evidence of this, I took my own mind off my own problem.

Lots of times I wouldn't like to say things on the intercom system to the skipper because you just didn't want the men around you to hear what you were saying. It might be misinterpreted or discouraging, when you didn't want it to be. Often I would write on a little slip of paper and say, "Run this down to the captain." We were on the deck above the bridge. I would quickly write a note, which said virtually nothing. This was just to send a message to Captain Ofstie by a runner from CIC, and half the time in those circumstances it was just to get the messenger's mind off his problem. Captain Ofstie understood what I was doing. We had an agreement between us. We had a few who lost control of themselves and started weeping, crying, praying, and things like that. Nobody minds people praying, but it's not quite a happy circumstance for men at their battle station. In that little CIC, which was primitive by modern standards, there were 12, 14 people. I don't want to magnify this. It was a human relations thing which was interesting to me. I found it in other circumstances in other times in the war, too.

The stress and strain, the long hours at sea, and being exposed to fire as the young pilots were all the time was overcome in some respects by letting the flight surgeon of an air group, or the ship, prescribe for a pilot who had come back from a combat mission, one of these small sample bottles of whiskey which the carriers had a plentiful supply of. They were used by the flight surgeons as a sedative for the nerves of the combat-weary pilots. It got to be, on the long watches at sea, that the flight surgeons were importuned to give these bottles of whiskey to people who sometimes didn't need them, but were recounting experiences that indicated they did. Sometimes they wouldn't drink them right away but would save them, and, when several of them got quite a number, they would have a party in their bunk room somewhere, which wasn't legal and was bad for ship discipline. On other occasions, they would use them as gambling stakes in card games. It became a bit of a sticky situation, as to how we could best get this back on the track.

We had a very fine senior doctor on the *Essex* whose name was Mac-Donald. He had a wonderful personality and was a very good psychologist. After talking our problem over, we evolved a program which proved effective. He said, "Let us say that anybody in the crew of the *Essex* could have a miniature bottle of whiskey if his next immediate senior in the line of command, even though he was a seaman first class and had a seaman second class working for him, would certify that this man had been exposed to a long stint of very hard work in disagreeable conditions, working on something that was difficult and required great physical endurance," then he could prescribe a bottle of whiskey for him. He would merely take him down to sick bay where the medical whiskey was kept, write out a prescription for him, certifying what it was for, and then watch him drink it in sick bay.

The last part was the catch, but it worked. We found this solved our problems and produced dividends. The practice was emulated by other ships later on to their benefit. We found that there were many men who deserved these bottles of "medical" whiskey who weren't aviators and hadn't been exposed to enemy fire, but needed a sedative just as badly. When they started to get some, which was helpful to them, the whole spirit of the thing changed. The aviators didn't mind it, except for a small vocal minority. The abuse of the privilege was given a 180-degree turnaround, and the total quantity consumed was considerably reduced.

Our pattern on most of the *Essex* strikes, with which I was concerned, was basically listening to the stories of our pilots and how successful they would be, making preparations for sending them off and returning them, taking care of the wounded when they came back, taking care of airplanes that were damaged, deciding whether to tell them to land in the sea or try to land on the ship. Damaged planes did sometimes land and made a crash on the deck, which had to be taken care of, sometimes pushed over the side. This was the routine which applied to practically all the invasions. Attacks by bombers on the ship were relatively infrequent. I don't think I can recall more than 5, 6, or 7 nights that we went through this, but it was always very impressive when we did.

There were other raids in late 1943, including Kwajalein and Eniwetok. But the most significant event of the new year was the raid on Truk, one of the largest atolls in the world. It's different than most coral atolls in that it has big mountains in the middle of it, quite a good deal of land area, and then a tremendous coral reef all the way around it. It's one of the largest protected anchorages in the world, and was long known as the headquarters for all the Japanese governmental activities in the southern Pacific. It was considered impregnable, partly because the Japanese advertised it as being that way. At least it had that aura in the minds of most of our sailors out there. So when it was learned that we were going to make a raid on Truk, everybody had their fingers crossed. As far as I was concerned, I never saw Truk even dimly on the horizon. Our planes attacked it successfully, sank a number of ships, and had very few losses.

The *Essex* received the Presidential Unit Citation, which was just one of those things for participating in a certain number of operations. Our air groups were always very successful. The real heroism, when there was any, was almost always in the person of the pilots who were sticking their necks out. A lot of them were lost. The crew on board ship, in the big carriers at least, were, except in the big carrier battles in which some of them were badly damaged, relatively out of the picture from bullet problems, bomb problems. At least this was the case in my time in the *Essex*. The *Essex* never received a bullet in her to my recollection, when I was on it. I think we did have a few machine-gun bullets in the attacks off Rabaul, but they were practically nothing. The pilots and the air crews bore the brunt of the fighting.

Carrier Task Force Doctrine—The Beginning

Vice Admiral Truman J. Hedding

Truman Johnson Hedding was born on 14 July 1902 in Morrisdale, Pennsylvania, son of Katherine C. and Dr. Benjamin E. Hedding. He was appointed to the U.S. Naval Academy in 1920, graduated and was commissioned ensign on 4 June 1924, and was designated a naval aviator on 24 November 1926. He received an M.S. degree in 1931 from the Massachusetts Institute of Technology. Subsequent service included extensive command and staff duties ashore and afloat, and he advanced in rank to that of rear admiral, effective 1 July 1951. Admiral Hedding was Bureau of Aeronautics Representative, Western District, from 14 October 1957 until his retirement, effective 1 January 1959.

During World War II, he assisted in fitting out the USS Essex and, from 31 December 1942 until July 1943, had consecutive duty as air officer and executive officer. In August 1943, he became chief of staff to Commander, Carrier Division 3, and participated in attacks on Tarawa, Kwajalein, Truk, the Marianas, Palau, and Hollandia and in the naval battle for the Marianas in

June 1944. From June 1944 to March 1946, he served on the staff of Commander in Chief, Pacific Fleet.

Admiral Hedding's decorations include the Legion of Merit with Combat "V," Bronze Star Medal, Commendation Ribbon with Combat "V," and the Presidential Unit Citation Ribbon with three stars.

Capt. Truman J. Hedding, 1947.

In August 1943, I reported to Commander, Carrier Division 3, Rear Adm. Charles A. Pownall, as chief of staff. While we were at Pearl Harbor getting ready for the Gilberts campaign, Admiral Nimitz realized that we would probably have to revise the tactical instructions for carriers. So he created a board with Admiral Pownall as the senior member of it. However, he very seldom ever showed up, so I more or less ran the board. We set up a lot of models in our headquarters basement and started learning to do things with carriers as we got more of them. We knew a lot about flying, and we'd learned a lot about tactics, but we had to learn to handle more carriers. We realized that never again would the carrier operate in support of the battle line. The fleet would be organized around the carriers, and the battleships and cruisers would be primarily for the carriers' protection.

Elements of the fast carrier task force rest at anchor in Seeadler Harbor, adjoining Manus and Los Negros in the Admiralty Islands.

So we developed a circular formation. It was just kicked around, and we used it later on and found it to be very effective, with one or two carriers in the center and then another concentric ring of alternating battleships and cruisers that provided tremendous antiaircraft fire. Then outside of that would be a circular screen of destroyers, usually a squadron of destroyers if you could get that many. They provided not only antiaircraft protection, but they provided primarily the submarine protection. Then we came to not only handling just one task group built around two or three carriers, we had 2, 3, and 4 task groups. That became quite a potent organization and became the fast carrier force. We had to draw up the necessary tactical instructions so the carrier task groups in operating wouldn't be running into each other. The basic thing that determined the formation was the wind direction, because the carriers have to turn into the wind to launch. During that time, we also developed the tactic of launching and recovering the fighter patrols and the antisubmarine patrols by a carrier positioning itself within the task group, and being able to turn into the wind and get their planes off and on before they got too far outside of the protective screen.

There were two methods; we called them Able and Baker at that time. We launched the aircraft by getting the carriers either to do it separately or we'd have to turn the whole formation into the wind. When we made carrier strikes we'd turn the whole task group into the wind. We continued to develop and refine the tactics as we got more and more carriers, battleships, cruisers, and destroyers. The fast carrier task force became bigger and bigger with more task groups. It was quite a job tactically handling the many task groups.

Then we learned something else. We always had troubles fueling. There were elaborate instructions on fueling. You had to have the wind just so much on one bow or the other, and you rigged all kinds of spring lines and breast lines to position the ships alongside each other. The poor tanker always had to make the approach on the big ships. It was a silly thing. I remember we were off Tarawa one time, and I said to Admiral Pownall, "Look, isn't this the silliest thing you ever saw?" Here came a tanker, with a cruiser alongside, making an approach on a carrier. "We all know how to fly formation. Let's set the tanker up there, and let everybody come up and make an approach on the tanker and just run the fuel lines across." He said, "Maybe that will work. Let's try it." We tried it, and we found that we didn't have to have the wind just right. We could even fuel down wind unless the seas got very bad. All we would do was run messenger lines across, a distance line, and fuel lines. It was very simple; you just flew formation, and it worked fine. If we hadn't done that I don't know what would have happened.

One of our big problems operating in the Pacific was that the wind was practically always on our stern, from the northeast. We were always traveling west. So every time we'd get going we'd have to turn around and go east to get the planes aboard or to fly them off. We learned a lot of tactics, not just the tactics of handling task groups and the task force. It was a very interesting business. Of course, one of the real good things about it was we developed real ship handlers. I guess we're all ship handlers; if you scratch any naval officer under the skin, he's a boat steerer whether he's an aviator or not. And we got people like Arleigh Burke to help further revise and refine these tactical instructions. We had critiques after every operation. Everybody would get up and say what we did wrong, and what we should do to correct our mistakes.

Below Decks on the *Saratoga*

Roger Bond

Roger L. Bond was born 19 June 1925 in Milwaukee, Wisconsin, and moved with his family to Los Angeles, California, in 1933. After graduating from Los Angeles High School, he enlisted in the Navy at the age of 17. He subsequently served at the Destroyer Repair Base, San Diego, aboard the destroyer Saufley, *carrier* Saratoga, *and* PCE(R) 858.

After discharge from the Navy, Mr. Bond attended the University of Southern California and graduated with a B.S. degree in Transportation and Foreign Trade. He has worked in the motor carrier freight business throughout his career, in Los Angeles, San Francisco, and, since 1970, in Minneapolis, Minnesota. He was Vice President of Traffic for E. L. Murphy Trucking Co. and Executive Vice President of Wiseway Motor Freight, both of St. Paul, Minnesota. Mr. Bond retired in March 1991 and lives with his wife in Minnetonka, Minnesota. He has retained a strong interest in ships, the United States Navy, and the sea.

Petty Officer Roger Bond, ashore in the Pacific, World War II. (Courtesy Roger Bond)

I reported aboard the USS *Saratoga* about mid-1943 and was assigned to the 19th Division, which was a labor gang under the master-at-arms. The air group usually flew off before we got into port, so, at that time, we would have no planes, or just a couple, aboard. One of our jobs was to paint the flight deck. When somebody tells you you're going to paint the flight deck, and you stand on a flight deck that is 919 feet long and roughly 100 feet wide, it's pretty hard to believe that you're going to do it in one day. We painted that flight deck with swabs. I call it gray white wash, and, by gosh, we got it painted by 4:00 P.M. The deck was wood, and it soaked it in pretty well. They used to paint the flight deck every few months when the planes weren't on it; they told me it didn't do any good to paint it with good paint because the wheels and the skidding just wore it off. This worked as well as quality paint.

I wanted to be a quartermaster, so, after an interview by the navigator, I was assigned to the 9th Division. We had to maintain the complete issue of charts from the hydrographic office. We had eight people assigned: three strikers, or nonpetty officers working toward the third-class rate, three third-class, and two second-class petty officers. We had two quartermasters on watch all the time under way; one was in steering aft, and one was in the pilothouse. When we were in port, we only had one on duty at a time on the quarterdeck, but we had to do most of our chart work in port. The charthouse was too small for us to do that kind of work at sea. So we would be up there working, and each quartermaster had certain portfolios or charts that he took care of. The commander would also be working or reading in there, and he would be around us. It was a very informal, easy association. I became aware of a lot of different functions of the ship; we worked in the nerve center of the ship, you might say. I had contact with all different branches of the ship, interacted with them, knew what was going on, where we were going, how we were getting there, and that sort of thing.

The island superstructure of the *Saratoga* was different from all other carriers except, of course, her sister ship, the *Lexington,* which was sunk at the battle of the Coral Sea. The *Saratoga* had a conning tower, which was immediately below the bridge. The conning tower was for use when the ship operated as a heavy cruiser with her 8-inch guns, which were removed in early 1942. Also, the bridge structure was small for such a large ship. The pilothouse was a pretty crowded place. It was perhaps 20 or 25 feet wide, and had to accommodate a helmsman, a lee helmsman, a quartermaster of the watch and his desk, a Marine orderly during the day, a boatswain's mate of the watch, a bugler, several phone talkers—to say nothing of the officer of the deck, a junior officer of the deck, and sometimes the captain would squeeze in.

I was almost the only nonrated man in the division, but the petty officers were great teachers. We had one little compartment and a storeroom up in the anchor windlass area where we kept all the flags, a sewing machine, and all the clocks. Two men slept up there, and that was considered their "cleaning station," which was changed every three months. The rest of us slept back in the compartment. These guys were intelligent men. They were good card players; pinochle was the favorite game in that compartment, and we had a lot of good conversation. The guys had been on a lot of different ships and seen a lot of different duties. It was an unusual group; I feel there were just so many guys that had been in the Navy a long time, and they inculcated this into the other people. The newer men joined the culture that was already there. But the atmosphere on that ship was that this was our profession, and we were interested in it.

In those days, most ports in the Pacific had a recreation beach. The ship carried beer, and you would go ashore and take the ship's beer ashore. You would have a couple of chits for a couple of cans of beer. So that was the basic recreation, because there was no interaction with the civilian community. They weren't interested in the sailors or anything else.

There were an awful lot of servicemen on these islands. There were a lot of ships there, and there was a lot of rivalry between them. I would say the rivalry between the *Saratoga* and the *Enterprise* was almost as great as the rivalry between the Americans and the Japanese. There was a lot of jealousy, some fights, name calling; two beers, a wrong word, and there would be a fight. They generally tried to keep the two crews apart.

During this time, early 1943, there was a lull in the action, with both the Japanese and the Americans sort of taking stock and building up their forces; both sides had lost quite a bit. I would say down there in late 1942, early 1943, we were still afraid we were losing the war in the South Pacific. We had this feeling that we were holding back; if anything unlucky happened and we would lose one of the important ships, then the balance would be tipped. On the *Saratoga,* in the spring of 1943, we felt we were the only carrier. We didn't know what the hell happened to the *Enterprise.* We knew the *Ranger* was on the East Coast, but we just felt that we were the only one.

For a while there, we operated with the British carrier *Victorious* in the New Georgia campaign. That was sort of fun. The *Victorious* was a pretty good carrier. I'd say it was about the *Wasp*'s size, maybe not even quite that big, but it was a pretty slick-looking ship. They were fine to operate with. They weren't used to staying out at sea quite as long as we were; they started running low on potatoes, so we loaded up a torpedo plane with dehydrated potatoes and sent it over to them. We got this message back: "We fried them; we baked them; we broiled them; how the hell do you cook them?" So we sent a cook over to show them how to cook dehydrated potatoes. I don't know that we were doing them a great favor.

One thing about the *Saratoga* was that the crew was quite a bit larger than what the Navy had anticipated the wartime complement would be. It just did not have the storage space for food. In the 1920s, when it was designed, they didn't think enough in terms of chill space. When we went to sea, they would have food stacked in the passageways, including a full load of onions. One of the things I never got involved in—boy, I'm glad I was never a seaman or fireman on that ship—was to get assigned to the breakout gang, because the breakout gang on the *Saratoga* went way down into those storerooms and they came up at least five or six decks to the mess hall and the galleys on the main deck, which was immediately under the flight deck. They would just put this case of something on your shoulder, and you would go just up, up, up. Those were the little things that showed you it was a ship of the "old Navy." They had more hard labor teams on older ships than new ships.

As another example right through the entire war, they had about 700 men sleeping in hammocks in the mess halls. Now that was not as bad a deal as it could have been because when those hammocks were stowed, you had big open mess halls. All the tables and benches were stowed in racks in the overhead and the hammocks in bins. I know at times at night we'd be going through there, maybe around the morning watch when you had wake-up calls to make. The overhead had all these humps hanging down, and you would have to sort of bend down to go through. Then all of a sudden you'd hear, "God damn it," and some guy picks himself up and crawls back in his hammock. With all the guys sleeping there, one or two were bound to fall out. You didn't want to turn over. In hot weather, I think the hammock was a little bit stifling. The secret to the hammock is to try to open the thing up by hanging your legs and arms down, because it would come up on the side of you when you were in it, and it would soak up radiant heat from the flight deck immediately above all day long.

The other compartments were what I call pretty straightforward naval compartments, with some exceptions. Since our hangar deck did not go to the outside of the ship, there were compartments between the hangar deck and the outside hull called wing compartments. All of these compartments were long and narrow. One of the outstanding characteristics of the ship was boat pockets along the side of the ship—four on the port side and one on the starboard side—where they stored the motor launches. Our compartment was just aft of one of those boat pockets. Another peculiarity was that our compartment was also a passageway. We had regular bunks against both bulkheads and lockers in the middle. Just before I came aboard, they had footlockers, which made it a little more open in the center of the compartment.

There were no wash basins or anything like that on the ship. Each man had a bucket; you would draw your water—cold water—and then take it to a steam jet, stick the jet in and heat it to whatever temperature you wanted. So you would soak yourself down with that and get into a cold shower. We had three big washrooms, and one was usually shut down all the time for cleaning and upkeep. Then the heads themselves were troughs; water flowed through the troughs and the stream ran through them off the side of the ship; in port and at sea, that's the way it was.

Since there were no wash basins, your bucket was used for everything, including brushing teeth and shaving. They had mirrors; they didn't want you to hurt yourself. The first thing you did was brush your teeth; then you shaved; then you sort of washed; then you'd go wash your clothes. We never had a limit on how much fresh water we could draw because the crew was very good in water conservation. The only time we ever got into any problem was when we were carrying passengers and we overloaded the system. But that was a remarkable thing that the crew was so mindful of the water. Of course, what helped was that the showers were cold, and with the buckets you just didn't tend to waste it as much. If you were caught wasting water, you were put on a list and when it came time to scale the evaporators, you were part of the work crew; that was, I understand, a very nasty job, especially in the tropics. There's not much ventilation, and it was hot working with that salt and getting it all over you.

To get our uniforms looking good for inspections and going on liberty, we would first rinse them in regular fresh water to get the soap out, then rinse them in salt water, which acted as a mild bleach and also gave them a little bit of body. Then you would roll the uniform tightly and tie it just like they taught you in boot camp; it worked out pretty well. Remember that a uniform is only supposed to be uniform. It doesn't mean it's supposed to be really sharp. The Marine's were sharp; the Navy's were uniform. If you could get it pressed in that climate, those creases would not stay sharp very long. The creases are inside out along the side so you're not dealing with a crease down the front, and the jumper, when it was clean, looked about the same in a few minutes, anyway. Quartermasters always wore whites on quarterdeck watch in port. The secret of getting them clean was not to let them get too dirty. If you wore them on watch, you didn't wear them again. You washed them, and in that way you could keep on top of it. You just didn't want to get dirty.

In colder climates, you didn't wash your blues much. When we could, we would send our blues to the ship's cleaners. Blues didn't show the soil, and you'd wear your undress blues on board ship, dress blues when you went on shore. You could scrub your stripes on your dress blues without washing the whole uniform. Take a toothbrush and a cake of soap and work a lather. But, again, don't let them get too dirty because you would never get the yellow all the way out and you would have to restripe them. Another thing to remember, the ship was full of rust. You wouldn't ask the crew to wear whites just generally aboard ship because it was too dirty. So our uniform of the day was normally dungarees.

The main mess deck was the aft main deck right under the flight deck where all the men in hammocks lived. Tables were lowered for meals. When I first went aboard for the first few months, we had "table mess," where you sat down as a division—larger divisions pretty much ate by sections—and the senior man ate at the head of the table. When the mess cook brought the meat, it went to him first. When it came down to me, and I was at the foot of the table, I never did get a piece of meat that was bigger than a quarter. Dehydrated potatoes were always mashed and sort of gray, and they varied in consistency with how carefully the cooks mixed them. But if they didn't get too much moisture in them, they were really pretty tasty. Put a lot of pepper on them, and then you could eat them. The time we were out 87 days, we were getting down to a very poor selection of food. There was one heck of a lot of beans and rice. One thing you could do aboard ship, you could tell what day of the week it was by what you ate for breakfast. A typical Saturday morning meal was cornbread and beans.

The brig was brutal. I never was in there, and I never wanted to be in it. The cells were four by four feet; the doors were a lattice of steel bands with an open basket weave. You couldn't really lie down; there was no bunk in the cell. You slept on the deck; you brought your blanket. When they gave you 10 days bread and water, you were fed bread and water, except you received a full ration every three days. Of course, Marine guards were there to make sure you followed the rules; in the day time you had to stand; there was no talking. If you misbehaved, they would give you an extra day. But there were a lot of guys on that ship that would rather spend the time in the brig than chipping paint, or breakout gang, or something like that.

The relationship between the officers and enlisted men on the ship was pretty good because there was a large percentage of people that had done a lot of duty in the Navy. The officers who were really running that ship were experienced officers, men that had spent five years as an ensign. They hadn't been rapidly advanced, and they really knew their stuff. The junior officers traveled under that umbrella. The enlisted men accepted the competence of the officers. There were also one hell of a lot of competent enlisted men on that ship, and the officers accepted the competence of those men. There was a sense of mutual respect.

As an example, the first time I ever met Rear Adm. Frederick C. Sherman, who flew his flag on the *Saratoga,* was on an outside ladder from the bridge down to the flight deck. It was about three decks. It had one little landing, and it was a narrow ladder. Boy, I remember the first time I'd ever gone up for watch on the bridge; I was late and I was tearing up that ladder. This little guy was coming down, and we met at that little bit of landing. I was taller than he and I saw over the bill of his cap; I saw two stars. I came to a halt and tried to move out of the way; I just about jumped off, you know. Sherman said, "Son, how long have you been in the Navy?" "About a year, sir." And he says, "Well, I've been in for 40 years, and now people get out of my way when I'm coming. And when you're in 40 years, they'll get out of your way. Do you understand me?" And I said, "Yes, sir."

On the subject of ship handling, as a quartermaster, I frequently had the opportunity to steer the *Saratoga*. In the first place, it didn't have a wheel. It had a little controller, like a trolley car. A quartermaster always steered when the ship was at general quarters, flight quarters, or special sea detail. You had to kick it hard to get it moving, and you had to anticipate and meet it hard because you'd swing past the course very easily. There was a lot of momentum. It was particularly tricky at slow speeds when you were entering port, particularly Pearl Harbor, which was pretty tight, and they didn't allow you to go very fast. One time we were coming in and the captain said, "Right 10 degrees rudder." I repeated as a question, "Come right, 10 degrees rudder?" because we always circled Ford Island to the left in a clockwise manner. And he said, "Yes, come right." After we were alongside, and I just was standing by the helm, the captain said, "I'm really glad you questioned me about that command because that shows you're involved." And he explained his reasons for ordering what I thought was an unusual course change under the circumstances. But he said, "I really appreciate the fact that the quartermaster is thinking with me, and is thinking ahead, and that's a comfort because it's perfectly possible for me to mean left and say right. Everybody could do that." He just didn't want me to just blindly follow orders, and I appreciated that. It was a nice personal touch, and it wasn't only me; he treated everybody that way. He seemed to go on the basis that everybody had a job, and he respected you and your job. Whatever rank that might go along with it was immaterial, and he was looking at you as his quartermaster, or his officer of the deck, gunnery officer, whatever task it was.

Incidentally, there was one steering wheel down in steering aft which activated hydraulic pumps, which, in turn, controlled two hydraulic rams attached to the rudder. Occasionally, just for practice, the officer of the deck would transfer the steering down to the steering aft to make sure the man on watch wasn't sleeping and that the system worked properly. I don't know how many revolutions of the wheel it took to change that rudder one degree, but I know you just spun it and spun it to get that rudder moving. You were pumping the oil to move those big rams, and you had to have a lot of mechanical advantage over that pump. When we were zigzagging, which was frequently, you would just about get started up and it would be time to change course again. It would be tough if you had to maneuver while under attack. Incidentally, the same man was on duty in steering aft both times the ship was torpedoed. After the second time, the division officer promised him he'd never have steering aft as a general quarters assignment again.

One of the interesting facets of life in the prewar Navy was that men often stayed in the same ship for years and years, and I discovered that when I was on board in the 1940s, there were two of the original crew from the late 1920s still there. They talked about the famous people that had been on the ship, places they had gone, transiting the Panama Canal. Those two were among the very few that were on there when they went through the canal. One time the ship ripped down all the lampposts along the sides of the canal as she went through. The next time the canal took them down before the ship did. I think that both of those guys were in the shipyards, too, and assigned to the ship quite a while before the commissioning took place. They talked about the thrill of it,

The USS Saratoga *squeezed through the Panama Canal in February 1928. The* Saratoga *survived hits by torpedoes, bombs, and kamikazes in World War II and was destroyed in the Bikini atomic bomb tests in 1946.*

because at that time, the *Lexington* and the *Saratoga* were the first genuine aircraft carriers, and it was a new thing. They never transferred off the ship because they just didn't see a reason to do so. That's like somebody that lives in a neighborhood; they just didn't see any reason to move out of the neighborhood. They realized that they were unique; they were in a special category, and they weren't going to give that up. I would guess they stayed on board until the ship was decommissioned after the war. From what I know about the Navy in those days, no one would order them off the ship.

One of the more interesting parts of the war during my tour on the *Saratoga* was the Indian Ocean venture. We rendezvoused with the British fleet in the Indian Ocean in March 1944 and proceeded to Trincomalee, a naval base in Ceylon, which is now Sri Lanka. Trincomalee was a large harbor with a very small town, several floating dry docks and navy installations. It was somewhat like Pearl Harbor and had several bays or arms in the harbor, but a much larger and more open entrance. The bays were restricted and tight, and the major ships tied to buoys fore and aft. The fleet there was built around the battle cruiser *Renown,* the battleships *Queen Elizabeth* and *Valiant,* the aircraft carrier *Illustrious* (the sister ship to the *Victorious),* and a number of heavy and light cruisers. Other Dutch, Australian, French, Italian, and American ships added up to a fleet of some 55 ships.

The French battleship *Richelieu,* a very advanced-model battleship, was part of the fleet. The French were not too friendly. The hospitality on the *Richelieu* was almost nonexistent, and there weren't any formal invitations. They were very jealous of some of the French technical innovations. For one thing, their main battery could be reloaded in the elevated position, whereas ours and other navies' had to be brought down to zero elevation for reloading. No American was going to get anywhere near those turrets, which we thought was rather odd since the ship was full of American antiaircraft guns and radar, which we'd put aboard.

I got an invitation by semaphore from a signalman on the *Valiant* to go to the Royal Navy canteen with him. The *Valiant*'s boat stopped by the *Saratoga,* and I hopped aboard. He was a kid from Croyden, just out of London, and we became pretty good friends. I have to admit I circumvented the American Navy censors by giving him my present wife's address, and he wrote to her. In the British Navy, they could say where they were and that sort of thing. As a matter of fact, their mail was postmarked through the Ceylonese postal system, with a stamp from Ceylon.

I remember going over to the canteen, and my friend, Lenny, was really apologizing for the fact that they had reduced the beer ration; they had just cut it down from six bottles to four. But in the American Navy the custom was two cans of beer ashore, and the British beer is a little stronger. When we got over there, we found out these were really quart bottles! I just cannot believe that those guys could drink eight quarts of warm beer in the tropics. But they did. So that was a very interesting place to go with all these nationalities.

The routine there seemed to be to go out on Monday and get back in Friday. They would then have inspection on Saturday and then have a regatta on Sunday. Of course, as you might expect, when we got there, the captain wanted to make sure we looked pretty good, so the first weekend we had regular captain's inspection. But then the rear admiral on the British aircraft carrier inspected us the next Saturday. Of course, he was in shorts and an open-neck shirt while we were all in undress whites with jumper; he took his time and looked each one of us over. At that time, the crew numbered about 2,200 to 2,400 men, so it took quite awhile. The next week the vice admiral of the battle fleet inspected us, and he, also, was in shorts and open-neck shirt and looked us all over, one by one. Then, believe it or not, Adm. Sir James Somerville, Commander in Chief of the Far Eastern Fleet, inspected us the next week, and he was in shorts and an open-neck shirt. So we really thought we had worked through the roster, and then we found out that Lord Louis Mountbatten, whose headquarters for the whole China-Burma-India theater were in Kandi, Ceylon, was coming down to look us over. When he arrived—I happened to be quartermaster of the watch—the first thing that struck us was he was not in shorts and open-neck shirt. The British have a uniform similar to the American naval whites with a choked collar, and that's what he wore. He came out on the quarterdeck of the *Saratoga,* which was located on the flight deck between the bridge structure and the stack structure. He went out on the flight deck and looked towards the bow, looked towards the stern, and he said, "They look very good. Now let's bring them all together in the shade of the stack."

That was his inspection. He just took one panoramic view and then got us all together in formation in front of a little podium they made there for him. He said, "Can you hear me?" Of course, you say that to a couple thousand sailors, and somebody's going to say, "No." So he said, "Well, just break ranks, come on in." And they crowded in. Then he started telling them about the war in the China-Burma-India theater, why the *Saratoga* had been requested, and why the war seemed to go slowly. I think that was pretty edifying for most everybody because we really didn't know much about it. He said that an Italian sloop of war had defected from Singapore and brought the information that there were five Jap carriers and seven battleships in Singapore. We were essentially trying to lure them out, or keep them neutralized.

The crew really thought Mountbatten was the greatest thing they'd ever seen from the British Navy. He, of course, said, "I just wish I could go with you." He said, "I know what you're thinking. I know, but I really do wish this. I can remember back when we were on destroyers early in the war in 1939 and '40, operating in the English Channel, and we would come in port after we had been tossed around that Channel. We would come in and get a little bit of fuel and food, and some gray-haired old bastard from Whitehall would come down and say, 'Go to it, lads, I wish I were with you,' and we would bare our teeth and say, 'Yea, you'll be in bed with your old lady when we're out there.'" But that kind of talk coming from that kind of man, a man you really identified with—they thought he was something. And I might say the British sailors also thought he was something, because they considered him a sailor, too. He'd proved himself as a ship's officer. Whatever he was doing now, that was all right because he had showed what he really could do, even though he was a bit accident prone. One of his jokes was when he took command of the carrier *Illustrious,* the King said, "Well, there goes the *Illustrious.*"

We were out in the Indian Ocean for a lot of flight operations "trolling for the enemy." We didn't get any strikes. Our first raid was on Sabang, a small island immediately north of Sumatra. I recall we did have a fighter shot down there; the pilot got out, and he was in the harbor in his small life raft. There was an English submarine stationed there to pick up any pilots who were shot down. They were submerged and saw that the Japanese were going to get out to the pilot before they got to him, so they surfaced and ran six miles on the surface to pick this guy up. They were under shore fire for the last several miles, but they got him out and submerged. They brought him out, and they didn't get back to port for a couple of weeks. But the fighter squadron had the entire crew of the submarine over for dinner on the *Saratoga.* It was not a large sub, so there were only about 60 men. They had all the ice cream they could eat. That always made a big impression on the English because they had no ice cream. Most of them hadn't had any since before the war.

We had a custom that, if the plane guard destroyer picked up a pilot in the water, when they returned him, we always sent over enough ice cream for the crew. This word spread around the British fleet. One day during air operations a plane came in very low and the landing signal officer jumped for the net below with such enthusiasm that he jumped over the net into the water. The British heavy cruiser *London,* several thousand yards across the formation, saw this, and they put the helm hard over, blew their whistle, and came across that formation, ships scurrying to get out of the way. They picked up the lieutenant, and now we had to furnish ice cream for 900 men. But we did; they got their ice cream.

There are always these rumors about drinking on board ship. I did see a little bit. I knew where there were at least four stills aboard the *Saratoga,* and I don't think I knew where all of them were. When they were arming the torpedo planes for strikes on Rabaul, they had a hard time finding 18 torpedoes that had a full charge of alcohol. We carried 80-some torpedoes, but they hadn't been used much and just been drained slowly over a period of time. The product of the stills was pure alcohol. The operators ran through cleaning compounds that were used on the guns, degreasing compounds, fruit products, etc. Most of the problem was just getting impurities out of the alcohol. The New Hebrides had a lot of lime trees on plantations. You could get a bucket and squeeze out this lime juice and then put alcohol in it. You couldn't taste the alcohol. You usually could get some ice aboard ship if you were willing to share the product. But I wouldn't say there was constant drinking. There was a lot more talk of it than actuality.

I do remember one Sunday when I had the afternoon watch. My relief was down in the quartermaster storeroom in the anchor windlass room. There was a hatch on the flight deck, the cover to it was open, and there was a ladder from the anchor windlass room up to the flight deck. So I thought, "Well, it's Sunday afternoon and it's hot, I'd better make sure he's awake." So I went down to check on him. There was a whole group of guys in there with a bucket of cold grapefruit juice. And they said, "You want some?" And I said, "Sure." It was awfully hot. So I drank down a full Navy cup. And "There's just a little bit more. You can have a glass of it." Almost another cup, and I drank that down and I said, "Well, I have to get back to the quarterdeck." So I went up the ladder to the flight deck. As I walked toward the quarterdeck, all of a sudden the superstructure moved; then it just started rotating. I just started going down, and I felt some hands under my armpits. My friends who had followed me caught me, and I woke up in the ready room in the superstructure off the flight deck. It was dark. I never had an experience like that before. It just came right out of left field—bong! Boy, I never drank very heavy anyway, but, you know, I was really surprised because you couldn't taste anything in that cold drink.

After several operations with the British, we were ordered to detach and return to Australia. On the day we left, we were steaming along in task force formation, and we pulled ahead, did a big turn, and strung our three destroyers out behind us. As we were pulling ahead, the British fleet had lined up in single file, and we came down alongside them about 100 yards apart. It was pretty close for big ships to be passing, and they had signal flags up: "Good luck, good trip," all plain language through the international flags. All the rails were lined with the crews. As we went by, we would get three cheers, and we answered. It was very, very impressive, with 55 ships in that task force spaced over miles of ocean. We were all pretty hoarse by the time we got through all the cheering, but that really left us with a good feeling. I would say that we had very good relations with the British during the time we were there.

When I reported aboard in 1943, the *Saratoga* and the *Enterprise* were holding the line in the Pacific, and in 1945, when I left the ship, there were so many carriers, the *Saratoga* didn't make a difference. It had completely changed. I think that for anyone that participated in the war, there were actually two wars. If you went out to the Pacific after, let's say, January of 1944, you had a completely different experience and viewpoint than those before, because it really was two different operations. I wasn't part of the one where we truly were losing, getting chased out of the place. I was part of holding the line. We just felt we were hanging on by our fingernails and didn't know what was going on. Today it's hard to believe you could be part of the Navy and know so little about what's happening back in the States and other places. Of course, those were wartime conditions. It wasn't on the daily news or the newspaper. The day in December 1943 in the Gilberts, when we sighted 13 carriers, was an awesome, awesome day.

1944: The Central Pacific Drive

The serious flaws in amphibious support doctrine and procedures that marked the assault on Tarawa were substantially corrected in the Marshalls campaign two months later. The Kwajalein operation became a textbook case that was repeated frequently as the Fifth Fleet continued its Central Pacific drive toward the Philippines and Japanese home waters. As the Marshalls campaign drew to a close, carrier planes struck the impregnable Japanese base at Truk, the so-called Gibraltar of the Pacific, on 17–18 February 1944, sinking 37 ships and heavily damaging shore installations. The Truk raid was also the occasion for the first night radar-bombing attack by U.S. carrier planes, carried out by TBM-1C Avengers from the *Enterprise*.

Plans for the remainder of the year committed Gen. Douglas MacArthur's Southwest Pacific Forces to advance along the north coast of New Guinea and, in mid-November, invade the southern Philippine island of Mindanao. In June, the Central Pacific Forces would occupy Saipan, Tinian, and Guam in the Marianas and in September begin seizing bases in the Palaus. Finally, in November, they would support MacArthur's invasion of the Philippines.

For the next few months, Marc Mitscher's Task Force 58 roamed the Central and South Pacific, striking the western Carolines, supporting MacArthur's landings at Hollandia on the north coast of New Guinea, hitting Truk once again, and softening up the Marianas for the invasion. On 14 June, U.S. Marines landed on the beaches of Saipan in an amphibious operation surpassed in complexity and magnitude only by the Normandy invasion eight days earlier. As it covered the assault with seven heavy and eight light carriers, Task Force 58 made all preparations to oppose a large enemy task force approaching from the west. On 19 June, the first day of what would be known as the battle of the Philippine Sea, Mitscher's carrier planes repulsed repeated air attacks by enemy planes shuttling from their carriers to the west to the airfield on Guam, to the east of Task Force 58. Over 300 enemy aircraft were destroyed in an eight-hour melee that was called the Marianas "Turkey Shoot." Enemy losses also included two carriers sunk by U.S. submarines.

Late the next day, the approximate position of the enemy carrier force was determined, and Admiral Mitscher decided to launch a strike at extreme range to the enemy fleet. After American pilots sank one carrier and damaged others, the return trip home became a nightmare for many pilots as they attempted to stretch their limited fuel supplies in a vain attempt to find friendly carriers in the darkness. Many ditched in the ocean, some in silence, others after sad, dramatic farewells over the radio; many finally saw the task force in the distance, as Mitscher issued his courageous order to "Turn on the lights." Pilots groped through the confusing pattern of lights of every description to land on any available deck; "home" was where they found it. By the end of the hectic night recovery, U.S. losses amounted to 100 aircraft missing in action, splashed near, or crashed on TF 58 decks. Extensive rescue operations the next day resulted in a final tally of 16 pilots and 33 air crewmen lost during the day's action. It was an unhappy end to what many aviators considered a less-than-successful battle—six enemy carriers had escaped to fight another day.

In the months following the Marianas occupation, the Fifth Fleet became the Third Fleet, under Adm. William F. ("Bull") Halsey, and Task Force 58 was renamed Task Force 38, still under the inspiring leadership of Vice Adm. Marc Mitscher. Strikes against Okinawa, Luzon, and Formosa and amphibious assaults against the Palaus and Morotai eventually led up to the invasion of Leyte, now set ahead from mid-November to 20 October 1944.

A major effort by the Japanese to disrupt the Leyte invasion led to the battles for Leyte Gulf, 23-26 October. On the 24th, a Japanese Center Force of battleships and cruisers was struck in the Sibuyan Sea by Task Force 58 planes, with the result that four battleships were damaged and the giant battleship *Musashi* was sunk. However, more would be heard from the Center Force later. In the early morning of 25 October, U.S. surface forces systematically destroyed a Japanese Southern Force in the battle of Surigao Strait, in what can best be described as a classic battleship gunfight. At dawn on the same day, hundreds of miles to the north, in the battle off Cape Engaño, Halsey's main carrier forces caught and destroyed the remnants of the enemy carrier fleet, sinking four grossly undermanned carriers in a one-sided victory. In the meanwhile, the enemy Center Force, after the temporary setback in the Sibuyan Sea, had broken through the San Bernardino Strait and attacked the three task groups of escort carriers protecting the invasion beaches. In the ensuing battle off Samar Island, enemy battleships and cruisers pursued the fleeing escort carriers in one of the most extraordinary battles of the Pacific war. Dramatically, and quite unexpectedly, when there seemed to be nothing that could save the American force from total destruction, the Japanese turned about and retreated, leaving behind a bewildered, battered escort carrier force. The *Gambier Bay* had been sunk by gunfire, and later the first blows were struck by the *kamikazes,* with the loss of the escort carrier *St. Lo* and damage to five others. Nonetheless, Leyte Gulf marked the end of the Imperial Japanese Fleet, for all intents and purposes. The two U.S. fleets which came to Leyte, the Third and the Seventh, stayed; the three Japanese fleets which fought in the battles were routed.

A key blow on enemy shipping in the Truk raid of 17–18 February 1944 was struck by a squadron of TBMs under the command of Comdr. William I. Martin. Bill Martin was a visionary who pioneered the development of night attack tactics in the carrier navy, and he recalls the less than enthusiastic support from his seniors as he tried to get his ideas accepted in the fleet. Four months after the success at Truk, Martin had the misfortune to be shot down during a dive-bombing attack on enemy shore installations at Saipan. After parachuting into the water, he was brought under heavy enemy fire from the beach. The compelling account of his escape and rescue reflects Bill Martin's resourcefulness, determination, and instincts for survival.

The story of the June 1944 battle of the Philippine Sea is told by three participants from completely different perspectives. The distinguished naval officer Adm. Arleigh A. Burke, then chief of staff to Vice Adm. Marc Mitscher, CTF 58, describes the battle from the viewpoint of an operational planner heavily involved in the decision-making process throughout the battle. His is a behind-the-scenes look at the historic moments that led to Admiral Mitscher's memorable decision to "turn on the lights" for the pilots returning from the strike on the Japanese fleet.

One of those returning dive bombers was flown by Lt. Comdr. J. D. Ramage, skipper of VB-10. Partly by reading from a booklet in which one of his young pilots, Lt.(jg) Don Lewis, shared his recollections, Ramage tells of the dive bombers' attacks on the enemy carriers and their harrowing return flight through the night to find their task force. As the lights of the task force came on, and plane after plane ditched in the water from fuel exhaustion, Ramage and Lewis finally found clear decks and managed to land safely. Ramage speaks for a great many carrier aviators who, at the time, were frustrated and disappointed in the failure to administer a final, crushing blow on the enemy carrier force.

On the other hand, fighter pilots had nothing to complain about on the day of the great Marianas Turkey Shoot, 19 June. Then Ens. Arthur R. ("Ray") Hawkins describes in vivid detail the view from the cockpit of a Hellcat as the combat air patrols of Marc Mitscher's carriers flew mission after mission throughout the day to counter waves of enemy planes approaching the task force.

Another pilot who got more than his share was Comdr. David McCampbell, who received the Medal of Honor for destroying seven enemy aircraft that day. He describes the tactics he used in aerial combat to become the Navy's leading ace with 34 victories. In a later chapter, he gives a matter-of-fact account of his unsurpassed feat of destroying nine enemy planes on one mission.

As a task group commander under Admiral Mitscher at Leyte Gulf, Rear Adm. Gerald Bogan was an active player in the infamous "Battle of Bull's Run," as Admiral Halsey made his impetuous dash up north to attack the enemy "decoy" force. Admiral Bogan was in a perfect position to observe and comment critically on the efficacy of Halsey's decision and the frustration and misunderstandings that led to the near catastrophe in the battle off Samar Island.

In that battle, Capt. Fitzhugh Lee and his escort carrier *Manila Bay* were in the southernmost of the three groups of "jeep" carriers and, in a masterpiece of understatement, he recalls the "unhappy passage of time" when splashes from the guns of an enemy heavy cruiser visible on the horizon rained down on his task group formation. Fitzhugh Lee remembers quite vividly his feelings of futility and deep concern as he sent a young torpedo plane pilot out for his third attack on the giant battleship *Yamato*. Later, to his great relief, he learned that the pilot survived the battle. In the weeks to come, the *Manila Bay* was the target of many *kamikaze* attacks. She survived a direct hit on the flight deck, and, through Fitzhugh Lee's superb leadership, survived to continue the fight for the liberation of the Philippines.

For every ace, there were dozens of "tail-end Charlies" such as Ens. Kent Lee, who, as the last man in the formation, kept his leader out of trouble and rarely had a chance to distinguish himself. Kent Lee had the unusually good fortune to begin his part of the war as a dive bomber pilot and then later fly as a fighter pilot in a Hellcat squadron. He seized this rare opportunity to shoot down one enemy airplane and, in general, enjoyed the world of fighter sweeps, dogfights, and infrequent night carrier landings.

Rescue at Saipan

Vice Admiral William I. Martin

William Inman Martin was born in the Ozark Hills of Missouri on 5 May 1910, son of Ada Inman Martin and Harry Martin. He attended the University of Oklahoma and the University of Missouri before his appointment to the U.S. Naval Academy. He was graduated and commissioned ensign on 31 May 1934 and was designated a naval aviator in 1938. Subsequent service included extensive command and staff duties ashore and afloat. He advanced in rank to vice admiral, effective 10 April 1967. He commanded the U.S. Sixth Fleet in the Mediterranean and was Deputy Commander in Chief, U.S. Atlantic Fleet, from August 1968 until his retirement, effective 2 February 1972.

During World War II, Admiral Martin commanded dive bomber and torpedo bomber squadrons operating aboard the USS Enterprise *and subsequently commanded the Navy's first night air group. His aviation specialty was instrument flight and airborne radar, and the application of these to night fighters and all-weather attack aircraft operating from aircraft carriers. Ad-*

miral Martin's many combat actions included the first carrier raids against the Japanese homeland and night attacks against shipping in the Inland Sea of Japan.

Admiral Martin's decorations include the Distinguished Service Medal with two Gold Stars, Silver Star Medal, Legion of Merit with Gold Star, Distinguished Flying Cross with two Gold Stars, and the Air Medal with two Gold Stars.

Left to right: Jerry T. Williams, Comdr. William I. Martin, Wesley R. Hargrove, USS Enterprise, *1944. (Courtesy NASM)*

On 13 June 1944, two days before the amphibious operations at Saipan, we operated against Japanese shipping, sinking everything we saw. The day these operations were to commence, a large part of our fleet was there and the number of air units to be put on the target to soften it were very large. Lt. Comdr. Robert H. Iseley commanded one of the groups that was to go in to strike at dawn, and I had the second group. My group was the northernmost one that took in Charan Kanoa airstrip and enemy air defenses that we knew about. Bob Iseley's group was taking the southern tip of the island, including Aslito Air Field, which later was named for him. Bob Iseley was killed during that attack.

We had planned this thing on tactical radio with signals back and forth about how to coordinate it. It was a coordinated attack approaching from the east. Our intention was to commence pushovers into our dives at exactly the same time so that the antiaircraft defenses that were between these two positions, which could fire either way, would be divided; they couldn't concentrate on one and then concentrate on the other. As we approached it and got within antiaircraft range, the antiaircraft bursts appeared in front of both of us at the same time. When he said he was ready to push over, so was I, and we pushed over into very steep dives. I was coming down as vertically as one can make it. My radioman called out the altitudes. As he called out 2,500 feet, the desired release point, I was on target, so I released. Immediately there was a terrific blast. A Japanese 5-inch antiaircraft shell hit my plane in the middle of the fuselage and burned the hair on the back of my neck. It was that close. I'll never know how I got out of that airplane alive because it takes just three and a fraction seconds to the deck. I pulled the ripcord as I released the safety belt. This let me get out just in time because the chute opened and didn't even swing before I hit the water.

The chute was torn; there were two panels badly ripped, and so I hit pretty hard. I was in four feet of water about 100 yards off the beach. There were lots of Japanese soldiers there; if I had known one of them I could have recognized him I was that close. It was very fortunate that I got out at low altitude; if I had descended slowly from altitude I would probably have been killed by enemy rifle fire, being a vulnerable target for several seconds. I looked up and large pieces of my plane were still falling, doing a "falling leaf." I was told my plane was chopped in two by the blast, and it was falling in flames. Just a few feet from me—30 or 40 feet—the forward part of the plane that I had just bailed out of was there burning, and I had to move away from it because gasoline was burning on the surface and was moving toward me. It was obvious the members of my crew were lost. They were probably killed immediately when the antiaircraft shell exploded. There were two—Jerry T. Williams, who was the radio operator and also the tail gunner, and Wesley R. Hargrove, who was in the turret. They were both killed, and their bodies were not recovered. This saddened me greatly; we had been on many combat missions together.

I realized that the "zip-burp, zip-burp" noise I was hearing was enemy rifle fire from the beach; they were not hitting me, but were very close. I stayed underwater then and was pulling in what was left of my torn parachute because I had an idea I might need it later. I had a one-man rubber boat, but I couldn't inflate it at that point; I would have been an easy target. I had to stay underwater except to stick my nose out for a quick breath and then move away from the beach. I was inside the lagoon, just south of Garapan Town. Garapan Town is on the northern end of the lagoon, and Sugar Mill is on the southern end of it. The Charan Kanoa airstrip was just inboard between the two. I continued to move out, away from the beach, from the small arms fire, and I realized I was in a position to observe antiaircraft guns that we had not known were there. We knew very little about that place. As a matter of fact, it was a very hot spot and the reports we had from reconnaissance were very sketchy. I learned later that our frogmen had tried to get in there but found it was too hot for them.

Gradually I moved out of there. It was about 500 yards out to the reef that enclosed the lagoon, and, when I was over halfway there, the small arms fire stopped, as I was beyond their range. When I got to the reef, I sat there realizing that I had gained intelligence that was of value. I took bearings on the southern coast of Saipan, as against Tinian, and was able later to know exactly where I was, and therefore my reports on the antiaircraft positions and other things of interest could be accurately located.

Don't think I wasn't frightened! As I was on my way out, I saw a boat approaching from Garapan Town, and I wondered then what I would do. I had a .45-caliber with me. Of course, it was wet; whether it would fire or not, I didn't know.

Only two of us were coached on the amphibious operation for the following day: Lt. Comdr. Bill ("Killer") Kane, the fighter squadron commander on the *Enterprise,* and myself. We had spent most of the previous week with Capt. Dick Whitehead and the amphibious people coaching us—preparing us to be air coordinators for the amphibious operation on the following day. We had all this knowledge, and this was what frightened me most; because of our rank, they would expect that we would know a great deal about the forthcoming amphibious operation, and they would use all kinds of torture on us to find that out, probably to the extent of killing us. I had decided that, if captured, I would use my gun and take as many of them as I could with me.

As it turned out, the next strike, strike Baker, came in, and they had been cautioned that someone had seen a parachute. Only one person had seen my parachute because it was open for such a short period of time. It was someone following me in the dive who thought he had seen it. So all the strikes in strike Baker were cautioned that there might be somebody alive there—and not to drop anything in the water. I was able to see where they dropped; they were dropping very accurately, and the enemy boat turned around and went back to shore.

Then later there was another enemy boat coming toward me from the Sugar Mill side, the southern end of the lagoon; it was about halfway there when our battleships and cruisers which had moved within range (about 30,000 yards) began firing at the beach—over my head. That's quite an experience! Each one of them sounded like a freight train passing over me. They had been instructed, as I found out later, that nothing should fall short. Their fire was extremely accurate from my point of view; nothing hit in the water near me, except for lots of shrapnel from antiaircraft fire falling around me. I finally got to the reef, as I have said, positioned myself, and sat there with just my eyes above water observing what was going on and making mental notes. There were no man-made obstacles in the water, just a lot of coral heads.

I soon left the reef because the Japanese spotted me. They opened up with something that seemed to me like a 40-mm. One shot was off to the left and short; it splashed water on me. The other was just to the right of me and long. So they had me "bracketed," and I wasted no time. I gathered up my parachute and ran across that live coral. It took about 15 steps to get completely across it, and then there was deep water on the other side. I had to move further out before I could inflate my rubber boat. When I thought I was far enough out that they could no longer reach me with small arms, I inflated the rubber boat, and it took some time to get in it; I swallowed much sea water so I was nauseated (it acts as a laxative too). I was throwing up and also had diarrhea suddenly, and cramps. The intelligence people who questioned me later said, "That's splendid, splendid; it acts as an effective shark repellent!"

Some time in the afternoon, planes from my own squadron and the *Enterprise* fighters came with the intention of finding a survivor, if there was one. I shone my mirror and that's what they saw; they came down and dropped another life raft to me, and I knew that I had been spotted. After that, I could relax because the wind was from the island blowing me westward—that's where our fleet was.

That was my first moment of confidence. I was confident that I was going to survive that ordeal, and all I had to do was sail toward them. So I pulled in my parachute and let out enough of it to act as a sail. The wind was breezy enough that I was kicking up a little wake as I sailed westward. When I got a mile or so from the island, a seaplane came in and landed close enough to taxi up to me. The pilot of that seaplane was from Admiral Spruance's flagship. He came to pick me up. I wanted to take my chute and my life raft with me, but he said, "No sir, Commander, you get in this airplane, we're going to get out of here real fast." He took his .45 and shot holes in the rubber boat; he was correct in doing it because otherwise it might have floated out and our ships would have wondered about it and spent some time looking for other survivors. So he very correctly sank it. I got in the backseat of the seaplane. It was the pilot's first encounter with enemy antiaircraft fire; he was very nervous. To take off, we had to head into the wind, which meant we were going right back toward the island and the enemy antiaircraft fire. He finally rocked it off, and we became airborne. That old SOC was very slow; fortunately, it was the first time that I, or anybody, had ever seen the Japanese overlead—their lead was far ahead of us. Usually their antiaircraft fire was behind, but the SOC was so slow they were leading it excessively. None of it hit us, and the pilot finally was able to turn away from Saipan and fly toward our fleet. We made a recovery on a sled towed behind the ship. It was the flagship of the fleet commander!

I was taken to Admiral Spruance, a fine gentleman. After I talked with him a few minutes, he turned me over to his intelligence people, who spent the next several hours questioning me. They briefed me on plans for the amphibious operations. Of course, I had previously memorized them. I had been shot down at Beach Green One, which was to be the first wave of our amphibious operation. As it turned out, the information I gained on the depths of the water, the obstacles, also the antiaircraft locations, turned out to be very helpful for their plans.

This was a very fine illustration of successful rescue operations. Actually, from the beginning of the war, this was a very comforting thing for the aviators because so much attention was put into improving rescue procedures, especially to improve picking up people that we knew had been shot down who might have been left behind at the end of the day. I know that Rear Adm. John Walter ("Black Jack") Reeves, Jr., whose flag was in the *Enterprise* the second year of the war, spent a great deal of time on the project of organizing seaplane rescue teams protected by fighters to go in close to the beach and pick up downed aviators that might be left behind as the task force left the area. It worked very well. I doubt if there was anything that concerned our planners more during an operation when our aviators were exposed like that and you knew you were going to lose some of them to antiaircraft; the planning for search and rescue was very complete and very efficient.

I was transferred by high line from the cruiser over to a destroyer that was to take me back to the *Enterprise*. The destroyer had also picked up a Japanese survivor who was a captain who had been aboard a ship my squadron had sunk the day before. One cheek of his buttocks had been shot off and he had lost a lot of blood, but our doctors worked on him, giving him the same treatment given to our own men. When I was transferred back to the *Enterprise,* he went there also, in a stretcher, while I was going over in a breeches buoy. We both went over together. He was queried by our intelligence people as I was when I got back. I know he got as good treatment as was possible to give him. This thing of shooting up enemy people in their parachutes and things like that—you would hear of isolated cases and maybe some went on, but I never saw it.

Night Is My Ally

Vice Admiral William I. Martin

I became very interested in instrument flying because I realized (after I had finished flight training in 1938) that I wasn't really a capable instrument pilot. This concern built up after I went to my first fleet squadron, a dive bomber squadron that was in the old *Lexington* air group. Every year we had to requalify as an instrument pilot, which meant that we would be checked by one of the senior pilots. The pilots who had graduated from flight training years before me weren't capable instrument pilots either. They considered they were doing very well if they could fly on instruments for a few minutes without spinning in.

I thought the training for bringing us up to speed as competent bomber pilots was very good for daytime, but for nighttime it was inadequate. It bugged me that we weren't able to operate efficiently in bad weather or at night. I had already decided when I was in flight training that this was what I wanted to specialize in, and, then when I went back as a flight instructor, after my first squadron tour, I was able to carry on that specialty and become a competent instrument flyer.

Because of this drive I had toward night and bad weather operations from an aircraft carrier, the principal thing in my thinking of tactics at that time was that pilots should have at least a basic capability to be able to defend our force or attack targets of opportunity, especially the ones that are found after the last of the daytime missions have returned to the carrier and the pilots tell about a "fat target" left undamaged. To be unable to go out and strike that target at night bothered me, so I started writing my ideas of what the tactics and the basic fundamentals of a standard night attack from a carrier should be. I took into account the problems of rendezvous, which are more complicated than taking off from a field because there are unpredictable interruptions. When an airplane goes "down" on the catapult, there is delay and you just can't expedite a rendezvous pattern before departure for the target. There are other problems involving the carrier. It is not going to be where it predicted it would be when you return. The ship must remain darkened. There are other complications, and I was thinking these things through. I wrote my first proposal on night tactics that we should be working on while I was in a dive bomber squadron aboard the *Lexington* before World War II.

I was not getting much encouragement. The fact is I was getting considerable discouragement, especially from some of my seniors. "We don't need it. We're doing OK without it." When I was ordered back to become a flight instructor at Pensacola, everybody who checked in at that time had to go into primary flight instruction, teaching the youngster to solo. I really didn't want to do that. I hid on the sick list for about a week until a vacancy in the instrument squadron opened up so I could become an instrument instructor. I know it wasn't an admirable thing to do, but I was determined to become an instrument flight instructor and a competent instrument pilot. That gave me a concentrated dosage of instrument flying as I was teaching it daily. Once I was permitted to take an airplane from Pensacola, Florida, to my home in Missouri for Thanksgiving vacation. I got into a bad weather situation which I really wasn't yet competent to handle. I was very lucky to get into Memphis without crashing. That further impressed me that, if flying was going to be my full career, I had better learn to do instrument flying well.

When I reported for duty aboard a carrier, I was disappointed because the aircraft carrier air groups were really not capable of carrying out simple night missions. Also something exciting was developed during my last year as a flight instructor—radar. By that time, we had radar in PBYs and in some of the large multipiloted aircraft. This was 1940–41. It was also in the summer of 1941 that two naval reserve airline pilots were being sent around the fleet to introduce naval aviators to what they called "attitude" instrument flying.

Prior to that time, we were doing what we called "needle, ball, air speed." The needle gave the pilot turn information; the ball told him if he was in a skid or in a coordinated situation during a turn; and the air speed was controlled by power settings for climb-out, cruise, or whatever speed you wanted to make, and it would determine the position of the nose relative to the horizon. It was not an easy thing to do; it took a long time to accomplish that, whereas with the gyro instruments the "attitude" system would permit you to use a gyro horizon, which would clearly indicate the plane's attitude. The directional gyro could be set from the magnetic compass to get exact stable readings. Some of the aircraft had gyro instruments, but the Navy originally considered them unreliable and wouldn't permit them to be used. We did find that with preventive maintenance these instruments became quite reliable, and we began to use them. In the first squadron I went to after my tour as a flight instructor, we took the masks off the gyro instruments and started using them routinely. We found that, if the gyro instruments were given proper preventive maintenance, they were reliable.

There were no books then on attitude instrument flying, so during the first year of the war I wrote the first instruction book. It was considered to be very good; I named it *Instrument Flying for the Carrier Pilot,* because there were certain aspects of it that were unique to the problems of operating from an aircraft carrier. I submitted it to the Bureau of Aeronautics and the first encouragement I got was from Vice Adm. John Towers' (ComAirPac) level, in 1942.

After an *Enterprise* deployment with a dive bomber squadron in 1943, I asked to be transferred to a torpedo squadron, because they were the only attack carrier aircraft that had radar. We had a few night fighter detachments at that time—four planes with radar per carrier, and some carriers didn't even have that. I was not interested in the technicalities of radar, but what it could do operationally was very important. It seemed normal to me that radar, which could provide eyes to see through weather and darkness, combined with competent instrument pilots, would be a perfect marriage. The things that you could do with just a few pilots who could handle the instrument flight part of it—taking off at night or in very bad weather, going from A to B, making an attack, and returning to A—gave additional capabilities that were really bonuses. We could paralyze an enemy airfield as long as we kept an aircraft near it. And there was the idea of keeping their antiaircraft people awake all night. A man who has been awake all night isn't going to be sharp on the guns the next day. So it would have some direct effects and some side effects that looked very attractive. I considered it valuable to distribute that information, to get the proposal out even if it might be turned down—just to sow the seed.

In late 1943, I was ordered to command Torpedo Squadron 10. We were training in Seattle, but eventually it was to deploy in the *Enterprise* where I had been previously. Assigned pilots turned around to go back with me. Because we were a torpedo squadron, we had to practice dropping torpedoes. We should have been the very best because by this time they were all competent instrument pilots and they could fly more accurately than those who were not trained in instrument flying. They became expert at flying by instruments and launching torpedoes under the most adverse conditions. I don't think a single one was dropped that was beyond the tolerances of the prescribed method. However, out of 30-some odd that were dropped, only one ran reasonably normal. This was a big discouragement.

In addition to the unreliability of the torpedoes, a plane during a torpedo attack is much more vulnerable than during high-level horizontal bombing. It's not difficult for the enemy to determine your altitude and speed because you

Under the leadership of Comdr. Bill Martin, the aircrews of Torpedo Squadron 10, flying TBF/TBM Avengers, pioneered the development of all-weather attack tactics in the Pacific. (Courtesy NASM)

are no more than 150 feet above the water. That's why we didn't drop any torpedoes later on when we were in combat except on one occasion. We couldn't talk our superiors out of it. The loading order was "torpedoes," so we took them to make an attack on a destroyer outside of Palau Harbor. There were 15 torpedoes dropped, of which only 1 scored a hit. Twelve SBDs also dropped 1,000-pound bombs, and the destroyer finally sank.

New Guinea was the first place where we showed the value of the all-weather preparations we had been making while we were in training at Seattle. The weather was very bad as the task force steamed toward New Guinea, to Hollandia. My pilots were able to get through there, and they took a number of aircraft from other squadrons with them. Some were able to get through to the target; others were not eager to penetrate that tropical front. The "tropical front" is a low cloud formation that wallows on both sides of the equator. It is not very turbulent, but there is no visibility through it. If you are flying through it at right angles, it takes about 10 minutes to penetrate it. We were able to fly through it and locate the target. We made repeated runs at Hollandia, catching many planes on the ground. Some enemy fighters were a problem, but we were able to penetrate the weather and make the attack visually. When we left Hollandia to return to the task force, which was east about 200 miles, it was necessary to fly on instruments until we had passed through the weather—an equatorial front. Planes from other squadrons joined up on my squadron to fly formation back to the carrier. That frequently happened when there was bad weather. The other pilots hadn't learned this new method of instrument flying we called the "attitude" system.

In February 1944, we were finally given permission by the fleet commander to make a predawn low-level bombing attack at Truk, which turned out to be a real classic. Truk was considered the bastion, the one that raised terror in every pilot's mind, because it was so heavily defended. There were 12 planes that attacked Truk from Torpedo Squadron 10 on 17 February 1944. It wasn't a designated "night" outfit yet, but we trained at night. The planes that went into Truk to attack shipping there were cautioned that there might be a Japanese hospital ship in the harbor. Each of the pilots had trained to make repeated runs until they were sure of getting a hit on a combatant ship. Radar displays at that time required an operator to do a great deal of interpreting. It was like learning a new language. Instead of it being a polar plot, looking down on it like a map, the cathode ray tube just gave indications that there was an object out there. After considerable practice, a radar operator could determine that there was a ship there and its approximate size. You related the blip on the radar scope to the image of the ship. We trained by making repeated practice runs over known targets. At Truk, we made repeated runs; some of the pilots made as many as four runs. They carried four 500-pound bombs. In Truk lagoon, there were little hummocks that gave a radar return that looked like a ship; there were some pilots who realized they were making a run on a hummock at the last minute and wouldn't drop; courageously they would go back and make another run. This explains why 12 planes got 13 confirmed hits—13 ships either sunk or burning and out of action. That number of hits is what might be expected from four or five times the number of day attacks in a similar situation.

The flak was quite thick, but, out of 12 planes, only 1 was lost to enemy action. This is one of the things about night work that adds a lot to the mystery of it: you never see what happens; you deduce the result from the little information that you have. I couldn't be sure that one of my planes was lost to antiaircraft fire, but in my own mind I was quite certain that he was shot down by the enemy.

I wasn't on that strike. I had a broken arm, and I went through the tests to see if I could manage the controls. Comdr. Tom Hamilton was the executive officer of the ship, and he put me up in the cockpit to see if I could operate all the controls. I couldn't do it well enough to pass his test, so I could not go on that flight. However, the pilots were so well trained and the tactics were straightforward, so they went out without me—the first time they had ever been out without me at night, but they did a terrific job. That helped along the selling of my proposal that we needed to have a specially trained night carrier and night air group.

I didn't want to miss that attack, but it was a great satisfaction to me that these youngsters were able to carry it out so professionally. They had become extremely competent pilots in utter darkness and in the worst of weather. They were the only ones who had this capability on the carriers at that time. Our land-based patrol aircraft were doing instrument flying all the time and were very good at it, but the carrier air groups were not. What it took to sell night and bad weather operations was a demonstration that, first, you could train the pilots to do it, and that the tactics we had worked out with this crude radar were effective. For example, in masthead-level bombing the radar operator would give a "mark" approximately over the target and the pilot would say, "One alligator, two," and push the pickle to release the bomb. I don't know who thought up "One alligator, two," but it was just the right amount of delayed timing to drop the bomb so that if you are at the proper altitude and on the proper speed you would hit a ship at the waterline. If you hit a ship at the waterline, a lot of water will gush in there, and it will sink quickly. If you drop a fraction of a second too early, you may still get a ricochet hit, but, if you drop late, you probably will not damage the ship. To do major damage and get the water inside the ship so it will sink, you must have the aiming point at the waterline.

After the attack on Truk, we began to get other missions on bad weather days. When the weather was really "stinking," that's when only we were scheduled to go. It opened up a lot of opportunities for us to do what we were trained to do, once we had that first success. The following year, in 1945, the Navy Department approved the proposal of designating at least one carrier as a "night carrier," and its air group was designated a "night air group." When we went out on that one, we were aboard the night-attack carrier *Enterprise,* and our group was called Night Air Group 90. Then we were made up entirely of night-competent pilots.

It worked out quite well because we would take over all the night duties of the task force, which would give relief to the day carriers. Where to position the ship when we operated on this kind of schedule took some experimentation—that is, whether we would operate inside the total task force formation or operate outside of it. At that time, I wasn't worried about the carrier division commander's problems. If we got outside the task force, we would try to get back in it before daylight for mutual protection. There was one period off Iwo Jima when we had planes in the air constantly, 24 hours a day during the period 23 February to 2 March 1945—174 hours—and the *Enterprise* was operating all night every night. During that period, the *Enterprise* had more landings than any other carrier in the task force because she was designated to take the daytime "cripples," the ones that were damaged, and the "stragglers," planes that came in too late to land aboard during the landing cycle of their own carrier. So the *Enterprise* during that period was going full tilt, day and night. I greatly admired that ship and her crew. They had unusual ability and great endurance. The commanding officer of the ship was in charge at night, and his navigator would take the captain's duties on the captain's bridge during the daytime. They formed two different teams that enabled the carrier to operate day and night.

Early in the war, the Japanese had more capability than we had at night, or at least they were flying more at night. Now I don't know what their operational losses were. They were operating from airfields that were not getting attacks at night and that sort of thing. Nothing was interfering with night operations at their bases.

The Japanese used flares at night as part of their night attack tactics. They had a technique of dropping flares on one side of the fleet and making their attacks against the silhouettes on the other side. It was not a bad scheme. However, at that point their instrumentation and their training of pilots was not good enough to carry it out well. At the battle of Midway, they had lost most of their first-line pilots. They never got as good again as they were at Midway. They weren't wiped out, but they weren't very good.

In any case, they became a threat to the fleet. There were contacts on our ships' radar screens frequently at night. That's why Butch O'Hare and John Phillips tried to devise a means of providing some defense against it, with John Phillips flying the torpedo plane that had radar and taking Butch O'Hare with two fighters without radars. The three would be the night fighter defense. It was a last resort to provide some defense. Even if it had worked as well as envisioned, it wouldn't have been very effective because the fighters at that time didn't have their own radar. They were operating on instructions from the torpedo plane that did have radar. Very early in those experiments, on 26 November 1943, the famous Butch O'Hare was shot down, probably by the tail gunner in the torpedo plane, who thought he was firing at an enemy plane.

There was a need for a capable defense. Some of our night fighter detachments were quite successful in night defense of their carrier. There were a few night shoot-downs before we had the designated night air groups. Our torpedo squadron wasn't the beginner of the night fighter defense team. We were the beginners of night-attack tactics.

It was very fortunate that some of us had been with the *Enterprise* from the first year of the war. She was already known as a great fighting ship and a ship of great endurance. There were a few men on that ship the last year of the war who were there when the war started. When it was decided to designate a night carrier, I think it was most fortunate that they selected the *Enterprise* in December 1944 to do this because she was a great veteran. The fact that several of us had been aboard before and knew the ship's officers and the ship's company was a significant asset for us because night operations are a great inconvenience to the entire ship. The eating hours had to be expanded, and the shops, parts, and spares had to be available 24 hours a day. There were some of the missions during this period— some of the day missions—when you needed to do some searching and some scouting when the weather was so bad they had to be conducted under instrument flying conditions; the night air group aboard the *Enterprise* did those.

I am sure that all the other carriers were happy to see a night carrier in the task force because it took over the night air operations for the defense of the fleet and the night searches, as well as the bad weather strikes. When the fleet was in the South China Sea in January 1945, we hit Cam Ranh Bay at night and Pratas Reef, which we knew had a large Japanese communications station on it. The weather was so bad that the night air group performed that operation.

The airplane we had to use for night attack, the TBF Avenger, was heavily loaded. It was at maximum gross weight to take off from the carrier. Invariably, it would settle at the bow at takeoff, which means it wasn't quite flying as it left the carrier. To configure this plane so that it was a reasonably safe proposition to operate at night, it was necessary to unload as much stuff as we could spare, like armor plate, in order to take more gas and full ordnance. While we were at San Diego, between deployments, we removed the whole turret assembly and the tail gun, which left us no defense except our forward firing guns. This would have been hazardous if we got caught by enemy fighters in the daytime, but at night we didn't consider that a real threat. We didn't consider antiaircraft fire as too much of a threat at night, either. The Japanese fire-control radar was not good.

Also, on the Avenger we took out all of the bottom armor plate. We would have taken out all the heavy armor plate that was back of the pilot, but that was just too complicated; we were getting into more weight and balance complications than we were able to deal with. We only had 10 days to do all these things before we deployed to the western Pacific, but we convinced Admiral Towers, ComAirPac, that the idea had merit, and he gave us priority to have the job done at the Overhaul and Repair facility before we left. I must admit the modified airplane was difficult to land because the center of gravity had been moved so far forward it was very difficult to get the tail down, but we found that by putting only 14 pounds of lead all the way in the tail it restored the center of gravity within workable limits.

The changes we made needed to be done to make this torpedo bomber into a reasonably safe aircraft operating from an aircraft carrier at night. We needed its additional endurance and range. It brought a lot of targets within our range at night that we couldn't otherwise have reached. Having additional endurance permitted us to go to Kyushu, Japan's main island, and stay over the target several hours at night, not permitting them to show a light, thereby grounding their aircraft during night hours.

I doubt that we would have succeeded if we hadn't had very capable and very dedicated young patriots that were willing to go out on a third consecutive deployment. None of them really *had* to go; they had completed two deployments. That's the way it worked out.

In January 1945, we performed a strike against Formosa, the northern end of which is the harbor of Kiirun. This was a remarkable mission. It was the longest range of any strike from an aircraft carrier at that time, and it was the kind of a strike that you couldn't do from a day carrier because it required going close to Japanese-occupied islands en route and returning. We had a very successful operation insofar as the damage we did to the enemy, but it was costly. Out of six planes, we lost three due to enemy action.

The purpose of the mission was to strike a concentration of Japanese shipping in Kiirun Harbor. We were able to hit them before they could get under way and escape us. It was a successful strike; they had no idea where we came from. The night operations gave them a lot of problems that they hadn't had before. Our idea was to paralyze the airfields—to damage them so they could not use them at night and therefore couldn't relocate their aircraft. It was their custom to redeploy at night to the fields from which they would be operating the next day. If we could hit those fields where most of the aircraft were, we could keep them paralyzed until our dawn fighter sweep would get into position, and then our day attacks would keep them from attacking our carriers. Once we commenced operating against the Japanese homeland, there were no strikes against our fleet for a long period of time—none from the airfields we had operated against at night.

Japanese effectiveness was declining at this stage of the war, whereas ours was improving, both as to our quality and our quantity. Of course, more new carriers were coming out the last year of the war, and we had four operating task groups of four carriers each. At one time, we had five, including the night task group. Our pilots were well-trained, and the longer they stayed in the operation the better they became. They were improving every day, and the Japanese fleet was not capable of countering our fleet again.

Spruance, Mitscher, and Task Force 58

Admiral Arleigh A. Burke

Arleigh A. Burke was born in Boulder, Colorado, on 19 October 1901. On 7 June 1923, he was graduated from the U.S. Naval Academy, commissioned ensign in the United States Navy, and married to Roberta Gorsuch of Washington, D.C. He served in battleships and destroyers, various staff assignments ashore, and received an M.S. degree in Engineering at the University of Michigan. Subsequent service included extensive command and staff duties ashore and afloat as he advanced to the rank of admiral, effective August 1955, when he became Chief of Naval Operations. Admiral Burke served three terms in that position before his retirement on 1 August 1961.

For the first two years of the war, he was assigned to the Naval Gun Factory. In 1943, he went to the South Pacific, where he earned the Navy Cross for extraordinary heroism as commander of Destroyer Squadron 23, the "Little Beavers," in actions against the enemy in the northern Solomon Islands area. In the latter part of the Solomons campaign, Destroyer Squadron 23 fought in

22 separate engagements with the enemy during a four-month period. He reported in March 1944 as chief of staff to Commander, Fast Carrier Task Force 58, Vice Adm. Marc Mitscher, and participated in numerous naval engagements until June 1945.

Admiral Burke's numerous awards during his 42 years in the Navy include the Navy Cross, Distinguished Service Medal with two Gold Stars, Legion of Merit with two Gold Stars and Oak Leaf Cluster (Army), Silver Star, Purple Heart, Presidential Unit Citation Ribbon with three stars, Navy Unit Commendation Ribbon, and many awards and decorations from foreign governments.

Vice Adm. Marc A. Mitscher (right) and his chief of staff, Comm. Arleigh A. Burke.

In March 1944, I was directed to detach from ComDesRon 23 and report to ComCarDiv 3, who was Vice Adm. Marc Mitscher, recently designated Commander, Fast Carrier Task Force. This whole business came about, I found out later, when Adm. Ernest King decided that every aviator admiral in important positions at sea had to have a nonaviator as chief of staff, and every nonaviator in a similar position had to have an aviator as chief of staff. The reason for that was that nonaviators, in the beginning of the war, had demonstrated that they didn't know how to fight an air war properly, and the same thing happened in surface battle when aviators had command of surface ship units. They didn't know how to use them properly.

I did know *I* did not want to go to carriers. I had experience in destroyers and surface warfare, and I thought that there was room for more surface combat in other areas than the South Pacific and I wanted to stay in surface ships. Nonetheless, my squadron eventually caught up with the Fast Carrier Task Force, and I went by highline to the *Lexington*. I didn't have any gear but a briefcase full of papers and a sea bag when I came across. I reported to Admiral Mitscher, and he said very little, except to offer me the use of his cabin to rest up. So I took a shower, went up to the flag bridge as soon as I got dressed, and said I was all set to go, I didn't want any sleep. The admiral said, "Well, you're on the job."

There was a strained period between me and the admiral, because neither one of us liked the idea. Admiral Mitscher certainly did not want me. I found out later, too, that Admiral Mitscher had protested taking a nonaviator as chief of staff; he had a good chief of staff, an excellent one, and Admiral King told him to do it anyway. He didn't want anything to do with me. He had made up his mind, I think, that he was going to bypass me; he'd keep me there as a figurehead; for surface actions and things like that maybe he would use me, but the normal chief of staff job he was going to do himself, and he certainly knew how. So I studied my tail off, and I asked questions. I talked to all the people on the staff, asked them how they did things, about their communications procedures, doctrines, dispositions, the whole ball of wax. I talked to the air group commander, who explained what airplanes did, how they formed up, what they had to watch, and their communications setup, the whole damned thing. Then I talked to the squadron commanders and some of the pilots. Although I didn't know it at that time, Admiral Mitscher had a very good system of talking to the senior pilots on a flight, every time a flight came back. That was very good, and I'd listen to them. I'd ease over to a corner. Admiral Mitscher would say "good morning" to me in the morning when I came up, and that was the end of it. He never sent for me. He talked to the junior people on the staff, but he never sent for me.

Well, I read all the instructions, all the plans for the coming strike on Palau, and they were voluminous plans. In looking at these battle plans, which were an inch-and-a-half thick, tremendous volumes and full of detail, I realized how complex this carrier war could be. They hadn't ever had a real carrier task force before; carriers had nearly always acted singly. When several carriers had operated together, it was sort of a mutual cooperation exercise. They would exchange information and ideas, but very seldom were there over two or three carriers at a time and they operated on an ad hoc basis primarily to avoid interference with each other's operations. On 1 March 1944, they had formed this fast carrier task force and put Admiral Mitscher in command. He had four task groups, totaling 11 carriers, and all the supporting ships, battleships, cruisers, and destroyers.

On our way to strike Palau, an incident occurred that helped to break the ice a little in my relations with Admiral Mitscher. On 29 March 1944, we got some very heavy attacks from enemy air from Palau. Torpedo planes were about to attack, and nobody had given any battle orders to the task force. So I went over to the TBS and directed the whole task force to come to a specific course to thread these torpedoes and prepare for attack. Of course, they could see it and were already prepared for attack, but I felt I had to check it. We didn't get hurt, although these torpedoes came close. Right after that little first attack, I went over to stand by Admiral Mitscher because I was sure I was going to catch hell. He probably hadn't said 20 words to me for the last three or four days, and he looked at me and said, "Captain, it's about time," which meant it was about time I did something. I'd taken charge, and that was all right with him. I knew then, if I were to become an adequate chief of staff, I'd have to make the moves, and they'd better be right the first time.

I did nearly all my work in flag plot or on the flag bridge. I lived in a sea cabin right next to the admiral's on the same level as flag plot. It didn't take over 10 to 15 seconds for us to hit the deck and be on battle stations when we got an unexpected surprise attack at night or when the staff duty officer wanted us on deck. I made a rule for the SDO that whenever the admiral was called I should be called, too. That admiral of ours did have some mighty good habits. He also had some strong convictions about what should be done by the task force and the task group commanders in battle and in normal operating procedure. One of his excellent ideas was to always operate as if battle were imminent—same idea I had used in destroyers in the Solomons—for that way we would always be ready for a surprise attack and it took no special operations to go into action.

Admiral Mitscher felt that the TG commanders should be experts in handling their air groups and their surface ships. They must use their own initiative and modify the standard procedures when such modification would be more effective and not interfere with the operations of the TF or other TGs. But the most important characteristic he required of his senior aviator TG commanders was that they must be aggressive and courageous. His confidence in his commanders was great and justified. But still, once in a while as the war progressed and some of the old commanders were relieved, Admiral Mitscher felt that a TG commander did not measure up to his responsibilities. Then he demonstrated his own high sense of his responsibilities; he relieved that commander at once and put in the most experienced standby commander in command of that TG. This always was the failure of a TG commander in battle. One failure to do the right thing in battle, and the commander was summarily relieved and sent home. A good combat commander must be ruthless in his demands that his subordinate commanders perform well in battle or be relieved by someone who could.

All the original TG commanders were battle-tested veterans and did perform extraordinarily well in the stress of battle. But later on a few failed for one cause or another. None failed because of lack of personal courage, but usually they failed because they did not use the forces at their disposal to the best advantage. Later, when this happened, it was my job, as chief of staff, to fly over to tell the unfortunate man who didn't measure up that he was all through, that he was relieved from command at that moment, and that he should take the first available transportation back to Pearl. Not one of them ever argued or objected. They knew why it had to be done. We did not broadcast this action, but, of course, others had seen what had happened, or didn't happen, and could guess what was going on. It was an onerous and unpleasant task for me, but a necessary one. I had to relieve a few senior people in destroyers in the Solomons for lack of combat ability, so I knew the necessity for such action. It must be realized that some men are just not capable of performing properly under heavy stress or great responsibility. That can usually not be determined before a man has operated under the severe conditions of hard-fought battles—and most battles with the Japanese were hard-fought.

All men who have been in combat realize this, and know that one of the fundamental requirements for winning battles is to have commanders who know how to use their force, have the initiative to press the attack home, have the knowledge to enable them to take the proper actions when things go wrong, and who are willing to shoulder the heavy responsibility for leading men into battle. Men who fight with skill, vigor, and a keen sense of duty must have competent commanders who are themselves inspirational. The responsibility to insure that subordinate commanders do perform with the requisite skill and judgment is one of the most important, and one of the most distasteful, duties of a combat commander.

I recognized within that first month that I was the chief of staff of a very demanding and a very expert battle commander, and I was commencing to build that great respect and admiration for him I came to have later on in our long association. At that time, perhaps that respect was a bit grudging—for he still did not like surface sailors much—and I still did not like my job much either.

He never said what he was going to do. I never knew his personal plans for the day. I could read what he was going to do later on, because I knew he was going to be up there before the planes were launched and he was going to stay there until they were all home, and he was going to be up there for every flight operation, he was going to be up there in every storm. He never left the level of the flag bridge, and I didn't either. I knew he would go in for his lunch, which was a sandwich. He usually did not eat his sandwich out on the deck in his deck chair, which was on the port wing of the flag bridge. He went in and had a cup of coffee and sat down. If he wasn't disturbed by a battle, he'd finish a whole sandwich.

On 18 June 1944, Rear Adm. J. J. Clark with TG 58.1 and Rear Adm. William Harrell with 58.4 struck Iwo Jima as part of the campaign to capture the Marianas. At that time, we were operating under Adm. Raymond A. Spruance, Commander, Fifth Fleet. Admiral Spruance was a surface officer and he handled the general strategy of the operation, but the tactical operations he left entirely to Admiral Mitscher, because Admiral Mitscher was the technical expert on carrier operations. Admiral Spruance knew that, and so Admiral Spruance, up until that time, gave just the most general orders, general directions, and there had never been any real differences of opinion between Admiral Spruance and Admiral Mitscher. They admired one another very much.

In the very early morning of 18 June, the submarine *Cavalla* had sighted an enemy task force due west of Guam, heading east. The task force was comprised of 5 enemy battleships, 11 carriers, 11 heavy cruisers, and a number of destroyers. It was a big task force. When we got the *Cavalla*'s dispatch, we made an analysis of what the enemy could do, and we decided in Task Force 58, the whole staff and Admiral Mitscher, that probably the enemy would come directly east for various reasons—fuel shortages, desire to bring our fleet into action, their tremendous carrier strength. They mobilized all the carriers they could get. We thought that they would probably want to attack us by surprise, and we didn't want to get hit at night. They were pretty good at night action. They'd never had a night carrier battle, but maybe they would try to mix it with those big heavy battleships of theirs at night. So we decided that they probably wouldn't play any games, and, if they did, the question was whether or not they would come directly towards Guam or whether they would go a little north or a little south. Of the two, the southern course, for them, was better than the northern course; because they could get back to their bases a little more easily, they could probably disrupt the Guam landings more easily than if they took the northern course. The only thing would be that, if they had another force coming down from Japan, that would probably throw the weight of their decision to the northern course.

We studied the situation and tried to figure out what we would do if we were Japanese, and we decided that the most probable action that they would take, not only the most logical one but the most probable one, would be to come directly east, toward us, and that, if they were going south, they would have headed a little bit farther south than straight east to begin with, so that they would use less fuel or gain more time, whichever they wanted. Since they had not done that, we figured that they would probably come directly east.

On the morning of 18 June, Admiral Spruance, who had also worked over all of these same data with his staff, said that if the Japanese took a southerly course, he thought that there was a great possibility that there would be discretionary attacks from either of our flanks. What he was afraid of was that the Japanese force, if it came south far enough and we did not detect them, would get in between us and Guam and thereby be able to knock the hell out of the amphibious force and the supporting force and we wouldn't be able to stop it soon enough, and that was his primary duty. He gave us specific orders then that we would advance to the west by the day as far as we could and we would retreat at night.

Well, what did that mean? The wind was from the east, so we could not make much advance by day because we had to have flight operations. The only way to have been able to gain much westerly would have been to break up the task force and let one task group handle all the air and the rest of the task force go west while that one task group operated to the east in about the same position and then catch up at night. That would have been an obvious circumvention of what Admiral Spruance meant, and also would be difficult tactically. We couldn't gain much westerly during a day. We would be lucky if we could gain 50 miles to the west. But we could gain a tremendous amount at night because we weren't conducting air operations at night. So we sent a dispatch back to Admiral Spruance and said that we thought the enemy would most likely head directly east and we could find them directly to the west, or nearly directly; and, if they did come south, we could put enough search planes over their possible route to detect them. We had submarines down there too which would also probably detect them, and so the probability of their getting into a position from which they could attack the amphibious force without our interception was very slight, indeed. Those aren't the words, of course.

So we asked permission to steam to the west all night, and we figured that if we did do that we would just about meet the enemy at daylight because we would be converging at a rate of perhaps 35 knots. They were making 15 or 20 knots, and we were making 15 or 20 knots; it would be 35 or 40 knots. If we went 20 knots and they went, maybe, 25 knots, and our relative speed was much greater than we anticipated, then we might meet at night and have a night melee. Vice Adm. Willis A. Lee, the battleship commander, didn't like that night attack business. He'd had a lot of experience with night attacks, and most of it had been bad. But we figured that with TG 58.7, the battleship task group, to the west and with their radars, with the scout planes that we could put up at night, the chances of their having a melee were very slight. We would detect the enemy before they came close enough for surface fire, and, if it was nighttime, we could change course to their course and just stay ahead of them. We could keep our distance from them at night.

We explained this to Admiral Spruance, and he said, "No, I don't think so. I think that we must not go west at night." We had another reason for wanting to go west at night. If we were operating west of the islands of Guam, Saipan, and other islands in the chain, with a great number of flight operations and light wind, it meant that we would have to go easterly all the time. If we had to get our ships to high speed with a low wind, we'd have to steam to the east for flight operations, so we would gain easterly during the day. We would have to thread those channels between Saipan and Guam and the other channels, and do it in battle. That is a ticklish thing to do and a situation we didn't want to get into because we might get two task groups in a narrow channel, where they both couldn't go through together, and one of them would have to stop flight operations to get to the westward in order to operate again. Consequently, it would be unable to protect itself with its own air, and its planes that were in the air would have to be landed on another task group. A very complicated sort of a business. We didn't like that.

We told Admiral Spruance all of this, and he said, "No, don't go west," so we did not gain westerly that night. In the meantime, Task Groups 58.1 and 58.4 had struck Iwo Jima and returned and joined the task force the afternoon of the 18th. So all the task force was there and had taken its combat disposition. Then we got a dispatch during that night from the submarine *Stingray* saying that the enemy was due west of us, so we thought that was pretty good confirmation of where we thought the enemy was. During the night of the 18th, we recommended that we come to course 270 degrees at 1:30 A.M. the 19th, and strike the enemy at five o'clock. We would launch a strike at five o'clock, and we thought we could do that. Admiral Spruance said, "No, we can't do that," for the very same reasons he'd given before. Of course, our intelligence reports could be wrong, and there could have been a decoy for us or a lot of things could have happened, but the chances were that there was a high percentage that it was correct. As it turned out, it was.

Then the submarine *Finback*, later on the same morning of the 19th of June, reported lights and aircraft, but it wasn't until morning at 8:50 A.M. that we received a patrol plane report of an earlier sighting at 1:15 A.M., which was a delayed report of the Japanese force, which confirmed the *Finback* and the *Stingray* positions. At about 1:30 in the morning, the enemy was about 330 miles, bearing 258 degrees, from us. So 330 miles is too far for us to launch. There wasn't anything we could do. We couldn't launch an attack against them. First, because the wind favored the enemy, they had the weather gauge. They could steam into the wind and launch planes and keep going on their landing course to the east, so the effective range of their airplanes was extended a large amount, depending upon the strength of the wind, and the wind was fairly strong. We would have to turn around to the east to launch or recover aircraft, which Admiral Spruance knew when he said "No" the night before. The enemy was given the advantage of being able to strike at their maximum range, which was beyond our maximum range even if we both had equal ranges in our aircraft. As it turned out the next day, the 19th, the enemy had done exactly what we thought. The next morning, of course, we were not far from Guam. We didn't make any early interceptions. We sent out predawn searches, but we didn't detect the enemy. Our patrol planes sighted nothing out to 600 miles from Saipan.

About 10:05 the morning of the 19th, we got a report, "Large bogeys bearing 265 degrees, 125 miles at 24,000 feet." Well, that was just what we were waiting for, so we launched all our fighters, the whole blooming works, some as a fighter cover, some to go out to meet the enemy, and we launched our dive bombers and our torpedo planes, to get our decks clear, and had them circle Guam. They were armed, but they circled Guam and dropped their bombs on enemy airfields or other targets, but they were not on our ships, so that carriers had clear decks. We were ready for a full-fledged air battle.

These bogeys came on in, large groups, tremendous attacks. They had concentrated most of their fighters and a good many of their dive bombers in this first attacking group. They were trying to get a surprise attack, and, if they'd been successful, they would have done a good job. But we detected them, and, of course, the first enemy they saw was our battleship force, so they attacked this battleship force, which just clobbered them. Our fighters were up there ready to meet them, and we just shot enemy planes down in droves, even the first attack. They were just devastated. You could tell that from listening to the radio conversations. That attack was blunted. A few planes got through, they always do, and they dropped some bombs near the battleships, some of them pretty close. A few got into Guam, but, by the time our defensive combat air patrol took on these planes, there weren't very many and the poor devils didn't have a chance.

These attacks continued all day long, heavy attacks, and the last really tremendous one was at about 3:00 P.M. and we got most of them. By that time, one of our intelligence officers, Lt.(jg) Charles A. Sims, was getting pretty excited because one of the circuits that he was reading was the Japanese air controller's circuit. One of their senior squadron commanders came over our force very high, just as high as he could fly, and he would direct the flights that were coming in. He would tell a fighter group to go south and then make an attack on our left flank. Lieutenant Sims heard his orders. That group was met by our fighters with an attack advantage every time. We read his signals all the time. They changed this air coordinator every once in a while when he started running out of gasoline, but the relief stayed on the same frequency. When the battle was nearly all over and we knew they didn't have any planes left of any significance—for we had a count of over 300 airplanes shot down at that time—the Japanese air coordinator was about to go home. I think he asked permission to return to his ship. Capt. Jim Flatley was the operations officer on our staff, and Jim said, "Let's shoot him down," and I said, "No, you can't shoot that man down. He's done more good for the United States than any of us this day. So let him go home; let him go. Don't attack him." So we didn't. He went home.

We got their aircraft, but we didn't get their surface ships. We couldn't reach them; they stayed out of range. They knew when they had the advantage of the weather gauge and they stayed right there, but they had lost all aircraft, so obviously they had to get out of there. And so Admiral Spruance said to attack the Japanese fleet tomorrow. Well, on the 20th, we were hundreds of miles away from them, but we started out, and we took a westerly course directly toward the enemy. At 4:47 P.M., we found that the enemy was on bearing 289 degrees, about 240 miles, too far away to attack. We couldn't catch up with them; we had to fuel pretty soon. So what do we do? We figured that one of our bombers could reach the enemy and have about 15 minutes over the enemy and get back, if he didn't have any trouble. But, at the end of that time, he would have run out of fuel. Admiral Mitscher said, "We won't be able to get him tomorrow, that's for sure, no matter how hard we try. So we will launch this afternoon. We know we won't get our airplanes back before dark." So we told the whole task force what we were going to do, and we launched as fast as we could. We gave the time of launching, and we launched a big attack.

As soon as they got into the air, Admiral Mitscher told all the ships to be prepared to put searchlights straight up in the air if it was necessary when they returned. It wasn't a last-minute decision at all. Admiral Mitscher did this over the intelligence circuits, so that the pilots wouldn't be concerned about it. The pilots did not know it, because that's a hairy thing and you don't want to worry them. Nothing was given to them ahead of time. But, after dark, when they started to come back, and they straggled in and they had varying amounts of fuel, we gave orders, "If you're short of fuel, land on any carrier deck. Any carrier, take any plane, no matter what mix-up you're going to have in the morning. We're probably not going to fight a battle tomorrow." Then he turned on the lights as a navigational aid, and we still lost a lot of pilots and a lot of planes.

Our pilots sank quite a few ships; they damaged quite a few. They did a good job on their strike. It was not a desperate strike, but it was just at extreme range capability. We were stretching our capability a little bit. And, of course, Admiral Mitscher was right. We could have clobbered that outfit the next morning if we had done what we wanted to do, but maybe the circumstances would have been a little different, too. His was a safe decision. It was a cautious decision, and where he was right was that those ships could never again get their pilots. They could never get the number of planes in those carriers again, and the pilots they had lost were their cutting edge. They didn't have time to replace them again. They had lost their cutting edge in Midway, and here they had gotten their second group of pilots and they'd lost them all.

This operation, the capture of the Marianas, was the first time that my ideas were incorporated in the planning. I discussed them with Admiral Mitscher, and during the planning stages he was cool to me, but he was also an unbiased individual, except in regard to aviation. If he thought the ideas were good, he'd say, "Go ahead." If he didn't, why, we discussed it some more, and sometimes he said he didn't think that would work, and if he didn't think it would work, it didn't belong there. During the operation, things worked pretty well. The systems that we had put in worked very well. Mostly it was decentralization. That was the biggest thing, to let the task group commanders do

Architects of the Pacific war (left to right): Adm. Chester W. Nimitz, Commander in Chief, Pacific Fleet and Pacific Ocean Areas; Adm. Ernest J. King, Commander in Chief, U.S. Fleet and Chief of Naval Operations; Adm. Raymond A. Spruance, Commander, Fifth Fleet.

those things that they could do, and we would do those things that the task group commanders could not do, which was coordinate their own operations. But we would not interfere or inject ourselves into their normal operations. That meant that we had to develop procedures for normal operations, so that all the task groups operated in the same general manner so that other task group commanders would know what each other was doing. That was the essence of all of these ideas—that, and simplicity, and not overloading the communications facilities, which were limited and which, if they were overloaded, would make control of a battle impossible. This pertained not only to surface ships but also to operations of air groups.

This was the general idea. There were a lot of things like that, and as the battle progressed, and things worked pretty well, Admiral Mitscher became more receptive, more tolerant of Burke, and, as ideas succeeded, then he started to talk, not just about the immediate operation, which is all that he had done before, but he'd talk about fishing. There's not always a strain on the bridge; sometimes there are long lulls, and he would talk about golf, things other than the immediate battle problems. After the tremendous success of the "Turkey Shoot," he was very cordial. During that period, he decided that I was trying to do a good job and that I could be his chief of staff all right. He realized that what I was trying to do was help him have the most effective battle organization there was.

I realized that he was probably the greatest air combat commander that the world had ever known until that time, because he had a sense of what to do. For example, with regard to fighter aircraft and the CAP, he had a sense of when an enemy was about to attack. "Burke," he'd say, "think we'd better launch some more?" "Yes, sir." I was floored when he first did that, but after a while I gathered what he gathered, that you had a feel that the enemy was going to attack and know what the enemy had probably got available, approximately, and that this was the time for him to attack. The Japanese are logical people, and so it turned out that way. He had a sense for that, because he'd had a great deal of experience in Guadalcanal and he'd been in aviation all of his life. He knew. Other people had experience, too, but this seems like a sixth or seventh sense that he possessed. Anyway, when this battle was over, he changed his attitude. Previous to that time, he would quite frequently tell the operations officer things, and I wouldn't know what he'd told him. He wasn't bypassing me, but he wanted to give directly to the operations officer his ideas, just discussing. After the battle, he talked with me *and* the operations officer, but he was talking to me. It was just a subtle little difference. The same thing was true when he would interview the returned pilots. He always said, "Wait a minute, let the chief of staff come over here and listen to this, too." Those sorts of little bits of things made all the difference in the world. We started to be real good friends then.

If I ever loved any man, it was Admiral Mitscher, and partly that was because we were initially antagonistic, not to each other but to each other's position, and I learned from him what a warrior really is. His personal qualifications, his personal characteristics I admired. He was a little bit of a fellow, a sandblower, who was a magnificent commander. He knew his pilots; he knew his job; he was skillful himself. He was not just a lovable man. He was a demanding man. He would praise his pilots but not excessively. If a man did a good job, he would tell him that was a good job he did and he was rewarded, but not much orally. There's a very narrow line there between not doing enough and doing too much, because, if you do praise too much too often, your praise doesn't mean anything to anybody. It was a combination that Admiral Mitscher had—being kind, and considerate of his pilots, and being absolutely ruthless if a pilot failed because of lack of judgment or guts. It was the same with his flag officers. The reason why that task force was so successful was that he required wonderful performance from his flag officers, his aviator flag officers. There was an occasion when I thought that a surface flag officer had failed to do his duty. He failed, and I asked Admiral Mitscher to send me over and detach him and he said, "No, that's not my job. I won't do it." I said, "Admiral, you're playing favorites with your aviators. You're requiring high performance of them, and you're not requiring it of your nonaviators." He said, "No, I'm not a nonaviator. I will keep the aviators up. You surface people, keep your own standards." So I went over to see Admiral Lee, who was the senior surface officer. He handled it a different way, but that man finally left, but not so that the force knew about it. You see, all the aviation flag officers knew damned well they were performing well as long as they were there, for if they didn't perform alright they were going to go.

Admiral Mitscher was wise, he was simple, he was direct, and he was ruthless. He demanded. So his staff was very alert, and to a man like that, people have childish, but very good, reactions. I mean every man has a simple reaction. You want to please him. You want to prove yourself, prove your ideas. You want to get a pat on the back; you want to be approved. You want to pull your share of the load. You want to do a little bit more than can be reasonably expected of you. He loomed so large in my vision, and this worked on the whole staff. So the staff would try to develop things, not for their personal aggrandizement—that's not the big purpose of it—but to improve the damned effectiveness. It's a delicate thing to say, because I don't mean that they were striving for personal recognition. It wasn't that. It was greater than that. The standards were so high it automatically drew everybody else up, and so he got a lot of ideas from other people. He didn't generate most of the ideas that made him an effective commander. Other people generated them, but he accepted them, and they generated them because of what he was. So he was fundamentally the instrument that developed those ideas.

This thing of striving to do your best and striving to do the best for the outfit, or have the outfit do the best, is what made that task force, the whole damned task force, so very effective. The planning was good, the operations were good, and the procedures were good, and it was good because if somebody had an idea that this doesn't work, this won't work quite right and maybe a little change there would help it, he could make that statement and it would be recognized, even if he's proved wrong. It was examined, at least, and they would ridicule even if they were wrong or something like that, but they wouldn't resent it. This was not only the top people on the staff but the other staff members because, really, the pressures on people are really the pressures of peers more than the pressures from the top. If you want to create pressure on a person, you create it through his peers. This tended to eliminate petty jealousies and so forth on the staff, and this is why the nonaviators and the aviators finally got on a team. Not because they said you've got to get on the same wavelength or be thinking the same way, but because they actually grew to do that. You can't order something like that, you can't direct it, but you can create it so that it will work.

"Pilots are the weapon of this force. Pilots are the things you have to nurture. Pilots are people you have to train, and you have to train other people to support the pilots." Of all the characteristics that Admiral Mitscher had, that was fundamental. He watched out for his pilots. He trained them well; he demanded performance; he made sure their equipment was the best possible equipment, that it was maintained well, they fought well, they had good leaders. He would rescue them; he did everything. Everything he did revolved around the effectiveness of his pilots.

Admiral Mitscher, during that war, became one of the best battle commanders the United States has ever had, and that was partly due to his demanding very high performance from his commanders and his willingness to peremptorily relieve those who couldn't, or didn't, measure up. Along with this was a deep appreciation and understanding of those commanders, and all combat personnel as well, who did measure up. With these two characteristics, it is no wonder he gained the respect, and then the love, of his command.

"Turn on the Lights"

Rear Admiral James D. Ramage

James David Ramage was born in Waterloo, Iowa, on 19 July 1916, son of David S. and Flora (Groat) Ramage. He entered the U.S. Naval Academy in 1935, was graduated and commissioned ensign on 1 June 1939, and was designated a naval aviator on 15 February 1942. Subsequent service included extensive command and staff duties ashore and afloat, and he advanced in rank to that of rear admiral, effective September 1967. Admiral Ramage was Commander, Carrier Division 7, from May 1970 until March 1972. He retired from the naval service effective 1 January 1976.

During World War II, Admiral Ramage served from March 1943 until August 1944 as executive officer and commanding officer of Bombing Squadron 10 on board the USS Enterprise, *participating in action in the Marshalls, Truk, Marianas, New Guinea, Palau, Philippine Sea, Saipan, and Guam. During the battle of the Philippine Sea, he led a fierce attack against the enemy fleet, personally scoring a hit on an enemy carrier. In September 1944, he assumed command of Bombing Squadron 98 and in August 1946 reported for instruction at the Naval War College, Newport, Rhode Island.*

Admiral Ramage's decorations include the Navy Cross, Distinguished Service Medal, Legion of Merit with three Gold Stars, Distinguished Flying Cross with two Gold Stars, Air Medal with six Gold Stars, Vietnam Gallantry Cross with Palm (2), National Order of Vietnam Fifth Class, and numerous other unit citations and commendations.

Lt. J. D. Ramage (left) and his Dauntless gunner, ARM 1 Dave Cawley. (Courtesy Rear Adm. J. D. Ramage, USN [Ret.])

During the battle of the Philippine Sea in June 1944, I was commanding officer of Bombing Squadron 10 aboard the *Enterprise,* flying the SBD-5 Dauntless. The first attack on the Marianas was extremely successful. We completely annihilated everything that flew the afternoon of 11 June, and started in on the regular softening-up process on the beaches on the 12th, followed by strikes on the 13th and 14th. The actual landing took place on the 15th, and it was very successful at the start, at least. About that time, we began to get some rumblings of the possibility of the Japanese fleet being in the area. We continued to strike into Saipan, and some of the other carriers were going into Guam. We were getting ready for the big "Turkey Shoot" on the 19th and the assault on the Japanese fleet on the 20th.

We were all down in the ready rooms wondering when we were going to get a crack at those Japs. We knew that Admiral Mitscher wanted to detach Task Force 58 and get out there and go after them. We all felt that we ought to go get them. However, we were kept close and continued to support the troops. On the 19th, about 10:00 o'clock in the morning, we launched all fighters, and we also had strike groups all loaded up ready to go in case somebody found the Japanese fleet. Our ship's radar picked up Japanese aircraft apparently at 100 miles to the west of us. For some reason or other, the Japanese decided that they would circle and get all the aircraft into one group rather than come on in, which gave us additional time to get everything in the air we wanted. Our fighters were heading on out after them. This was the day of the big Turkey Shoot. I don't know the exact count of enemy planes shot down, something over 300 airplanes, but it was a big day. We could see an occasional flamer going on down, while we in the strike groups were airborne and holding about 15 to 20 miles back east towards Guam. Of course, we didn't have any fighters with us, they were all up topside. I put my dive bombers into the fluid four formation rather than in the tight six-plane division that we used, because I thought possibly some of these people would break through and we might be able to get a shot at them. After about two or three hours, we received a message to go on in and drop our bombs on the Orote Peninsula, to see if we couldn't keep the field at least temporarily knocked out in case some of the Japanese got through and tried to land on Guam.

We got over there in time to see several shoot-downs. It was kind of interesting because our F6Fs were right down at treetop level chasing these guys up and down the landscape. I don't know if anybody landed safely. I think there were some Japanese pilots that either force-landed or actually were so scared, they just landed right in the water, but it was a real massacre. So they ended up that day with their whole striking force gone, plus a pretty good percentage of their fighters that they sent along as escort.

So we were ready for the big battle on the 20th, which became known as the battle of the Philippine Sea. On the morning of the 20th, we finally began to get some kind of contacts, and in the afternoon of the 20th, Stu Nelson, who was in VT-10, did locate the Japanese fleet. We'd been in the ready room all day and we had the flight all planned. We had completely gone through all of the best ways to save gas, to see how much we could get out of the SBDs. There really was nothing that we had overlooked in being prepared for this. We'd been at sea for five months at the time and had quite a bit of combat, and we certainly felt that we were ready to go. The one thing that we didn't know was that as it got later, that we'd probably come back at night, which didn't bother us because we were all night qualified and there wouldn't be any problem with that.

Finally, about 4:20 P.M., we got the word to launch. I had with me the 12 SBDs, I think only 5 torpedo planes, and 12 fighters. We had been briefed that it was a long distance out and the fighters and torpedoes would take off first as they always did, get themselves grouped, and we bombers would take off and immediately make a 180-degree turn because the prevailing wind was from the east and the targets, of course, were almost due west. So I would make a turn immediately and slow down, and the other bombers would simply fly up and join me on the way. We called it a running rendezvous. Everything worked out fine.

We finally got all the bombers together. I was flying along about 5,000 feet and climbing, when all of a sudden I got smoke in my cockpit. I thought, "Oh, God, I'm on fire." Here's my big day and here this damn thing is happening to me. Dave Cawley, my rear-seat man, said, "I think it might be just spilled oil." He said that one time previously the plane captain had spilled oil around the engine and when the cylinders got heated up, the oil burned off. That's apparently what happened because within about three or four minutes, the smoke cleared out. I wasn't going to turn back anyway.

What I'm going to do here is read from a booklet that was put out by one of our pilots, Lt.(jg) Don Lewis, to tell about the strike. I'm doing this because of my mother's admonition that self-praise stinks, and I'd rather have somebody else say something good about me than try to say it myself. So this is from Don—we called him "Hound Dog"—Lewis's account of the strike on the Japanese fleet on 20 June 1944:

"That afternoon at 1615 [4:15 P.M.], with beating heart, I manned my plane and wondered for the hundredth time of the merits of this poor, old, tired-out SBD Dauntless dive bomber, if it still had anyplace in the war where planes were slow if they cruised at less than 250 knots. I'm ashamed now of my doubts. I was to have ample proof before that day was out that tenacity and the ability to keep going can sometimes make up for speed and show. Of course, the behavior of the plane depends a lot on its pilot, its crew, and its squadron. It can be handled rough, and it will probably balk. We handled ours gently that day.

Ens. Don Lewis, pilot, and Gunner's Mate John Mankin, with most of the rest of VB-10, succeeded in landing on a friendly carrier the night "they turned on the lights." (Courtesy Rear Adm. J. D. Ramage, USN [Ret.])

"My crew consisted of one John Mankin, once a good citizen of Wyoming. He was both radioman and gunner. He represented, I thought, the best there was. I had confidence in the other squadron members. I felt that they, too, were the best, and I know to this day that my story would be a lot different if our skipper had merely gone by the rules. Lieutenant Commander Ramage, our skipper, was different. Sometimes in this business the rules are inadequate and things happen so quickly there isn't time to consult an admiral's committee about some new ones. They have to be made right on the spot. The skipper made quite a few that night. The Jap losses which we had helped to inflict and the fact that 12 pilots and 12 air crewmen went up that night and all returned to their ships speaks more for his leadership than anything I might write here.

"My regular place in the division was flying number two position in Lieutenant Bangs' division. He had at one time been an instructor in Pensacola for Wayne Morris. By 1630 [4:30 P.M.], all of our planes were in the air. We were rendezvoused with Comdr. Bill Martin's Grumman Avenger torpedo planes, this flight being led by the exec of the squadron, Lt. Van Eason; our Hellcat fighter escort was under Comdr. William ('Killer') Kane, destined to become an ace with five planes to his credit as a result of this day's work. At last on a heading of 290 degrees and throttled back to the maximum to ensure the most economic fuel consumption, we started out after the Jap fleet."

I [Ramage] can interject one thing here; we thought at that time that the Jap fleet was out 260 miles, and after we were launched, we got a correction in the position report. Nelson's position was one degree off in latitude in the wrong direction. In other words, it was about 60 miles farther out. The radius of action of the SBD was about 250 miles, and if it was as plotted, about 260 miles, it wasn't a bad chance to take. But when you add on the extra 50 or 60 miles, which takes you well out over 300 miles, it becomes pretty much a one-way mission as far as SBDs are concerned. I now go back to Lewis' story.

"Our navigation boards told us it would be 250 miles at least. I burned out my left auxiliary tank, 52 gallons gone already, I thought, and we were scarcely at the halfway mark. We were then at 6,000 feet, and it was 1800 [6:00 P.M.]. I could see more air groups from some of our other carriers to one side and, of course, headed at the same target. I felt good to see them there. At least, we were not doing this alone. I heard a contact report from a TBF scout plane piloted by Lt. Robert S. Nelson, apparently over the Jap fleet. He gave their strength as consisting of three separate task forces, one consisting of six fleet oilers plus a number of destroyers, another containing battleships and more destroyers, and a third, containing the carriers, in which the search plane said there were seven, three large and four small.

"At 11,000 feet, I put my engine in high blower, adjusted my oxygen mask, and called my gunner to see how he was doing. John said he was cold. For days while we had been about the ship, I had been too hot, but now because of the altitude, the pure oxygen I was breathing, and the nervous drain on my energies, I was beginning to feel cold too. Not even the heat from my engines seemed enough to kill the chill. We were now at 14,000 feet. I had just run out of gas on my right-wing auxiliary tank. It was 1845 [6:45 P.M.]. I was thinking to myself that, if we would only go into our dives right now, my chances of a hit would be the best, as with my gas tanks evened off, the plane would trim up just about perfectly. I wanted to have as many things in my favor as possible, as I knew that once over the target, there would be quite a few things decidedly not in my favor. At any rate, I decided to keep my two main tanks of fuel, approximately 150 gallons, exactly equal up to the moment I actually did nose into my dive. I imagine some of the other pilots of my flight were worrying about the same thing, as it meant changing tanks every five minutes.

"It was now almost 7:00 o'clock, and we had already covered 225 miles. I thought of my gunner again and knew he was almost frozen to death. The backseat of an SBD is a pretty exposed place, and he must make it even more so in order to keep his guns ready for quick use. I think the real credit of naval aviation goes to those rear-seat gunners. Their job is the hardest and requires more downright nerve and guts than anything I can think of.

"We were at 15,000 feet when I heard our fighters tally-ho the Jap force. The first report gave their positions as 15 miles to our port. This force consisted of six fleet tankers and a half a dozen destroyers. The TBF had sighted them now and even as their report was given, I could see several thin strips of white far below, which were the wakes of those ships. They were moving fast with everything they had. Even at this altitude, I could tell that.

"I heard my skipper on the air. '41 Sniper to 85 Sniper. We will not attack. We will not attack. Where are the Charlie Victors?' I think he must have been exasperated that anyone would even suggest that we would come 300 miles to dump a load of bombs on a few oilers when there were carriers around. I started to get squared away. I took notice where the wind was from in relation to the direction we were now heading. I changed my gas tanks again, checked my bomb release, flipped on my gun switches and bomb sights, and did as many things as could be done this much in advance of the dive.

"Then I heard another contact report. More ships had been seen still further north about 20 miles. There were many cruisers and destroyers, some battleships, and best of all, and my heart turned over when I heard this, seven carriers—four small CVs and three large CVs. I started to get ready in earnest now. I was scared. I couldn't really believe this was happening to me. I went over my checkoff list again, closed my formation. In a few minutes, I could see them. Yes, even as I thought this, I could make out several black forms ahead, way below and partly concealed by some clouds. They were already starting to maneuver. Some were going in circles, others were zigzagging. Their formation was well spread out, just the opposite battle procedure from our task force. '41 Sniper to all bombers,' I heard my skipper call again. 'The first division will dive on the largest CV. The other sections will dive on the small jobs unless the big one is still not hit. Out.'

"We were beginning to spread a little now. From 15,500 feet, we started what was to be a high-speed breakup into our dives. Three carriers I could see plainly trying to make cover under a cloud. Another large one, I'm sure of the *Shokaku*-class, was on my left without a cloud near it. We had 200 knots now. I checked everything. Once more my gas seemed to be evened up, the plane well trimmed. When I came back to low blower because of the natural decrease in power at this altitude, I had lost a little distance. Tip Mester, the other wingman in my section, filled in quickly, keeping the interval between planes just about right. We had agreed before the flight to make a close-in diving interval as that keeps the men on the gun crews on the deck below taking cover most of the time, so quickly does one bomb follow another. This then is the way I would try to keep it. I glanced quickly at my altimeter; I saw 13,000 feet. For the first time now, I took notice. AA fire. I couldn't help thinking how unlike our ships those Japs were, for I knew we would never let two divisions of dive bombers get us near as we were now without sending out every available fighter and throwing up a virtual barrage as well. I saw a pair of our fighters on the other side of my cockpit. One of them was Lt.(jg) John Shinneman. He had been just off my starboard, watching the other bombers steepen up into their dives. Now he would go down with me. I was the last plane to dive, and I knew there was little chance of anything besides an F6F Hellcat getting on my tail. There were great black puffs all over now and smaller white ones, looking for all the world like small balls of cotton.

"Things started to happen fast. It was a blur from here on in. Now it was 10,000 feet. I was starting to overspeed and then overshoot the carrier I had picked out. That meant the last thing on my checkoff list, dive flaps. I pushed the actuator, glancing out to see if they had operated successfully, saw a plane smoking horribly away on my port, wondered if it was one of ours. I heard Japs talking on our radio frequency. They were counting, then more talk. They were excited. Who wasn't? I heard someone tally-ho again, 'Enemy aircraft, 4:00 o'clock, Angels 5.' It seemed to take an eternity. Never had a dive taken so long. The wind was from my left. I was overshooting. I corkscrewed toward the left and then back again. It helped. The carrier below looked big, tremendous, almost make-believe. I had a moment of real joy. I had often dreamed of something like this. Then I was horrified with myself. What a spot to be in. I must be crazy. I was straight up and down now in my dive. I was right in the middle of all those white puffs, and for the first time I could see where they were coming from. From each side of the carrier below seemed to be a mass of flashing red dots. It had been turning slowly to port. It stopped, and I noticed a larger red flash, which was a bomb hit on the side and well forward, but unmistakably a hit. I figured it must have been scored by 'Banger,' as we called Lou Bangs. The carrier below had stopped moving. Who could ask for more?

"I thanked whoever it was who laid on the last one, as it had stopped the carrier right up and down in my sights. I kept trying to move my point of aim to the right to allow more for the wind. First I could move so that it rested squarely on that side of the carrier. That wouldn't be enough, I knew, but it was too late to do any of the violent maneuvers necessary to move it more. I could allow for the error in one other way, however, and that would be by going lower. The last time I glanced at my altimeter it registered 3,000 feet. Stopped below, the big carrier looked even larger. It was completely enveloped in a sort of smoke haze. It was hard to stay in my dive this long. Under some conditions, a person can live a lifetime in a few seconds. It was time. I couldn't go any lower. Now! I pulled my bomb release, felt the bomb go away, started my pullout. My eyes watered, my ears hurt, and my altimeter indicated 1,500 feet. Too low, I thought, but what had I done? I turned back to see that there was more smoke and flame on the same side as the first hit, the first hit I had seen, only this was way aft. That could be mine, but even with my low pullout, the wind had apparently carried it way to the starboard side. I experienced a momentary disappointment. I had expected much more of a conflagration to follow a direct hit on something as vulnerable as a carrier. Then I remembered that our section carried semiarmor-piercing bombs, which would, of course, pierce the flight deck and burst below. My ears still hurt. I had already closed my dive flaps and had 280 knots, but I couldn't seem to go fast enough.

"There were ships all about. They were all shooting far above the carrier, which was dark with smoke and its own AA. I saw a plane burst into flames and then slowly float downward. I saw a smaller carrier off my other wing with its flight deck a mass of flames. A torpedo plane flying at only a few thousand feet left a vicious path of black smoke and dark flames before it plunged into the sea. I wondered if I would get out of this yet. I had felt good and a little surprised after pulling out of my dive still unhit. Now I had to do it all over. For a moment, I was almost panic-stricken. Everywhere I looked, there seemed to be ships with every gun blazing. The sky was just a mass of black and white puffs, and in the midst of it planes already hit, burning and crashing into the water below. It's strange how a person can be fascinated even in the midst of horror. I'd see orange bursts from some ships, a moment later a billowy puff would blossom out too nearby, a second later another, still nearer. They were getting the word. I was employing the wildest evasive tactics possible. I would be down low on the water and then pull up quick and pick up hard rudder one way, hold it for a moment, then kick rudder the opposite way. I had decided it didn't make much difference which way I went. Our prearranged retirement course was 090 degrees. I would take that. Any direction I went, I would still have to run the gauntlet.

"I saw now the Japs' advantage in spreading out their formation of ships. I would no sooner exceed the range of one ship than I would fall into the sights of another further along. I seemed to spend an eternity in the midst of their AA. I began to think that real low on the water was the best place. I flew there for a few seconds, a temporary lull. Suddenly a tremendous geyser suddenly ahead, another to starboard. I pulled up quickly and realized that a cruiser was using its large deck guns to drop shells in front of us, hoping we would run into some of the columns of water, even if the shell itself did miss. There were other planes all about now. I saw a Helldiver flying low over the water as I had been a moment before, lose a wing and disappear almost instantly without either smoke or fire, scarcely a ripple on the sea below.

"I found myself with a cruiser on one side and a destroyer on the other. Resulting crossfire was effective. I believe they were closer to getting me than any of the other little yellow men I had been a target for. Some of the shells burst so near the concussion would lift my plane a few feet higher in the air. A few times I was surrounded by black bursts, and I could hear the hollow metal sound that concussion made when it came against the metal fuselage. The Japanese should have had one more SBD Dauntless to their credit that day, and if it had been our gun batteries, they would have. I saw a bomber, one of our own, it was Lt.(jg) William Schaefer, and his rear-seat man, Santuli. I joined up on him. My own gunner called, 'Jap fighters, high starboard.' I looked to my right and saw half a dozen fighters fighting off in that position, even as I watched. I saw one literally blown to pieces in the air and another catch fire and slowly descend, disappearing in a cloud. Schaefer and I joined on some other planes. We were about out of the AA now, except for an occasional burst. I began to feel better. These were planes from the *Lexington*. I wondered where my own bombers were. There was no other interference from the Jap fighters. They had apparently been well taken care of. My attention was taken by a tremendous explosion far off on the horizon. I looked, seeing the remains of one of the fleet tankers, which we had seen going in. Some other group had decided to concentrate on that task force after all.

"I stayed with this group of planes for 15 minutes. It was rapidly getting dark. I took stock of my gas and immediately decided that I would have to leave this formation. Much as I liked their company, I knew I would never make it back at the engine settings they were using. I had 32 inches of manifold pressure and 2,100 RPM, and I could barely stay up with them. I couldn't help wondering if they would make it back either. John called and pointed out another formation of bombers way to starboard. I broke away and joined them.

It was our own air group. I counted them like a mother hen counting her chickens. There were eight and I would make nine. We had come with 12. Well, I would not try to think about that now. Perhaps they had joined with one of the other groups. I joined up with number three position on Lt.(jg) Hubert Grubiss. 'Grube' gave me a smile and started wiping his brow as though he were hot. He probably had been shortly before in more ways than one. I felt better. Our skipper was using his head. We were conserving what little fuel we had left, for it was quite dark already, and we were still a long way from our ships. I could only imagine what would go on when we did get back and 200 planes started trying to make night landings, some of them for the first time, aboard a dozen carriers.

"We ran into a few rain squalls. It was now pitch dark. I turned on my lights, dim, ate an apple which I brought along, and then readjusted my oxygen mask, as I was feeling tired and my eyes were seeing things that weren't there. The pure oxygen, even at 2,000 feet, would both relieve fatigue and help my vision at the same time. Apparently there were many of our planes that day who hadn't used their fuel economically. The results began to show. It was 8:30. I heard one pilot tell his rear-seat man to get ready for a water landing. I heard a fighter pilot call his wingman and say he had been hit in one tank and was going down. The wingman called back and said that he would land with him. I saw a group of lights to my right getting lower and lower, then there weren't any more. Apparently a whole section of planes had been low on gas and decided to land together, thus giving a greater chance of being picked up. I heard some pilot, apparently lost, calling desperately for a carrier. His base was too far away to pick him up. Finally he called again, he was out of gas, bailing out. Then silence.

"Another hour had passed, making the time after 9:00 o'clock. I was worrying about my own gas. I had three of my four tanks completely dry and a good deal gone from the last one. With good luck, I might make it back. My eyes were tired and my back was stiff, my head ached, and I was hungry. In short, I had had enough for that day. Everyone felt the same way, I could tell by the loose formation, but we hung on. Every few minutes now I could hear a plane falling, calling its wingman, its base, announcing it was going in, then silence for a little more. At 9:20, I thought I could see star shells off the starboard, but I wasn't sure. There was also lightning around. A moment later there was no mistaking it. They were star shells, and the searchlights as well. We were still a long ways off, but it made me feel good. I realized that a tremendous concession was being made in our favor. I heard pilots express the opinion that the admirals looked upon the fliers as quite expendable, and I suppose they must be to a certain extent, but I shall never again feel that they wouldn't do everything conceivable in their power to bring a pilot back. I know there were subs about the fleet that night, and enemy planes had followed us back, for one actually got in the landing circle for one of our carriers, and yet when we approached the outer screen of our fleet, it seemed that almost every ship had a light of some kind on. In the utter darkness, the intensity of some of the lights was blinding. The largeness of the carriers seemed to stretch off into infinity. It was a demonstration I shall never forget.

"Every group seemed to get over the fleet at the same time, and, of course, everyone being low on gas wanted to land immediately. We were told to land on any base available, that is, which had a clear deck. The skipper found a carrier landing planes; the first two sections broke up. I could see them break away and head down for the landing circle. It was a little before 10:00 o'clock now. I figured I had about 15 minutes more fuel, then I would have to make preparations for a water landing too. My best bet, I thought, would be to circle, for I was at 1,500 feet, and try to spot a carrier not only with a clear deck but with no one in the landing circle, for I thought if I once put my wheels and flaps down and started operating at full power, the little gas I had left would be gone in no time. Some carrier was on the air, their deck was clear, they said, furthermore they would signal their position by two flashes from their largest searchlight. That was what I was waiting for. I watched for the signal. Finally I saw it off to the left. I felt good again. Perhaps I would make it after all.

"When I drew near, I saw one plane in the traffic circle. I started to get squared away myself, mixture rich, wheels down, shoulder straps tight, and so forth. I made my turn a little way ahead. I could just barely see the lights of the ship. The plane I had noticed before was in his cross leg. I saw his lights steadily approaching for his final turn into the groove, then there was just blackness where he had been. He had gone through all the incredible experiences of this day and night, and then scarcely a minute before he would have been safely landed aboard, his gas had run out. I checked my own gas again. Even my last tank registered empty. It was 10 minutes after 10:00. I felt I had enough gas left for three passes at this ship. I was in the groove now and could plainly make out the long line of lights down the flight deck. There was a signal officer to the left. He looked grotesque, like a mechanical man with arms of light where the electric wands were that are used for night carrier landings. I was near enough now to pick up his signals. My heart stopped. He was waving me off. I was mad, frustrated. I would land anyway. Still I couldn't. He was under me now. As I gunned it, I heard the engine gobble up still more of my last precious gallons. I called him everything I could think of. Well, perhaps he was right. Maybe I had been too low. I would try again, and this time concentrate what energy I had on making my approach perfect. Just the right speed, just the right altitude. Once again I was in the groove. Another wave off. I was really mad now, but as I went by, I saw the reason. On the deck just after the island structure was a plane on its back and thoroughly cracked up. They couldn't land me without wires or barriers. I pulled up my wheels and flaps, throttled back as much as possible, and gained a little altitude. Perhaps a destroyer would pick me up in the water. After such a day, I was too tired to have much concern now over a mere water landing in the middle of the Pacific enemy waters. I think this must have been the attitude of most of those pilots that night who actually did make water landings, as a surprisingly high number of them were made successfully.

"I decided if I could find a carrier shortly, I would have enough fuel for one pass. Surely, I thought, there must be one carrier with a clear deck around. I saw more lights further ahead. I gained on them slowly. Yes, it was another carrier, and what luck, I was approaching from its stern. For a moment, my impulse was to let my wheels and flaps down immediately and come right in for a landing, a very unorthodox procedure. I decided against it, mostly because I had lost sight of the landing signal officer. I went by the port side and looked down. He was giving me the wheels-down land signal. The deck looked clear. It was a big carrier of the *Essex*-class. I got squared away once again. This would be my last chance, as I must be at the very end of my gas. Again I was on my cross leg and got in the groove, picking up the landing signal officer. He was giving me a high and fast. I dropped my nose, took off a little throttle, picked up with a little back stick pressure, and now I was right over the ramp, and there it was at last, the cut. The deck looked big after so many landings on our smaller 'E.' I dropped my nose and guided her down, felt the hook catch a wire. It was all over.

"I was taxiing on the deck following the plane director's lights, cutting my engine. I heard myself talking as in a dream. Everyone seemed friendly. What carrier was this? The *Yorktown*, I was told. Another plane was coming in to land. There had been accidents that night. I was told to clear the deck quickly. I felt tired but elated. From the side, I watched this next plane land. It was an SBD also, and a good landing followed. I saw the number on the side; it was the skipper's plane. We were glad to see each other. It had only been seven hours since I had seen him last, but it seemed like a year. He had done a swell job that day. I told him so, but he scarcely heard me, he was so glad just to be back. I was grateful to my old SBD, still the most dependable plane in the fleet, grateful to my skipper for a fine job in leading us out and back, to every admiral and captain who willingly took 1,000 risks to help us back, and last but surely not the least, to my God who knows when a fellow needs help."

I [Ramage] would like to add my own observations to those of Don Lewis. As we approached the Japanese fleet, I would say about 20 miles out, when we were still in a fairly tight formation, we got a tallyho on a number of Zeros. My gunner, Cawley again, said Zeros at 4:00 o'clock. But because of our fighter escort, and VF-10 was darn good at this, they would not in any way ever leave a strike group in order to shoot down an enemy airplane. They hung right in there, and every time the Zeros would start an attack towards us, Killer and his guys would nose into them, and then the Zeros would go on back. They weren't very determined on getting us before the time of breakup.

It was getting dark, but there was plenty of visibility, and the Japanese ships were making high speed, so the wakes were very visible. As I dived, the Zeros began to come after me, and I think two of them went down with me, one in particular, and with my dive breaks out, he zipped past me so fast that I could hardly see him. Cawley called out to me that he was coming and was trying to shoot at him. Cawley was afraid he'd hit us, and it could be very possible that he might have been a kind of *kamikaze* plane, as far as trying to knock me out of the sky, because he missed me by a matter of just a few feet right in my dive.

It didn't disconcert me too much. There wasn't anything that was going to stop us. The antiaircraft fire was coming up, and it was shallow, that is, going under my belly. A dive bomber coming down is nearly vertical, and it's awfully hard to shoot straight up. Most of their stuff was going beneath me. It was a very nice, clean dive. I picked up the carrier easily. I went much lower than we normally did; we wanted to make sure we got a hit. I put my pipper on the port bow, which was the way I figured the ship's motion and the wind at the time.

During the retirement, my trusty colleague in the backseat would call out, and I would respond to what he said, "Go up" or "Go down," depending upon where the enemy was shooting. When we finally joined up, there were still some Zeros in the air, and they were, of all things, doing slow rolls and various stunts around the area. I don't know exactly why. This was not unusual for Zeros, but they were doing it even at this time when the whole world was falling apart on them. Kane and his fighters by this time were right with us, and they knocked down two or more of them. We had absolutely no problem after that.

I might talk a little bit about the return to the ship because I was very unhappy with the air discipline of some of the other air groups that were there. We went back at slow cruise, of course, because we planned it that way. But a lot of them became frustrated and so forth, and I think they went into the water unnecessarily. Some of the people actually dived into our carrier decks when they got wave offs, and showed poor air discipline, knocking carriers out. When I broke up our formation, I had a lot more with me than just the SBDs and the TBFs of Air Group 10. I had quite a few stragglers, as I was the last one out of the target area. They all joined up, so I don't know how many planes I had. We came back directly over the *Enterprise* because I wanted to get back to my own ship. On my first approach, I could see that somebody had gone into the *Enterprise,* and they had a wreck on the deck. I then departed. We'd broken up by that time. It was kind of every man for himself. I was lined up for a straight-in approach on a CVL, and was coming on in, when just ahead of it I saw one of those large, fat fleet carriers ahead. So I just kind of pulled my nose up and dropped it again and made a pass at the *Yorktown.* Getting aboard the *Yorktown* was great, but it was a real unhappy situation because they had an SB2C squadron aboard, and I think every one of them went in the drink.

There's a negative side to the turning on of the lights. In spite of what a certain admiral has to say, the operation was planned in the afternoon by Arleigh Burke, who was Admiral Mitscher's chief of staff. He had separated the task groups to a greater distance, and they had prepared ahead of time to turn on the lights, so it wasn't a spur of the moment operation. It was a well-considered plan. The drawback was that if the signal had been for carriers only to turn on their lights, it would have been absolutely perfect, but in that mass of ships down there, it was very, very difficult to tell the carriers from other surface ships. There were literally hundreds of lights all over the place. It could very well be that many people made passes at ships that weren't carriers.

We lost 97 planes, including, I think, 43 out of the 51 SB2Cs, so that's an 85 percent loss rate. In Bombing 10, of our 12 planes, we actually only put one in the water, Lou Bangs. We brought them all back, and we got Lou back. Killer Kane went in the water again that night, so he'd been in twice within a week. He had black eyes under black eyes when they finally sent him back from the destroyer by highline. The recovery rate on these downed crewmen was very good, about 80 percent.

I spent the night on the *Yorktown,* and it was rather an unhappy time. As I say, they lost a lot of their aircraft, and it was quite an unhappy situation. One interesting thing is that Capt. John Crommelin, who was chief of staff to the carrier division commander aboard, came down to the wardroom where I was having a late dinner, and asked me about the strike. He was quite exuberant. He said, "Well, we finally got to them." And I said, "Captain, I think that these reports that you're getting are very exaggerated. I think we got two carriers out there." There were other carriers beaten up, but it really wasn't that good. I just didn't want to have the same thing happen that happened in the past, where the senior officers got carried away with the idea that this had been a great, great victory. It was a victory, there's no question about it, when we tied it all together, but it wasn't the way it looked at first. I told him that I really didn't think that it was that big, and he really looked at me a little askance. I think he wanted to believe that it had been the big day the way the reports were coming in, but I also think that he believed me because I had known him from the previous *Enterprise* cruise. And it turned out that I think my figures were about right. Of course, we didn't know about the submarines doing the great job they did at the same time, and they got two more carriers, so it was a decisive victory, particularly when you consider the Turkey Shoot the previous day.

One of the controversial points about which there was much discussion at the time was the matter of the attack on the enemy oilers. We, being in the SBDs, were coming along late on the way in and late on the way out, so when I sighted a strike group of SB2Cs getting ready to go on to the oiler force, I said, "Unknown air group going on the oilers. What are you trying to do, sink their merchant marine? Their carriers are up ahead about 20 or 30 miles." Heck, you could see the antiaircraft fire up there, it was all over the place. Later on, I understand that the strike group commander claimed that the reason he went on them was because he was low on fuel. What the hell, so was everybody else! However, he did, and the following morning when I did get back to the *Enterprise* and was debriefing Rear Adm. "Black Jack" Reeves, I noted that, and he was really mad, because specifically the target was the carriers. There wasn't any consideration of any other type of ship.

After the battle was over, we stayed around the Marianas for a little while and continued to furnish close air support at Guam. We headed back to Eniwetok, and the whole fleet was in the harbor. I got a message from the flagship, which was the *Lexington,* that Admiral Mitscher wanted to talk to me. I went over there, cap in hand, of course, and went in to his cabin, where he had several of his staff members. I can remember looking at that man, he was such a slight little person, and whereas I had seen him before at awards ceremonies, the thing that impressed me so much was the way he looked at me. I felt as though that man thought that I was about the greatest thing coming, and I felt that way about him, there's no question about it. In spite of the fact that he had to commit his pilots to this really almost one-way mission, he really felt for us, and I think that he was just a great, great person. But after discussing the strike and other matters, he said, "It looks like you and Ralph Weymouth [he was the skipper of the other SBD squadron of the fleet on the *Lex*] got in and got out, and probably got a lot of hits. What do you think of going back to the SBD for our bomber plane?"

I pointed out that in my opinion the SBD was still a finer airplane, and the pilots could certainly do it. There was a discussion that ensued with the supply people, and it finally became just a matter of discussion, because we couldn't get spare parts and other support items. So when Weymouth and I flew our squadron aircraft off into Eniwetok, that was the last of the SBDs on the strike carriers.

The one thing about this battle, it was the last big carrier battle. Although the Japanese carriers, or what were left of them, did show up in the northern attack force in the Leyte Gulf affair, they really had no airplanes. They were simply decoys. Again, Task Force 38 and their planes took care of all of them. But this was the last big carrier battle where both sides really had at each other.

I did have the opportunity several years later to talk to Admiral Spruance about the battle personally, and he was very honest about it. He said, "I know of the criticism [of not releasing Task Force 58 earlier]. However, you have to look at the information that I had at the time." He said, "I didn't know exactly where the Japanese fleet was, and I knew that they had a habit of splitting their forces, and I also knew what my mission was, which was to seize, occupy, and defend the Marianas. As such, I certainly didn't want any end run into my amphibious force." So I think even the most steadfast of aviators, including myself, will recognize that Spruance's decision was correct. It was safe. But Spruance was honest about it. He said, "Maybe I was wrong, but that is the way I saw it and that is what I did."

The Marianas "Turkey Shoot"

Captain Arthur R. Hawkins

Arthur Ray Hawkins was born in Zavalla, Texas, on 12 December 1922, son of Alva M. and Gillie B. (Russell) Hawkins. He attended Lon Morris College in Jacksonville, Texas, had cadet training at the Naval Air Stations, Dallas and Corpus Christi, Texas, and was designated naval aviator and commissioned ensign 1 January 1943. Subsequent service included extensive operational and staff duties ashore and afloat, and he advanced in rank to that of captain, effective 1 July 1963. Captain Hawkins was placed on the retired list, effective 30 June 1973.

During World War II, Captain Hawkins served as navigator and gunnery officer of Fighting Squadron 31, which was based on the USS Cabot. *He participated in all naval engagements from the Marshall Islands operations to the fall of the Japanese Empire, and was awarded the Navy Cross three times for extraordinary heroism in aerial combat against the enemy. He was credited with shooting down 14 enemy aircraft, sinking various enemy ships, and assisting in the sinking of the Japanese battleship* Ise.

In addition to his Navy Cross awards, Captain Hawkins' numerous decorations include the Distinguished Flying Cross with two Gold Stars and the Air Medal with three Gold Stars.

Capt. Arthur R. Hawkins, Fighter Squadron 31, USS Cabot, 1943–45.

I reported to Fighting Squadron 31 at Atlantic City in mid-1943 to start training for deployment with Air Group 31 aboard the light carrier *Cabot*. The air group consisted of 24 F6Fs and 12 TBFs by the time we reported to the *Cabot*. We went aboard in September, went on through the Panama Canal, and arrived in the Hawaiian Islands in November for training before deploying for combat. At that time, I had not operated from an *Essex*-class carrier, so to me it was routine to operate off a smaller CVL. The deck was much narrower. You had to be lined up coming in; there was no way to be off center and make your landing. So the length of the ship had nothing to do with difficulty of landing aboard, since the landing area was about the same length as the landing area on an *Essex*-class carrier. But the width was certainly much less on a CVL, since a CVL was built on a cruiser hull. With all that flight deck added on top of it, it had a tendency to roll much more than the *Essex*-class, so in rough seas, you were fighting a pitching and rolling deck. Other than that, our ship's speed was greater than the *Essex*, with our clean-cut cruiser hull and the cruiser engine still in it. She was good for 32 to 33 knots quickly. I mean it would come up to speed much faster than the wide-bottomed *Essex*-class.

The operations were different in that, since we were a smaller unit, the air group knew the shipboard people, whereas on the *Essex* you could be there for a year and not know who the first lieutenant was. But, in our case, it just seemed that you knew you were more of a family-type affair than aboard the larger ships; the camaraderie was much better, I thought, than on the *Essex*-class. Other than that, a CVL pilot was always a CVL pilot; they were proud of it. There was a little feeling that we could do a tougher job because of the size of the ship. A CVL pilot would come in on an *Essex*-class carrier and would ask which runway to use—just to put the needle into them, you know. "Right or left runway? Which one?"

Our first campaign was the Marshalls, in the latter part of January 1944. However, my first kill didn't come until 29 April, on our second raid on Truk. I was on standby, in the cockpit on the catapult. A flight of torpedo bombers came in from Truk to hit the ships. They came in low on the water, and CIC didn't pick them up until they were about 15 miles out. I was on the starboard catapult, and, as they launched me, the ships opened up with antiaircraft fire. As I went off the cat, I turned into the flight coming in, and there I was head-to-head with a Judy coming in. So I opened up on him and splashed him there, then pulled up in sort of a quick chandelle, getting my gear up and what have you, and turned and followed the remainder of the raid on through the force while 18 destroyers, 2 cruisers, 2 battleships, and 4 carriers were firing at these planes coming through, and here I was following them. It was one flight I'll always remember; let's put it that way.

But I did get through; I didn't get hit. Luckily enough, I was a little higher than they were. They were right on the water dropping their fish at the ships, and everybody was shooting. We had a few ships shoot up each other in this particular case. I followed them all the way through the force, out the other side. The pilot who went off the other cat had turned and gone around the back of the force; I joined with him on the other side, and we pursued them while under radar control. He got one more of the planes that went in. That was on 29 April, predawn.

It was about time I ended up with something, after almost four months of combat. Of course, just following that was when the big "Turkey Shoot" came about. As you know, the Jap fleet was coming across at us from the west. Their plan was to launch from their carriers way out, hit our ships, go on into Guam,

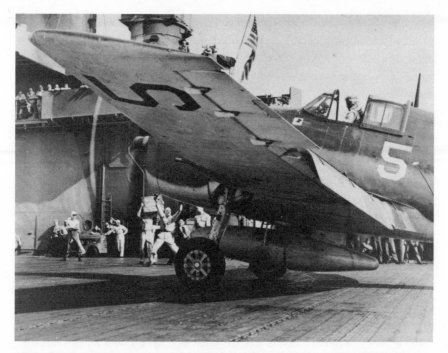

*Without question the most successful Allied carrier-based fighter of World War II, the
F6F Hellcat also performed well in the bomber role in the late stages of the war.*

land, refuel, and hit us on the way back to their fleet. That particular day, 19
June, I was with my division on combat air patrol at 25,000 feet, sitting there
waiting for them to come. The first wave that hit the ships was fighters; they
came in ahead, with the bombers coming in later. It must have been a flight of
40 or 50 that came in the first wave, mostly fighters. There were some Judys
with them but not very many in the first wave. Our division was vectored out to
hit on the first wave. We were in perfect position about 3,000 to 4,000 feet
above them, and as they came in, we dove into them from above. My division
accounted for 13 airplanes on that particular hop; I got 3. They hit us in about
four waves that day. Actually, it was so timed that when we finished and were
getting low on fuel, we could not land back on our own ship. I landed on the
Monterey that day, and so did my flight. They refueled us, replenished us,
rearmed us, and back in the air we went as soon as they could get back in the
wind and launch again.

By that time, the last wave had come through. Of course, the ships had
launched all the planes they could get in the air; cleared the decks. They had

launched bombers, everything, and they had sent the bombers all over to orbit out near Guam, just to get out of the way and leave the decks clear for the fighters to be able to cycle through the deck while this was going on. We had fighters over protecting the bombers as they were circling. Well, all the enemy planes, if they lived through the dogfight, headed for Guam to land. The fighters were over there protecting our bombers that were out in that area, and here came all these Japanese planes into the Guam air field to land—low on fuel, low on everything, and they were in the traffic pattern, with our fighters nearby. I think one guy got about six or seven that day in the traffic pattern. It was a bad day at Black Rock for the Japanese.

I think it was so one-sided for a number of reasons. It was a desperate effort to start with. We were in the middle, with Guam on one side, and the Jap aircraft had to fly over us into Guam. They had launched at maximum range, figuring they could do it because they had a field to land on to refuel. Their communications couldn't have been too good, because we had just beaten the hell out of Guam with bombs, strafing, and everything, and it just was not a good plan to try to land there. On that particular day, the weather was such that contrails were being formed at 20,000 feet. Usually, you didn't see them down that low. Radar was just not needed that day; you could see a flight coming in 30 miles away because they were leaving contrails. You have never seen anything like the dogfights going on over the ship; it was just a maze of contrails. So that hurt them too; there was no surprise at all. Also, they had to come in high to conserve fuel as best they could. Radar was able to pick them up. We were ready for them, that's basically what it amounts to.

That night, one of the Japanese airplanes got in our pattern and wanted to land aboard ship. He came all the way up to the stern before they realized it was a Zero. He went off to land in the water somewhere, I guess, but he didn't come aboard. It was just a very, very poorly planned endeavor.

Doctrine for a Fighter Pilot

Captain David S. McCampbell

David McCampbell was born in Bessemer, Alabama, on 16 January 1910, son of Andrew Jackson and Elizabeth LaValle Calhoun McCampbell. He was appointed to the U.S. Naval Academy in 1929, graduated 1 June 1933, and was designated a naval aviator in 1938. He served in a variety of shore and sea duty assignments and advanced in rank to that of captain, effective June 1952. Captain McCampbell was assigned to the North American Air Defense Command at Colorado Springs, Colorado, at the time of his retirement on 1 July 1964.

During World War II, Captain McCampbell was a landing signal officer aboard the USS Wasp *when she was sunk by enemy submarine action on 15 September 1942. After shore duty in the United States, he joined the carrier* Essex *in February 1944, and while commander of Air Group 15 shot down 34 enemy aircraft in the Marianas and Leyte Gulf battles. He was awarded the Medal of Honor for his prowess as a fighter pilot in the June 1944 Marianas*

"Turkey Shoot," and in a single sortie on 24 October 1944, during the battle of Leyte Gulf, he downed nine Japanese aircraft plus two probables on a single mission—a feat unequaled by any other American pilot in any war.

Captain McCampbell's decorations include the Medal of Honor, Navy Cross, Silver Star Medal, Legion of Merit, Distinguished Flying Cross with Gold Star, and the Air Medal with Gold Star.

Comdr. David McCampbell, Commander, Air Group 16, leading Navy ace in World War II.

We had our own group tactics when I was the commander of Air Group 15 on the *Essex* in 1944. I wrote up a doctrine for air group actions, which went something like this. In a coordinated strike, once we were in the air, we used the running rendezvous. I would take off, and then I'd make a half-circle and slow down so the other people, as they took off, could cut in and join up. If they didn't get joined up, then they could tail in behind me as I headed for the target area, and then get joined up on me—the fighters, torpedo planes, and the bombers. That's one reason we preferred the deck load launch instead of the full air group launch. With the full air group, you would have to circle and circle until they all got off and joined up. The deck load launch allowed us to be usually the first at the target. Once we got over a target area, the fighters went down first on the target, followed by the bombers and the torpedo planes at the same time. The torpedo planes, of course, were low on the water, whereas your bombers came in overhead. The fighters, after strafing or dropping bombs, rendezvoused and gave the bombers and torpedo planes protection while they were rendezvousing with the fighters. The initial strafing run was designed to get the enemies' heads down before the bombers came in, and was the best way of getting the fighters in the whole action. They would make one run when the air group was operating, and then get to the rendezvous point to make it safe for the bombers and torpedo planes. As an example, on 25 October 1944 during the battles of Leyte Gulf, our fighters went down first, provided a rendezvous, and then shot down three or four Japs.

I exercised my functions as the group commander by radio primarily. Usually, I would lead the fighters down into the initial attack, but if I had the mission of directing two deck loads, I didn't go down with them. I would stay up and tell them what to attack and when to attack. The reason I didn't go down with the first strike was that I didn't want to get hit and have to ditch or go back and land on the ship. Then, in between strikes, my wingman and I would get out of the active area, and then come back for the second deck load strike and/or other air groups, as in the battles of Leyte Gulf. Generally, when we got about halfway home, the fighters would take off and get out pretty far ahead of the bombers. We were out of the combat zone and headed home, and the fighters would land first. They would all be landed, normally, by the time the dive and torpedo bombers came home, just to expedite things. There was another reason, a good reason. The fighters, it turned out, were better on landings than the other planes. We had fewer landing accidents. In fact, we didn't have any in the fighters during the whole combat tour, so they could expeditiously get the fighters aboard and then take on the bombers and torpedo planes.

I taught my fighter pilots to do their navigation in the ready room. They knew they were going out to attack a target in a certain place geographically, so you plot the course to your destination, and just turn around when you get finished with a mission, and fly the reverse. I said, "Now the ship won't likely be in the same spot that you took off from." But we had what was called a YE-ZB system, which consisted of the ship, with the YE, like a "pie plate," which they put on radio. It put out a signal, like AA, the first 15 degrees of the compass, and every 15 degrees thereafter would give you a different signal, like, FF, ZZ, and so on. When we returned to the ship, it wouldn't always be in the same position; it would be somewhere within about 60 miles, depending on the length of your mission and time. I said, "You can pick up this signal from the ship, and then you change course as necessary and head for it."

During a shakedown cruise before our combat tour, we sent the fighters out on different quadrants, usually two to a quadrant, and tested reception range versus altitude. We found out in this experiment that we could pick up the coded signals from the ship at 6,000 feet about 60 miles away. At 8,000, you could pick up the ship about 80 miles away; and then on down the scale. At 40 miles out, you could pick it up at 4,000 feet. So this gave us a system that we could use in returning to the ship; your altitude determined how far out you could expect to pick up the signal. When the ship was following radio silence, they would still use this YE-ZB system. They changed that pie plate every day, so you had different codes in different quadrants.

Most of the aircraft combat action reports were edited by me. The three squadrons would make different determinations of what they attacked and what damage they'd done. I would try to put it all together so it would be consistent if there were any deviations. There was a natural tendency to be optimistic in claims, and I usually made the final determination. I turned down a lot of claims where there was no evidence. Where they had evidence, either visual or photo assessment or some other means, then I'd allow it. The main source of intelligence was having another pilot visually see the action. Initially, when we went out there, we had camera guns, and we did not use the camera guns for two reasons. The first good reason was that the pilots had a tendency, as occurred on one or two occasions, to follow a plane down that was smoking and circling to make sure he hit the water or the land. They would forfeit their altitude to go down and get a picture of him blowing up or crashing. This was, I considered, for the birds. He's not only breaking up the flight formation, but also he's forfeiting his altitude, which is a tremendous advantage in these fighter-versus-fighter engagements. The second reason was that the cameras were very cumbersome, and it was difficult to correlate the film with the actual action. Two planes may be firing at the same plane that they knocked down, and also, we had considerable difficulty with vibration. When you're firing a gun, you get considerable vibration in the camera. I see a lot of good photos that were taken mostly by the *Yorktown,* because they had a special camera gun crew on board, and they even had color photos. But we didn't have that; we had the initial installation. So we took the camera guns out and discarded them, I think shortly after the Marianas "Turkey Shoot" on 19 June 1944. They just weren't satisfactory for the purpose they were designed for.

I think I tended to have somewhat of a conservative outlook on claims for destruction of enemy aircraft. We didn't give credit for destroying planes on the ground, for good reason. The only organization that gave credit to destroyed planes on the ground was the Eighth Air Force. The Marines didn't do it; the Fifth Air Force didn't do it; the Navy didn't do it. You generally came down from high altitude to strafe planes on the ground; you may be hitting all right, but it doesn't mean you've destroyed them. One air group had a pilot come in with 123 bullet holes in his plane, but the plane wasn't destroyed, and that was air-to-air combat. The only way you could positively claim one destroyed would be photographs taken right afterward, because if a plane's sitting on the ground, you don't know how many different people have attacked that same plane. I never followed a plane down to see if I'd destroyed it because I didn't want to sacrifice my altitude, and I taught my pilots not to do that. In other words, you've got an advantage, you want to keep that advantage as long as you can.

As far as air-to-air combat was concerned, there were a few basic precepts that we followed. Generally, it would be a good idea to get the leaders; it may throw the rest of the pilots off a little bit, disrupt the formation. We made a practice, if they headed toward our ships, we hit the leaders first, if you could. Most of the Jap planes were highly vulnerable, because they didn't have self-sealing wing tanks or seat armor. We learned very early that if you hit them near the wing roots, where the fuel was, they would explode right in your face. So after that, all of us learned to shoot for the wings instead of going for the pilot or the engine, and it turned out very successful.

I don't think that we had as much need for the Thach Weave as the F4F had, because we had more nearly comparable performance characteristics to the Zero. Thach specifically devised that with a plane that had inferior characteristics. It was one of my propositions that I imparted to my pilots that fighters should never be put on the defensive initially. So we used a more aggressive attitude. Our fighters would fly in formation above the bombers and torpedo planes, if we were on an air group mission, and generally a little out ahead of them, so we could catch anything that was coming in before they got to the bombers and torpedo planes.

I viewed all enemy pilots as equal, because you could never know when you might run into a real topnotch fighter pilot. So I always gave them the benefit of the doubt of being a good pilot, and I engaged him in that fashion. In other words, I expected him to give his best, and I gave my best. That didn't make me more cautious. I knew that I was a pretty good shot, so I was just doing what I had trained to do. There's no way you can tell whether he's good or poor until you engage him. If I found that he had a tendency to run, maybe I would be more aggressive. If he was more combative, I'd be less aggressive and pay him more respect.

I shot down 13 different types of planes. The Zero was by far the plane that I met most frequently in air-to-air combat, and I guess that was the one I had the most respect for. Although I shot down different types, I considered the Zero superior to the others. We had combat action as high as 22,000, 23,000 feet. The Zero was better in maneuverability, rate of climb, up to 18,000, basically, and from there on, the F6F began to get equal and then get better, the higher you went. An interesting thing worth mentioning is the bore-sight pattern of the guns on the Hellcat. Back in training in the U.S., one of the people who had a little combat down in the Solomon Islands didn't like the gun performance, which had a pattern called the Bureau of Ordnance gun-sight pattern. So he went to work and developed a pattern for 1,000 feet. At 1,000 feet, the six guns would concentrate into a 3-foot-diameter circle, and he could get 92 to 94 percent of the shells in that 3-foot diameter circle at 1,000 feet. Now that contrasted with the Bureau of Ordnance pattern, which had the six guns firing parallel all the way out to infinity. What this amounted to was very concentrated fire at 1,000 feet, where the bullets would cross each other, so you still had basically the same pattern for strafing which you do at much further distance. We found that most effective for shooting down planes. We would start firing in earnest at about 1,000 feet; you may open fire a little further because in flying along, it's difficult to judge 1,000 from 1,200 feet or even 1,500 feet. But at that point, you had a very concentrated fire.

About the only special technique we had for avoiding antiaircraft fire was not to go too low. We tried to do most of our strafing, if it was a heavily defended spot, to start pulling out at 1,500 feet. So we would go down as low as maybe 700 or 800 feet at a strafing line, and then pull out—a little high for strafing, but not too bad. The gun pattern would accommodate it at that distance. So we had pretty good success. We claimed, although it is not official in the records, that our air group had destroyed 442 planes on the ground, while we had 318 in the air officially.

■
■
■

The Battle of Bull's Run

Vice Admiral Gerald F. Bogan

Gerald Francis Bogan was born in Mackinac Island, Michigan, on 27 July 1894. He was appointed to the U.S. Naval Academy in 1912, was graduated and commissioned ensign on 3 June 1916, and was designated naval aviator on 16 March 1925. Subsequent service included various squadron, ship, and shore duty assignments, as well as extensive command and staff duties as he advanced in rank to that of vice admiral, effective 2 February 1946. He assumed command of the First Task Fleet on 8 January 1949 and remained in that command until his retirement, effective 1 February 1950.

During World War II, then Captain Bogan was commanding officer of the USS Saratoga *from October 1942 until April 1943, operating in the Solomon Islands campaign. Shore duty followed until January 1944, when he became, in rapid succession, Commander, Carrier Divisions 25, 11, and 4, operating in the Pacific. Following the Saipan operation, he became Commander, Task Group 38.2, and was awarded the Navy Cross for extraordinary heroism in*

action against Japanese forces in November 1944. Admiral Bogan served as a
task group commander in Task Force 58/38 until the end of the war.

In addition to the Navy Cross, Admiral Bogan's awards included the
Distinguished Service Medal with Gold Star and the Legion of Merit.

Vice Adm. Gerald F. Bogan,
Commander, Carrier
Division 4, 1944–45.

After Formosa came the second battle of the Philippine Sea, or, as MacArthur
insisted, the battle of Leyte Gulf, in June 1944. I was Commander, Task Group
38.2, flying my flag on the *Intrepid*. We were divided into four groups: Rear
Adm. Frederick C. Sherman, Commander, Task Group 38.3, and the *Lexington*
were up north; Rear Adm. R. E. Davison, Commander, Task Group 38.4, was
well south, and Vice Adm. John S. McCain, Commander, Task Group 38.1, had
just started back to Ulithi to refuel and resupply. We sent an armed scouting
force to the west about 7:30 on the morning of 24 October 1944, and about 9:30
they saw this central force under Vice Adm. Takeo Kurita, Commander First
Striking Force. Admiral Kurita had already lost two cruisers to submarines, the
Dace and the *Darter,* the day before off Palawan. Then Davison was called
north, although he didn't join in time, and my group made several air attacks

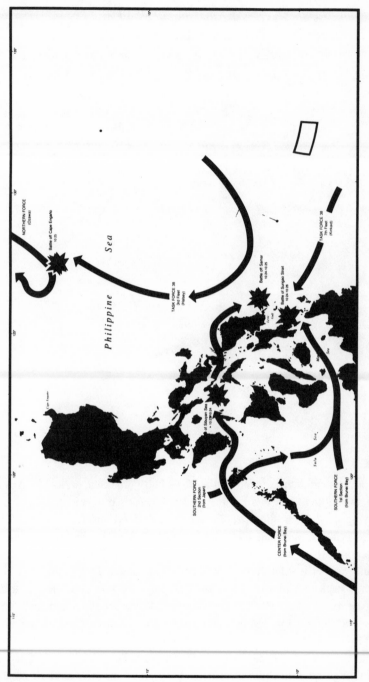

The battles of Leyte Gulf, 23–26 October 1944. (Courtesy NASM)

throughout the day, as this central force came back and around through the Sibuyan Sea.

Admiral Sherman's Task Group 38.3 also sent one very heavy attack at about 3:00 P.M., and I don't know whether it was as a result of that or cumulative effects from previous attacks, which caused the *Musashi*, a sister ship of the *Yamato*, to slow down, and the rest of the enemy force then turned around for a few minutes to cover her. Halsey got that report and thought they were retreating. In my group was the *Independence*, which carried a night group, and we kept surveillance over the central force until about 11:00 P.M. on 24 October, when we were too far away to do it anymore. Meantime, Halsey had ordered all three groups, Davison, Sherman, and myself, north at 25 knots to attack what turned out to be a decoy force. There were 17 ships in it, and we had 64. I then talked to Captain Ewen in the *Independence*, and he said that the enemy force was on a course of 060 degrees and were coming out through San Bernardino Strait, and navigation lights in the strait were turned on for the first time.

I thought that Admiral Halsey was making one hell of a mistake. I had this message all ready to send him saying, "Recommend Form Leo (which was Task Force 34, Admiral Lee's force of fast battleships). Leave my group in support and let the other two groups handle the northern force." But when I told him about the light business, somebody on his staff said, "Yes, yes, we have that information." That was a brush-off, as far as I was concerned, and I wasn't going to say any more. I doubt very much if it would have had any effect, because Admiral Halsey talked to me time after time later and justified his decision to go north. Commodore Arleigh A. Burke, chief of staff to Vice Adm. Marc A. Mitscher, Commander, Task Force 38, tried to get him to recommend something to Halsey, but Mitscher, who felt the tactical command had been taken away from him, said, "If he wants plans or information from me, he'll ask for it." He did nothing.

Then about 1:00 o'clock in the morning of 25 October, Admiral Halsey ordered a search made from the *Independence*, in my group, for the northern force. Admiral Mitscher protested, saying he thought that, if the planes got up in the air, the Japanese radar would discover them and change course. Halsey said, "Launch the search." The search was launched, the Japs did discover them in the air and did change course, and, instead of this gun duel which Halsey had envisioned early in the morning, it was nearly 8:30 A.M. before we could even catch them with planes. By mid-afternoon, we had sunk all four carriers.

Adm. Chester W. Nimitz, Commander in Chief, Pacific Fleet, sent this message to Admiral Halsey, "Where is Task Force 34?" There was a little padding on the end which some kid put on, "The world wonders." That just turned Halsey on his ear. "God, why is Nimitz sending me a message like that?" So, at 11:30 A.M., we formed Task Force 34 with the battleships and my group in support and started back to the Philippines, refueling destroyers at 14 knots until they were filled. Of course, Kurita had knocked off the action about noon and had gone west again, and nobody ever knew why he turned around, but he did. He'd sunk one little "jeep" carrier and two destroyers, and had he continued he could have wiped out the landing force at Leyte Gulf.

Halsey justified that decision to me by saying, "I thought that was Vice Adm. Thomas C. Kinkaid's [Commander, Seventh Fleet] responsibility to guard that strait, not mine." It's a long story, and it will never be resolved, except that I'm clear in my own mind that it was a great mistake on Halsey's part. Between the Seventh Fleet, Kinkaid, and the Third Fleet, Halsey, there was no direct communication and there was no direct chain of command. Halsey had orders to aggressively support the landings at Leyte, and here was a big force coming through which was about to destroy those landings and he did not provide support. Also, while Kinkaid had launched aircraft searches that morning, he had left open a sector which was not searched, through which Kurita had come, and he didn't see him until there they were astern of all these little carriers. Kinkaid misinterpreted a dispatch from Halsey, a dispatch that said, "Be prepared to form Task Force 34." Kinkaid assumed that Task Force 34 had been formed, which, of course, it wasn't because it was a preparatory message, not an executive message, and he never did send an executive. In other words, I wanted to form it the night before—we were going north—and come back and stay out there with my task group in support, and let the six battleships and the cruisers, Task Force 34, handle these Japanese coming through. It could have been a slaughter. It could have meant the end of Japanese naval power right there. Completely.

It was extremely frustrating. My staff and I discussed this thing for 45 minutes, because I didn't think that the message that Eddie Ewen, the skipper of the *Independence,* sent out was sufficiently strong to alarm Halsey to all the implications. I called Ewen on the TBS myself, and he said, "Yes. They're on course 060 degrees, navigational lights are on, they're coming out through San Bernardino Strait." One of Halsey's justifications was that he overestimated the reports of damage that the pilots made on this force during the afternoon of the 24th. Well, unless you're right there and see the picture, you don't know. You can only tell how many hits you've made, and you don't know how strong the ships are, what they can take. Anyway, he died thinking he did the right thing.

Escort Carriers at Samar Island

Vice Admiral Fitzhugh Lee

I assumed command of the carrier *Manila Bay,* a *Casablanca*-class escort, or "jeep" carrier, in September 1944. The *Manila Bay* had just had some minor repairs done to her when I took over in Pearl Harbor. I was surprised to find that the skipper had left before I even got there. This was rather unusual to me in my previous experience in the Navy, but I soon found it was routine in wartime.

I might say a word or two about the Kaiser jeep carriers. The United States built 109 of these carriers from June 1941 through June 1944, including 76 for the U.S. Navy, and 33 for Great Britain. They were built on production lines on the West Coast, and the majority of the workers who constructed them were women. They tell many fantastic stories about the rapid building of the ships. One of them was about a lady who was christening one. She missed her swing with the champagne bottle and was told, "Stand here for another 40 minutes, and we'll have another one ready." This was apocryphal but not too far from being representative of the actualities of building those ships.

For this reason, we were constantly finding, as the operators of the ships, that they had some peculiar characteristics, and sometimes rather makeshift arrangements in places that broke down when least expected or when least desired. The *Manila Bay*'s main engines were Skinner Unaflow turbine engines. These were unique to a small class of ore-carrying ships on the Great Lakes. Inasmuch as they had a plant there that was manufacturing these engines, and they had to use all the plant capacity they could in wartime, it was decreed they would keep on making Unaflow engines up there and would put them in all the jeep carriers. They weren't too bad but they were unique in design and no ordinary machinist or engineman—the products of our wartime technical schools—had any knowledge of how to operate them. So they were always troublesome. We found many engineering difficulties which sprung from the nonstandard design and the lack of spare parts. Our chief engineer was a man in his late fifties who had been a chief engineer in merchant ships all his life, but he'd never seen a Unaflow engine and thought they were terrible and should never have been built.

Another characteristic which was disturbing was that the gauge of the metal used in constructing the ships was very light. They crinkled and crackled like a tin can when the ship rolled or pitched and yawed in heavy seas. To go through a typhoon in one of them, which I did, was an experience. The noise of the ship just creaking and cracking, coupled with very heavy rolling, was quite unnerving to people who hadn't been to sea before, as well as to many who had been, such as I. In the battles for Leyte Gulf, several of the 8-inch shells of the Japanese cruisers attacking the small aircraft carriers went in one side of the carrier, through the hangar deck, out the other side, and on off into the water. They exploded when they finally hit the water because the water was harder than the sides of the ship. Of course, the shells were fused to go off only on a heavy impact. They were armor-piercing shells designed by the Japanese to hit armored warships.

We proceeded directly from Pearl Harbor in the *Manila Bay* to a place called Manus, in the New Hebrides, where the forces were being assembled to make the amphibious landings on Leyte Island in the Philippines. Manus was an out-of-the-way spot. We stayed there for several weeks as they assembled the forces there. There was nothing to do but welter and swelter in the heat for quite a while. While at anchor in Manus an ammunition ship, the *Mt. Hood,* was anchored fairly near us loaded full of ammunition. While dispensing some of it to the ships in the harbor, it blew up; it was one of the major disasters of the war. It damaged quite a number of ships besides itself and the one that was alongside, both of which practically disappeared; only fragments were found. The explosion was a whopper, and the *Manila Bay* was anchored probably about three or four thousand yards away. I was in the wardroom with some other officers when it happened. We all thought at first that someone had fired our one 5-inch gun, which sits on the stern as the main battery. When it is fired, it is quite apparent that something big has happened; the whole ship jumps. So when it jumped from the explosion, we all thought somebody had fired our gun. We knew it shouldn't have been fired, and we were frantic. We all started rushing for the stern to see what was happening. When we got on deck, we found people looking at the mushroom cloud, just like the atomic cloud, that went up from the explosion.

Before proceeding to the invasion of the Philippines, let me take a moment to set the scene, so to speak. The southern part of the Philippines consists of quite a number of islands which enclose the Sulu Sea. There are only two exits to this sea into the Pacific—one is called the San Bernardino Strait, which is to the northward near Luzon, the big island, and the other one is the Surigao Strait between Leyte and Mindanao at the southern end of the Philippines. The plan was to land on the Pacific side of Leyte Island, which is central, and between the two straits. If this were successful, we were to proceed northward, playing it somewhat by ear, but taking our forces through the Sulu Sea around to the China Sea side of the Philippines, going up past Manila and making a second invasion about 90 miles north of Manila at Lingayen Gulf. The troops at Lingayen would then fight their way south and recapture Manila.

The Japanese had been in occupation of the Philippines for quite a time. They had many air fields ashore there. They were just starting the use of the *kamikaze* pilots, whom they had trained for some time. We had heard vague reports of their doing something like that. We thought it might happen, but we didn't know really if it were true; at least I didn't. We suspected that it wasn't because it was a hard thing to imagine that anyone could train a sizable force for such a purpose.

Their major forces, knowing we were coming in to the Philippines, were concentrated in northern Borneo and the southern Philippines under Vice Admiral Kurita. He had the job of preventing our invasion. He elected to do this by sending part of his force northward through the San Bernardino Strait, and part southward through the Surigao Strait to attack our ships off Leyte. The part that went out from San Bernardino was to join up with some reinforcements that were coming from Japan, which were the ragtag of what was left that could do anything in the Japanese home waters, including two large ships which had been modified into semiaircraft carriers. They really weren't carriers and were incapable of acting like one in a meaningful way. These forces were coming south, and Kurita's northern forces would join with them.

This would he a major force which we had to oppose, and the people coming through the Surigao Strait would have to be opposed locally just off the island of Leyte. There were some 18 jeep carriers in the forces assigned to General MacArthur for this campaign. They were divided into three carrier groups. In the support of the first landings in Leyte, our ships were there giving close air support to the troops. There was nothing to attack ashore because the Japanese didn't know where we were going to land. They couldn't put any permanent forces ashore in the spot to oppose us really. The minute we got there and until we got a few airstrips going, we had to supply all of the close air support for the landings in Leyte and Samar.

Kurita's forces were somewhat depleted on their way out by submarine attacks in the Sulu Sea. They had poor communications with their homeland, so all Kurita knew was that he had to join up with this other force and do the best he could to sink as many ships that were engaged in landing troops in the Philippines. The first phases of this battle were almost routine for us. We just sent off planes engaged in close air support for the Army troops that were going ashore in routine unopposed amphibious landings. It wasn't until we got positive word of the approach of these Japanese forces that we knew that we were in for a major battle. At least, I, as the skipper of one of the jeep carriers, had my first knowledge of it then.

On the day we were attacked, 25 October 1944, we were in three circular carrier formations in a north-south line, with about 7 or 8 miles, maybe 10 miles, between groups. We could just see the group to the north of us, and we could not even see the third group, which was even farther north over the horizon. We were the southernmost group, and my group was the one that was the least attacked by the forces, which actually turned out to be those under Kurita coming out of the San Bernardino Strait. He came out with the super battleship *Yamato,* which was probably one of the most lethal fighting ships ever made. It was a super battleship, the sister ship of the *Musashi.* There were only two of them, and they were as heavily armed and armored as any ship ever built. Kurita had a couple of heavy cruisers, which were the first to come through the San Bernardino Strait and headed south towards us. The first, almost, that we knew of them was only an hour or two before they started shooting at our jeep carriers, who were more or less sitting ducks. The Japanese ships had speeds of up to 27 or 30 knots. Our maximum with our Unaflow engines flowing as fast as they could was

Evading shells from Japanese ships can be seen from the deck of the escort carrier Kalinin Bay, St. Lo, *and another CVE during the battle off Samar, 25 October 1944.*

hopefully 18 knots. And when you went that fast for long you had the fear that something would break and you'd have to slow up.

As soon as we knew of their presence, every effort of the jeep carriers was to damage or sink these ships with our aircraft, and also to put as much distance as we could between the attacking ships and ourselves, which meant that we turned to a southeasterly heading and went as fast as we could. We did all our launching and landing airplanes after that regardless of the direction of the wind by simply going as fast as we could away from the Japanese. This was not good, but I can't recall any takeoff or landing accidents that were caused by insufficient wind across the deck. Everybody knew it was for keeps; they were on their toes to do the best they could, and they did.

We, of course, started sending off groups of airplanes in reasonable tactical groups—everybody in good shape and all set. But after the first attacks were made and we lost a good many of the planes, there was much confusion as they came back. The actual procedure, as I saw it from my bridge, was that it was every pilot for himself; he landed on any carrier he could find, he got some more ammunition, and went back to deliver it against the attacking ships, then came back and tried to find a landing deck open to land on and be loaded again. This went on for quite a number of hours.

There were shells fired from heavy cruisers into our carrier formation. None of them hit the *Manila Bay,* although the splashes fell between our escort destroyers and us. We could just barely see the top of the cruiser's mast that was firing at us over the horizon. It was disconcerting because they kept shooting for some time, and you didn't know when the next one was going to hit you. As the time went on, it became apparent that unless we could sink the ships, we were all going to be sunk by their guns, because there was nobody else around that could help us. So it was a rather unhappy passage of time with nothing seeming to change much. We obviously weren't sinking these cruisers and the big battleship *Yamato*. Time was on their side.

I might add that the fighter airplanes that were embarked in these little jeep carriers were the little F4Fs. They were good small fighter planes but had practically no capability against anything like a fighting war ship. The torpedo planes were the Grumman TBMs, "turkeys" they were called. They could carry a torpedo and bombs. The most useful weapon they could carry was a torpedo, against these ships. However, we ran out of torpedoes before we lost all the planes that could shoot them.

It was my unhappy experience—I remember this more vividly, perhaps, than almost anything in the war—to have a torpedo plane, who wasn't one of our air group, land on my ship. He had made two attacks on the *Yamato* with torpedoes from his own ship. The doctrine was you loaded him up again and sent him off. He was pretty shaken up because he had watched his pals get shot down and he had made two passes and done his best. We had just one torpedo left. I had to tell this young man that he had to take that torpedo and go back and make a third try. I wasn't too sure that I was doing the right thing, but we didn't have any other pilot on board. Ours were all flying. So we loaded him up, and I gave him a fight talk on the bridge and patted him on the back and said, "Go out and do your best." He did make a third run and he landed on another ship and he survived, I heard later. I was quite moved by this at the time. I thought after I had sent him off that if I'd scouted around I probably could have found a volunteer who was good enough at flying that kind of airplane who could have taken off and done it. And I hadn't done that; afterthoughts do you no good. But it worked out all right as far as his making his effort and doing the best he could, and we'd done the best we could.

None of the Japanese ships was sunk, and some of our ships had been. We were on our way to being wiped out fairly soon unless something happened, and there was nothing in prospect that could happen that would help us much. Then the completely unforeseen did happen. Admiral Kurita, for reasons completely unknown to any of us at that time and for many months afterwards, suddenly turned around and went off to the north. He could have easily, with the ammunition available to him and the circumstances at the time, sunk all the escort carriers, probably. Maybe if we had scattered he couldn't have found all of us, but he could have sunk quite a number. But he did turn back, and subsequently after the war he said that he had a complete lack of communications; he got garbled messages and thought he was supposed to join and reenforce the ships that were coming down from the north. It was a misunderstanding. I don't think the Japanese ever forgave him, but we were glad that he did what he did.

That was really about the extent of our participation in the battle. I was awfully happy to see the way all our ships performed. We didn't have any basic troubles. All the pilots did their utmost, and there was nothing that I knew of that didn't reflect the greatest credit under the most difficult circumstances on the part of all hands. It made me feel good.

Our task group commander was Rear Adm. Felix Stump. He was quite a colorful character, and he spent all of this long period of the battle with his microphone in his hand talking to all us skippers on his six carriers, giving us all kinds of encouragement, sort of like the football coach running up and down the sidelines shouting signals to the players on the field. Really he didn't give us any tactical order during the whole thing, except to say what the basic course would be and go as fast as we could, and we did that the whole time. Since some of the ships were able to go a little faster than the others, we got strung out in a long line for awhile, and I think Admiral Stump got worried for fear that his short-range radio words of advice weren't going to reach all his skippers; that was the only thing that phased him. But that was surmise on my part.

In such circumstances, I think the Navy, rightly so in many ways but mistakenly in others, finds it difficult to reward everybody according to his performance, and the principal commanders are given awards in the name of the performance of the ship as a whole. It can happen that the commander might have been something of a dud but had wonderful people working for him. One of the things in a situation like that is that most of the crew on an aircraft carrier, 90 percent of them I would say, are down below. They can't see anything, they don't know what has happened, and they don't know what's going on very much.

We had, early in the game, established a battle watch station for our supply officer, who sat up on the bridge; he was the emcee for the operation. He talked over our loudspeakers to all the crew down below, telling them what was happening. He didn't have any words of good advice or tell them to do this or that unless he was told to tell them. If that happened, his mike was cut off and mine or somebody else's was used. He had the job of trying to paint the picture to the poor fellows slaving down below to keep the ship going, get the ammunition coming up, and doing all the hundreds of other needed things. This was used in many ships. We started it in the *Essex,* but only after we had been operating for some time, and were very pleased with it. A lot depends on the personality of that guy on the microphone. We were fortunate in the *Manila Bay* in having a lieutenant, our supply officer, who was a young politician from San Francisco. His father was the mayor of San Francisco. He had a good knack of choosing topics to talk about and a good voice. He phrased things to encourage but still tell the truth, and had a wonderful sense of humor.

We were able to recoup quickly from the attacks of the Japanese ships, losing only two of our jeep carriers. The ships coming through Surigao Strait had been completely destroyed almost by our own opposing battleships, so they posed no further threat to us, for which we were very happy. We were aware of the fact that a Japanese force was expected from the north. We knew it was supposed to have Japanese carriers and that it was a threat to our forces. I believe we were aware that Admiral Halsey had gone to oppose those forces. I personally was not aware, or have no recollection of the fact that he had, in going north, uncapped or left unwatched the exits from San Bernardino Strait, thus permitting the Japanese ships which attacked us to come out unopposed. We couldn't have done anything about it at the time if we had known it, but it was only in the aftermath when all these things were straightened out as to what had happened that we became aware that the ships had come through unopposed.

After our troops were firmly established in the central Philippines, the escort carriers were returned to the harbor of Manus in the New Hebrides to reorganize and get rested for the next step in the invasion.

"Use Your Best Judgment"

Captain David S. McCampbell

During the battles for Leyte Gulf, we sent in a large fighter sweep over Luzon on 24 October 1944. As I recall, we sent over 24 fighters for this fighter sweep, and I didn't make that. The admiral had called me up to the bridge and specifically told me after the Marianas "Turkey Shoot" that he didn't want me taking part in any more scrambles or purely fighter-type missions; he wanted me to lead the deck loads of fighters, bombers, and torpedo planes on missions. So I didn't get in on that fighter sweep. But then a couple of hours later, we got notification by radar that an enemy flight was coming in on us. We only had seven planes left flyable on board. We were in the middle of loading bombing and torpedo planes for a strike. I was in the fighter ready room when I heard this announcement of a large raid coming in, and I called to the air officer and asked him if he wanted me to take part in this flight or not, knowing that there were only seven planes ready to go, mine included. He said, "Yes, the group commander is to go." Then I buckled up, was getting all set to go, and the next word came down shortly, "The group commander is not to go on this flight." So then I started taking my gear off, when shortly afterwards, word came down, "The group commander is to go."

So, after much confusion, when we were told to man our planes, my plane was on the catapult, ready to go, except it wasn't full of gas. I looked at my gauges and saw that my main tanks were only half full, and the belly tank was full. Of course, the first thing you do when you get in combat is drop that belly tank. So they launched me with the other six planes, and we made a running rendezvous. Shortly after I got off, the first fighter director information I received was that the enemy was 22 miles away at 14,000 feet. The direction was 290 degrees, which was later changed to more like 298 degrees. We intercepted them, and five of the fighters went down to attack the bombers, leaving Roy Rushing, my wingman, and I topside. We first made a couple of attacks on the fighters, and they quickly went into a Lufbery circle, so Roy and I just preserved our altitude, got up about 2,000 feet above them, and circled, figuring that some were apt to come out of this Lufbery circle, and then we could go to work on them. So we each had a cigarette, and in about 8 to 10 minutes, they broke out of this circle, and headed for Manila. I don't think they ever sighted our task group at all. They got strung out, and later formed up in a nice, neat formation, real tight, and that's when we went to work on them.

We had the altitude advantage all the time we attacked the Japanese. We zoomed down and would shoot a plane or two. Roy and I each would take one; I'd tell him which one I was going to take, if it was to the right or to the left. That allowed him to know which way I was going to dive, which gave me freedom to go either way I wanted. I would pick out my plane, then he'd pick out his. We'd make an attack, pull up, keep our altitude advantage and speed, and go down again. We repeated this over and over. We made about 20 coordinated attacks. After Roy and I had gotten about five, I took out my pencil and started marking them down on the dashboard. I had one slot for the ones I shot down, and the other for the ones he shot down. I'd cross them when I got to five, and that way kept score.

I have been questioned about smoking a cigarette at 18,000 feet. You can do it, because both my wingman and I did! It's quite simple. You just pull the oxygen mask away from your face, put in a cigarette, and light it. You get the cigarette lit, put your mask back on, and periodically pull the mask away, take a puff on the cigarette, and then put your mask back on. You do this until you finish your cigarette, then throw the cigarette butt out the window. You crack the cockpit hood a little so the smoke will go out too.

In the meantime, a third fighter pilot, Albert Slack, joined up on us, and he made two attacks, getting a plane on each one. Then he said he ran out of ammunition, and he went back to the ship. Pretty soon, Roy called me and said,

"Skipper, I'm out of ammunition." I called back and said, "Well, Roy, I've got a little left. Do you want to go down with me for a couple more runs, or do you want to sit up here and watch the show?" He said, "Oh, no, I'll go down with you." Roy Rushing was an outstanding wingman. He would stick so close sometimes I'd have to wave him back to give me a little more freedom to operate. Hell, he'd get within three or four feet between his wing and my wing! It wouldn't have hurt me, I don't think, if he'd hit me flying formation. It'd disturb me, no doubt, but it kind of cramped my style as far as maneuverability. So I'd just wave him back and loosen up the formation. We set up a communication system, a dot-dash type thing. If I had something to tell Roy, generally I'd just pound on my dashboard. I would pull him close in, and then I'd go ahead and pound on the dashboard—dit-dot, dit-dot, whatever, and communicate that way. He would do the same if he had to make an answer. So that cut down on radio communications tremendously. I also didn't concern myself with the details of recognition, but it was up to Roy to identify what I had shot down. I was not anywhere near as sharp on recognition as he was, so I'd take his word for what I shot down. He was always that close to me when I was in air-to-air combat.

So he followed me down for a couple more attacks. Then I looked at my gas gauges, and I saw I'd emptied one main tank, and I was working on the second one. By then, I was out of ammunition, getting low on gas, so I called him and said, "Well, we'll go back to the ship. I'm getting low on gas." By now, having followed this flight away from the task group towards Manila, we had gotten pretty far away. I'd estimate maybe around 100 miles, give or take a few.

When it was time to go home, I counted the remaining enemy aircraft. There were 18 left. Roy and I had gotten 15, and the other pilot, A. C. Slack, who joined us for a couple of runs, claimed 2. So the 18 and the 17, that comes to 35, and Roy and I claimed 3 probables, so that brings it up to 38. It's pretty close to the 40 that I estimated. I think they were probably *kamikazes,* because the very next day, the *kamikazes* started operating against the "jeep" carriers down off of Leyte. It was first reported officially as *kamikaze* attacks, but there were a number of instances out there during the war where they thought they must have been *kamikazes* because they went right into the ship. But whether they were or not, I don't know.

The 40 I estimated, I had reported back to CIC before we attacked. The fighter director officer was John Connally, who later became Secretary of the Treasury, Secretary of the Navy, and Governor, for two terms, of Texas. I called him and said, "Rebel base," which is the code name. "My wingman and I are up here alone with about 40 fighters. What do you suggest that we do, attack them or not?" He came back and said, "Well, use your best judgment."

So we headed back to the ship, and when I picked up the homing signal, I figured I was about 65 miles away, which turned out was about right. I called the ship, when I first got the YE signal, and told them that I was returning to the ship, was low on gas, and asked if they could take me as soon as I got back. They said, "Oh, yes, come on in." So we pressed on toward the ship; we passed the *Hornet,* and they started shooting at Roy and me. I counted 12 bursts from the 5-inch guns. Fortunately, they were all behind us. They also directed their combat air patrol on us. I saw him coming down, and I called on our frequency. They must have been on the same frequency, although they weren't in the same task group. I said, "For chrissake, call off the dogs! We're friendlies!" I don't know whether that got to the combat air patrol people or not, but anyway, somehow they got the word, maybe by recognition. We also passed the *Princeton,* which was in the throes of sinking.

When I got over the ship, I found they had a flight deck full of planes; I knew that to launch all those planes would take a good 20 minutes, and I didn't have that much gas left. So I called the ship and told them that, and the admiral called the *Langley* and directed them to launch nine torpedo planes, so they could give me a clear deck to land aboard, which they did. When I saw the deck was clear, I came around and made a pass, but he didn't cut me on the first pass. They still hadn't cleared the deck properly for landing. So I made a quick turnaround, came back again, and he gave me the cut, and I landed safely. But when I tried to come out of the landing gear, I gave it near full gun, and the engine konked out on me. So I ran out of gas on the deck. They had to push me out on landing gear area, and I found out later that I had exactly six rounds of ammunition left in the starboard outboard gun, and they were all jammed. But it worked out all right.

I went down to the fighter ready room. I remember the air group commander came back from a flight. I was in the ready room, having a sandwich and some milk, and he was all excited. He said, "Dave, I just got five planes! How many did you get today?" I was almost embarrassed to say, "Well, I think I got nine. You'll have to wait and talk to Roy Rushing." No, I told him I think I got 11, with a couple of probables thrown in there; that took the wind out of his sails. But then shortly thereafter, the admiral directed the *Langley* to launch me on a low combat air patrol by myself, no wingman, nothing. We started getting a lot of low-flying torpedo planes, so they sent me out about 20 miles from the ship at 3,000 feet. I circled out there, doing left-hand turns for about an hour and a half or two hours before they would take me back aboard the *Essex.* So that completes the day for me. Roy Rushing, who had plenty of gas, got down okay on the *Essex.*

Kamikazes in the Lingayen Gulf

Vice Admiral Fitzhugh Lee

The landings at Lingayen Gulf were set for 9 January 1945. As part of the invasion armada, the *Manila Bay* was to go through the Sulu Sea, south of the island of Mindoro, and on to Lingayen Gulf. Mindoro is just south of the island of Luzon and was heavily defended by the Japanese, with a lot of air fields on it. Our passage in the carrier *Manila Bay* through the Sulu Sea was pretty hairy because it was our first experience with *kamikazes*. We were all very jittery. Some of the ships in our vicinity were attacked, and one or two of them sunk, as I recall. They seemed to be attacking ships like cruisers and destroyers and tankers, which were good targets for them rather than the carriers at this time, which was a happy situation as far as we were concerned. We were on a constant alert for any Japanese air raid alarm, and every time anybody thought he saw a speck on a radar screen, everybody had to rush to general quarters. We wore ourselves out, almost, being ready for things that we really couldn't do much about. The *Manila Bay* was not attacked by *kamikazes* in the Sulu Sea, although ships in our formation were attacked. Some were damaged, but none sunk.

However, as we approached Lingayen, after we passed Manila on the way north, the *kamikaze* attacks became more frequent on our ships, and they were attacking the "jeep" carriers particularly and successfully. The ship next to us in our formation was the carrier *Ommaney Bay,* and on 4 January it was hit by two *kamikazes*. She was close to us, and we didn't know whether they were aiming at us or the *Ommaney Bay* early in the attack, but they hit her and sank her. She sank with a large loss of life. Many people were left swimming in the water, and in the subsequent rescue operations we brought aboard the *Manila Bay* about a 150 or 175 people from the crew of the *Ommaney Bay.* We put down boats and picked them up. Other ships were doing the same thing. They were all trying to rescue all the people we could find. The ones we were bringing back in boats had to climb up a rope ladder from the boat into the ship. Some of them were wounded and burned, and we had to put them in stretchers and hoist them up.

After that rescue operation was over, we had another 24 or 36 hours of steaming to get to the site of the landing at Lingayen. I got together all of the principal people we had rescued who had any positions of responsibility or capability of observation in key spots in the *Ommaney Bay* and asked them to tell me all they knew about what had happened. I think it was the hangar deck officer who told me that they wouldn't have been so severely damaged if they hadn't had a terrible holocaust. The whole hangar deck caught on fire almost simultaneously because every plane in it was filled with gasoline and armed with bombs to go. The hangar virtually exploded in flame and damaged the ship so much it sank pretty quickly. The hangar deck officer was fortunately blown off clear and survived. I said, "Didn't they sound the sprinkler alarm?" He said, "It happened so quickly that we couldn't do it." I said, "If you had had the sprinklers going when it hit, do you think it would work?" He said it would help. So I got my principal officers together, and we concocted a system that if I felt we were about to be hit, almost certainly, I would punch a button that would instantly turn on all the sprinklers in the hangar. Then if they missed we would turn them off; we would have done a lot of damage to planes and things, but it might have been better than losing the ship.

The next day our formation was attacked several times, and another ship was sunk. Two or three *kamikazes* attacked us specifically. They came across the water, close to the surface. They were small planes, Vals I think they were, and had quite small bombs. They were only about 25 or 30 feet off the water. They came out of the late afternoon sun, and we didn't get them in our optical sights, although we had them on radar for quite a little time. Many ships were shooting guns at them, but none of these three was hit. Others were shot down, however. The tactic which most of the *kamikaze* pilots seemed to be using in that area at that time was to come in low, get under the radar, and then, when they were about 300 or 400 yards from the ship, they would zoom up in a large arcing maneuver which would take them up to about 300 feet or so, and then they would come down in an almost vertical dive on the ship. These three planes did this, and they all aimed themselves at the *Manila Bay*. As they came down in the vertical part of their dives, they fired their machine guns at us too, and they apparently were firing at our bridge, at least the one that hit us was. When the Jap planes went into their final dives and were heading right at you, you could see the flames coming out of their machine guns and knew they were shooting at you, though you couldn't hear them. Then there was a slight lapse of time, and you heard an awful racket around the bridge. These were the machine gun bullets hitting the steel of the ship, and it made an awful clatter before you realized whether or not you were hit. But that was just a matter of a split second or two. Then there was an awful loud bang when the bombs and the gasoline in the airplane all exploded, and that was deafening. In fact, it did deafen several people who suffered ruptured ear drums. Of course, other ships around us were firing their guns, too.

Only one of the three hit us squarely, and he did a great deal of damage. The second one almost missed. He hit the side of the walkway nets and some of the radio antenna boom sticking out from the stern, and we had a little bit of damage there. He went into the water right alongside the ship and exploded, damaging the hull a little bit aft, but not seriously. The other, although he made a beautiful big zooming dive, missed us by about 50 or 100 feet and didn't do any damage to us at all.

The one that hit actually crashed into the flight deck just at the base of the flight deck island structure. He went right on through that deck and into the next compartment, which was a part of our CIC and radar control rooms, and then on into the hangar deck. Part of him went into the hangar deck, and part of him stayed on the deck above in the CIC. When he started on this loop down, he started firing machine guns. The two people standing on each side of me were hit by machine gun bullets that went through their shoulders and upper chests, although neither of them fatally. I wasn't hit. I knew we were going to be hit so I punched the button, and the sprinkler system in the hangar was turned on, which is undoubtedly what saved the ship because a big fire started, but it was fairly quickly put under control and stopped. If it hadn't been for the loss of the *Ommaney Bay,* and the chance to talk to her survivors, we wouldn't have done that.

When the plane and the bombs exploded, everything exploded right under-neath us on the bridge. I had to go by eyewitness accounts later on, but all of us on the little top bridge of the ship were thrown up into the air. We were well off the deck. I think I went about four or five feet off in the air. I landed more or less on all fours, on my feet and my hands in a crouching position as I came down on the deck. On the flight deck about 20 feet below me was what we call an airplane tow bar; it's a long steel bar with little wheels on it that is hitched to an airplane, and the forward part has a hook that attaches to a tractor that pulls the airplane around the deck. Those tow bars are about 15 or 20 feet long and about 4 or 5 inches in diameter, and they aren't light and feathery. They're made of steel pipe. This thing had gone way up in the air, and it came down partly on top of me, so I was hurt on my back. It bothered me for some time, but it wasn't really a wound or anything. Also, the flash from the explosion took away almost all the hair, eyebrows, and eyelashes, and burned the exposed skin of almost everyone on the bridge. We had our helmets and flash masks on, but there were exposed places which were burned. Just a very severe sunburn is all it was—a terrific sunburn.

I mention all this to explain a ceremony held a few days later when we were passing out all the Purple Heart Medals for the wounded. I think there were about 18 killed and about 70 wounded by this particular explosion. Anyway, we passed out a large number of Purple Hearts. Everybody kept asking me why I didn't get a Purple Heart. I didn't get one because the qualifications for getting a Purple Heart stated you had to be wounded, and in order to be wounded you had to have your skin punctured. My back was sore and black and blue for weeks, but my skin hadn't been punctured anywhere, so I was ineligible for the Purple Heart, while some people with little tiny scratches got Purple Hearts because that was the letter of the law.

The pilot of the plane that went into our hangar deck and exploded was blown out of his seat and back up through the hole in the flight deck he had created by his crash. He landed some distance away on the flight deck, virtually intact, but pretty badly banged up. He was very dead, but he wasn't terrible mutilated, so we inspected him. It was quite interesting because he wore the ceremonial trappings that the *kamikaze* pilots used. He had a Japanese flag wrapped around his waist with some inscriptions on it saying in effect, "This life was given for the fatherland," and in very high sounding terms apparently. He had a scarf tied around his head which had a lot of good luck inscriptions and parting good wishes from friends such as, "You're going off to die, fella, good luck," that type of thing. He had a small Japanese military sword tied around his waist which was purely ceremonial because there was certainly not much occasion for his having to use it. The military sword of the Japanese naval officer is only about 18 inches long; it's sort of like a long dagger. It's a badge of authority, not a weapon, just as we use our swords in the U.S. Navy. He had no uniform, just a flight suit. He was a young boy.

The national ensign, the battle flag of the *Manila Bay,* which was flying from our bridge properly when all this started, was quite unusual as a national ensign because all that was left of it was the little canvas strip that binds the pole side of the flag with the brass grommets in it. That was all that was left. All the rest of it had been burned off by the hot flame of the explosion, so the flag itself had disappeared; little bits of burned strings coming out of this canvas binding were all that was left.

All of the electric wires for ship control of these little jeep carriers were in a shaft that came from the power sources down below through a big tube that went to the bridge in the island structure. They also went into a secondary battle-control station, which is an alternate command post in case the bridge is wiped out. In the case of the jeep carriers, this alternate is back on the stern. When the bomb went off, it severed every wire to the bridge, and, when the other plane hit at the stern, it damaged most of the communications back there. The effect was that nobody inside the ship could talk to anybody on the bridge, where almost all the control personnel were, and nobody could talk to the executive officer who was back at the stern. From that moment on, we had to run everything by messenger around the ship to take whatever messages were necessary to fight fire and so forth. This was a terrific handicap. Also, we had no radio with which we could talk with anybody else.

They got the fire out fairly soon, and we repaired the hole in the flight deck, which was on one side of the deck. The essential parts of the ship were virtually undamaged from most points of view, so for the rest of the engagement at Lingayen we were able to operate our airplanes, although with crude and makeshift arrangements. We were very proud of the fact that we could and did. Oddly enough, we found that one thing that had been damaged and was most dangerous to our aircraft operations subsequently was that the flight deck had gotten sort of a bubble in it due to the explosion in the hangar below. It made a slight mound, not more than six inches high, in the forward part of the flight deck. When our little planes took off and rolled over this mound, the attitude of the plane was changed as it went over it, destroying part of the lift, and slowing the speed that the planes should have had when they got to the bow. We almost always flew the planes off the ship, never catapulted them. We found that planes that we thought were going to go sailing off into the wild blue yonder were falling over the bow and just barely staying above the water for about 150 yards before they could get real good flying speed. We had to take out some of the load to compensate after we almost lost two or three planes. I regret to say that I, as the skipper, was pooh-poohing this, saying, "It's ridiculous. That couldn't be the cause of that little thing. It's just poor pilot technique. Try harder next time." But they were right and I was wrong, and we did remedy it later on.

We established communications with the other ships by using the radio in one of our airplanes on the deck to talk to the task group commander. We only had one low-powered circuit, and we had to operate with that one circuit all the way. We did contribute air support until the end of the landing operations at Lingayen, and, when these were completed, we came out with the other carriers and all went back together as far as Leyte.

I was awfully proud with all that went on in the ship. Most of the people down below couldn't know exactly what was happening, but they knew that plenty of awful things were happening. Some of the ship was in darkness because light cables had been cut, although in many places they weren't and we did have electric lights. We were soon able to start rerigging and making repairs. But in all of those very trying circumstances, with most of the ship in uncertainty as to whether or not we were going to sink like the *Ommaney Bay* had, we didn't have one case that I ever found of anybody leaving his station, trying to come up topside, stopping doing what he was supposed to do. This I think was in part due to the supply officer, Lieutenant Lapham, who kept telling everybody what was happening. He wasn't able to for awhile, but he went down and rigged a temporary cable to the loudspeaker system of the ship, and we were soon able to get his microphone going. He started from that moment telling people below decks what was happening in a most encouraging way. I went down and talked on that circuit a little while myself, but most of the time it was just this one young officer who was the big factor in keeping up morale.

I remember the first message we were able to send to Admiral Stump, our boss. Our code name for the ship for the voice radio circuit was "Circus," and our message said, "Circus performance interrupted for awhile. Have two rings operating, expect to have third ring operating soon." During our trip back through the Sulu Sea, there were still an awful lot of Japanese airplanes, including *kamikazes* around, and it was a painful trip for us in the *Manila Bay*. We had no radar of any kind, and we'd become very dependent on radar to be aware of enemy attacks. We hadn't any good radio that was really dependable.

We still had our little airplane radio to use to talk and listen to, but this was a crude rig and not the same at all as having your regular radio communication equipment.

We were put in the rear part of the circular formation which the task group cruised in. In other words, if the carriers were traveling north, we were on the southern rim of the circle. The other ships were supposed to stay clear of us if we didn't keep formation very well. Ordinarily we always kept formation at night by radar, and you saw whether you were out of formation and getting out of position. We had no radar, and, on a dark night with no moon, we could see nothing. I didn't like it and I kept slowing up and getting far behind, and most of our communications, I seem to recall, were arguments with the task group commander. I signaled, "I want to stay behind." He replied, "No, you've got to stay up because of danger of submarine attack." I got to the point almost where I thought I would rather have been sunk by a submarine than to have the uncertainty of a collision with our own forces at night. We had radio silence so our messages had to be restricted to flashing light and semaphore in the daytime with only emergency signaling at night. Staying up all night and worrying about how you were doing became a big strain for all the deck watch. It seems silly in retrospect; I guess I shouldn't have worried about it, but I did.

We were also isolated in effect, in many ways, from the news. We only had a few radios that could copy on the broadcast, Morse code, and there were no net broadcasts by voice. So we knew little about what was happening about the invasion of the Philippines, whether good or bad. Anyway, it was a long voyage back to the Surigao Strait and out into the Pacific again. From Lingayen Gulf down through the strait, it was about three days. Near Leyte we anchored for a day or so and then joined another carrier that had been damaged considerably in the Lingayen landings. The two of us went back to San Francisco for repairs at reduced speed because the other ship had hull damage.

Once we were out to sea, we weren't in any difficulty. If the ship isn't operating planes, there are many people who have little to do in the way of passing ammunition, moving planes and gear around, fixing up this and that, fueling the planes. They don't get tired; mostly they get bored. The engineering people and the deck watch standers work as usual. It took about 20 days across the Pacific, and I got a lot of reading and writing done. In San Francisco, I was detached from the *Manila Bay,* and in April 1945 reported for duty as public relations officer on Admiral Nimitz' staff in Guam.

Tail-End Charlie

Vice Admiral Kent L. Lee

Kent Liston Lee was born in Florence County, South Carolina, on 28 July 1923, son of R. Irby and Hettie Floyd Lee. He enlisted in the U.S. Navy on 15 August 1940, became an aviation cadet on 12 November 1942, and was designated naval aviator and commissioned ensign on 7 August 1943. Subsequent service included extensive command and staff duties ashore and afloat, and he advanced in rank to that of vice admiral, effective 29 January 1972. Vice Admiral Lee was Commander, Naval Air Systems Command, from 31 August 1973 until his retirement on 1 November 1976.

From 1943 to 1944, he was assigned to naval air stations in Florida and then joined Bombing Squadron 100. In June 1944, he transferred to Bombing Squadron 15 on the USS Essex *and on 19 August 1944 was assigned temporary additional duty to fly with Fighting Squadron 15. He participated in numerous strikes against enemy positions and shipping in the Marianas, Bonins, Palau, and Philippine Islands during the period 19 June to 24 September 1944.*

Detached from Bombing Squadron 15 in December 1944, he joined Bombing Squadron 151 until September 1945.

Admiral Lee's awards include the Distinguished Service Medal, Legion of Merit with Gold Star, Air Medal with two Gold Stars, and numerous foreign decorations.

Ens. Kent Lee, 1943. (Courtesy Vice Adm. Kent Lee, USN [Ret.])

In June 1944, I joined Bombing Squadron 15 on the USS *Essex* in the Pacific as a replacement pilot. The air group commander was Comdr. David Mc-Campbell, who, during the course of this particular cruise, shot down 34 Japanese airplanes and was subsequently awarded the Medal of Honor. The captain of the ship was a man by the name of Ralph Ofstie, who later became Deputy Chief of Naval Operations for Air. The executive officer was David McDonald, who later became the Chief of Naval Operations.

My commanding officer in VB-15 was Comdr. James H. Mini, in my view at the time, the world's best commanding officer. I thought VB-15 was an exceptional squadron. I had a very good basis for comparison, because, as I will relate later, I also flew with VF-15. The first thing Commander Mini did was put us in a training program. Lieutenant Bridgers spent a number of hours with us on the airplane, the Curtiss SB2C Helldiver, to make sure that we understood all the systems, safety and survival procedures, and problems they'd had with the airplane. This training took a period of a week to 10 days with the squadron. It was a very thorough checkout, even though we had qualified in the SB2C at Pearl. The instructors were squadron pilots who had some combat experience. We got a fair amount of survival training: bailing out, parachuting to the water, how to survive once you hit the water, the life raft. The officer responsible for a particular part of the squadron—whether maintenance officer, flight officer, operations officer, ordnance officer, or survival officer—was in charge of that segment of the training. Commander Mini made sure we were thoroughly qualified and checked out in every area. In all the years I was in naval aviation, I think he was probably the best administrator as a commanding officer that I ran across. He had a thorough grasp of what training was all about and how vital it was. Commander Mini was not one of our outstanding aviators, which David McCampbell was. But, even so, we need a lot of Commander Minis in our Navy, because they make the place go.

I thought VB-15 was a very cohesive unit. They had a lot of squadron spirit, a talented group of officers, and they did a creditable job. We had a lot of squadron briefings, which covered intelligence and every other aspect of the operations coming up. It was probably the best-informed squadron in the fleet, the best trained, and the best organized. After every flight, there was always a very good critique—what went right and what went wrong.

We didn't fly for the first week or so while we went through this training period. Our first flying was done in the Guam area. At that particular time, the ground forces were invading Guam and Tinian, bypassing Rota. Our job was to fend off any Japanese that came around, to give close air support to the men ashore, and to run missions of opportunity, such as railroads and shipping. We did that through June and July 1944.

We were given detailed maps of Guam, Saipan, and Tinian. We were taught how to use a grid system to designate specific locations ashore. We would fly over to Guam and go into orbit until the ground controller called us in on a specific target. He would describe it to us, give us the coordinates, and, when we had the target in sight, we would attack it.

The first couple of nights before I went into combat, I didn't sleep very well. As you can understand, I was very uptight and nervous. And—as normal, I think, for most people—you go through this until the time you man your airplane and rev up the engine, and then all of that nervousness leaves you. At least, it did me. And I found that was true throughout World War II. The night before the first flights following a period of rest and recreation, I was always very nervous and didn't sleep very well. Once we manned the airplanes, revved up the engines and were ready to go, it was all business. I don't ever remember being very nervous about that.

We had a lot of coordination with the rest of the air group. If the target was defended, we always went in what is called a group grope—torpedo planes, dive bombers, and fighters all went together. The fighters provided fighter cover, the dive bombers went in high to make a dive-bombing run, and the torpedo planes went in low to make glide-bombing runs. With a few exceptions, the torpedo planes carried bombs, because it wasn't often that we had an enemy ship to torpedo. The TBF Avenger wasn't a dive bomber, but it could make 40-degree glide-bombing runs and do pretty well, about as well as the SB2C in glide bombing. The SB2C was a better glide bomber than it was a dive bomber.

In mid-August, after my first combat tour, our part of the fleet went into Eniwetok Atoll for rest and recreation. During this time, the commanding officer asked for volunteers to check out in the F6F Hellcat and go over to VF-15. There were seven volunteers, and I was one of them. We moved ashore to Eniwetok Island, lived in tents, and checked out in the F6F. I got 12 flights in eight days, two field carrier-landing practice flights, and the other six pilots got about the same. Then we went back aboard ship as fighter pilots and joined VF-15.

I was absolutely amazed at the contrast between VB-15 and VF-15. We got absolutely no indoctrination and no training in VF-15. We had enough experience in VB-15 to know the things we ought to learn. So we had our own little training sessions, more of a do-it-yourself thing, because the commanding officer and the department heads organized nothing for us. We were assigned to various flights, and the first day out of Eniwetok all seven of us were launched. I got four carrier qualification landings in the F6F in one flight. That was the extent of our training. We then went to sea as fighter pilots.

Our first combat out of Eniwetok was on 8 September 1944. The Marines were to invade Peleliu on 15 September, and I was sent over to bomb and strafe. We made an attack in our assigned area, dropping bombs, and strafed. As we pulled out, my section leader, Lieutenant Kramer, was hit in the right wheel well. We pulled up to 2,000 or 3,000 feet, and I told him that he was on fire and to get out. But he never opened the canopy, never made a move. He just rolled to the left, and went right in. His only combat flight in the F6F was at Peleliu. Of those seven VB-15 pilots that went over to VF-15, we lost two of them, Ensign Gaver and Lieutenant Kramer.

After Peleliu, we took part in the initial raids in the Philippines. We stayed in that general area of the Pacific for about 30 days. We were involved in air-to-air combat with Japanese planes, hitting shipping, hitting military installations, and whatever was needed in softening up the Philippines for MacArthur's invasion, which was to come off fairly soon.

I'm going to describe three or four events during the course of this. One of the things that a fleet normally does is send out scout planes. We were in the vicinity of Formosa, and these scout flights were usually made up of one SB2C and one F6F Hellcat. They went out 250 to 300 miles at 2,000 or 3,000 feet looking for the Japanese fleet or planes. The idea was that the scout bomber was a better navigator. I happened to come from the VB squadron and thought I was a pretty good navigator, but the fighter and the SB2C were paired together because these were long search missions. The primary job of the SB2C pilot was navigation. The F6F pilot was to fight any combat necessary, and, of course, they could both attack freighters and the like. At that time, it was considered a pretty good combination. We could put wing tanks on and go out to 300 to 350 miles maximum, and every day searches like this were sent out.

On 12 October, I was sent on one of these. We were out perhaps 200 miles. As we were nearing the end of our sector, I spotted a Japanese Betty, a twin-engine bomber with a turret on top of the fuselage. I alerted my SB2C partner, and told him, "Let's catch that Betty." Well, the Betty had sighted us, and he had made for the clouds. I went to full power, and the SB2C, of course, couldn't keep up with me. I was going to give him a shot at it too. SB2Cs didn't get many chances to shoot a Japanese plane. But the SB2C couldn't keep up, and I didn't want to let the Betty get away. Before I could catch him, he'd gone into a cloud, and I went in right behind him. He came out the other side of the cloud, with me right behind him. I started right on his tail, but he opened up with that turret. I could see the tracers going by me. So I decided that wasn't such a good idea. By then, I was running at full power. I pulled up to an altitude about 1,500 feet higher than the Betty, on his right side, and made what aviators call a high-side run and pulled in on him at about a 30- to 40-degree angle from above and the side.

The F6F had six .50-caliber machine guns, and they always worked—the best armament the Navy ever bought. I turned all six guns on, and, when I got within range, I let all six go and hit him in the starboard wing root. His wing root and engine caught fire, and he then spiraled down to the ocean. The plane hit the water; there was a big flash of fire, followed by black smoke. I followed him down to the ocean. The SB2C pilot could see the smoke and came to join me. We made one circle and then resumed our search, but we didn't see another Betty that day. The adrenaline was flowing freely. Having cornered this Betty and shot him down first pass, I thought I'd accomplished a great deal. The SB2C pilot was just about as excited as I was.

We were in the Formosa area during this period. One of the first things that was done when entering a new combat area was called a fighter sweep. The first thing in the morning, a big flight of fighters from each carrier was sent in on the attack. They would fly over and sweep the airfield, trying to catch the enemy airplanes on the ground. It wasn't often that VB-15 replacement pilots in VF-15 got to go on fighter sweeps. Fighter sweeps could be good hunting. The senior pilots claimed their rights. VF-15 pilots were a very aggressive lot, led by Commander McCampbell, Riggs, and Duncan—very good pilots, very aggressive. I'll have to give them credit for that. VF-15 had 26 aces—pilots who shot down five or more Japanese planes.

Anyway, on 13 October 1944, for one reason or another, I was assigned to a fighter sweep, fourth man in our division of four planes. There were 30 or 40 F6Fs altogether on this fighter sweep. There was always cloud cover over Formosa especially on the east side. Most of the built-up areas in Formosa were on the western side; mountains were on the eastern side. We crossed the mountains above the cloud cover and dropped down through the broken clouds—and it was perhaps eight-tenths or nine-tenths cloud cover—and attacked airfields. There were Japanese fighters flying around just beneath the cloud cover. It was very difficult to spot them. I don't think we shot down any Japanese planes that were in the cloud cover.

Our mission was to destroy anything that was movable—tank trucks, vehicles, people, airplanes—on these airfields. That we did. Coming away from the airfields, we were attacked by these planes that had been flying around in the cloud edges. My division leader, of course, was using lots of power and flew into the clouds, which everybody was doing, and I was supposed to hang onto him. I lost him as he went into the clouds. When you're flying wing on another pilot, and not looking at your own instruments, when you lose him, you've lost your point of reference. It's very difficult to regain your orientation from the instruments in your cockpit.

The next thing I knew, I was pretty much out of control, dropping out of those clouds. I could see those Zeros heading for me. I got my plane straightened out, went to full power, and right back into those clouds. I must confess I wasn't much of a hero that day, but I think the true heroes are those who know when they're licked and live to fight another day. I climbed into the clouds, went on through, and rendezvoused with my flight back over the ship. We were heading for home when this happened, and I knew how to get home, obviously. The other pilots thought I had been shot down.

We had two methods of navigation from a carrier. Method number one was a plotting board. Each airplane had a rack for a plotting board. A plotting board is a navigational device for plotting course and speeds, called dead reckoning. You estimate the wind by reading it from the water, and after many flights over water, such as we had in the Pacific, you got pretty good at dead reckoning, good enough so that you could get yourself home most any time because you always knew approximately where you were.

The second device was what was called ZB. The 360-degree sector around the ship was divided into pie-shaped segments, and a different letter of the alphabet was sent out by radio in Morse code in each segment. For instance, from dead north to 015 degrees might be AA today. Pilots were issued a little wheel which would show what the sectors were for the day, and if a pilot tuned in ZB, got a Morse code FF, he would look for the F sector, and then could determine where the ship was. We always tuned in our ZB coming home from flights to make sure we were coming in the right sector.

Now the other reason this was important is that we had assigned sectors, and they were different every day for approaching the ship. Today we might approach the ship from sector M. Tomorrow it might be sector F. This is because of possible attacks by the Japanese. Any airplane that didn't come in the assigned approach sector was shown no mercy; it was automatically shot down. So the pilots had a very good reason for tuning in their ZB and making sure that, first of all, they knew where the ship was, and also to come in the right sector. This was varied every day—every day a different wheel, and different sectors—but it was a very effective system.

On another day, 5 November 1944, four F6Fs were sent over Manila to bomb and strafe. Our assigned area was the waterfront this particular day. This was when the invasion was in progress down south in Leyte. We arrived over Manila, and, lo and behold, there was a Japanese destroyer out in the stream doing 20 or 25 knots, obviously hoping to escape, as we came onto the scene. We each had one 500-pound bomb. Of course, our six .50-caliber machine gun magazines were filled. We dived on this destroyer, and the three people in front of me released their bombs, and all three missed. I figured I had him. I had him right in my sights, pickled the bomb, and nothing happened. I pulled out, and my division leader saw I hadn't dropped my bomb, and I could just see what he was thinking: "That dumb-ass ensign." So I persuaded him, "Let's make another run. Let me drop my bomb."

I double-checked all my switches, and we went in again on this destroyer. He was smoking a little bit where we were hitting him with the .50-calibers. Another run, released it—was just positive that I had a hit—pulled out, no explosion. About that time, the division leader had had it. So we didn't make any more strafing runs on him, and the three bombs had missed. We then made some runs on our shore-based targets and headed back to the ship. I tried to jettison my bomb, which is the procedure because you don't like to land aboard with a bomb on, but it wouldn't jettison. So I got back aboard ship, inspected the airplane with the ordnance man. The bomb rack was not hooked up. Otherwise, I would have gotten myself a destroyer.

I think the other exciting event of my combat tour in the *Essex* happened during the battle of Leyte Gulf. You might remember that we were landing in Leyte Gulf when the Japanese launched a two- or three-pronged attack on us. They sent some carriers down from the north—carriers without airplanes, for the most part—as decoys. Admiral Halsey bit. We had literally dozens and dozens of amphibious ships landing troops in the Leyte area, and the Japanese, meantime, were sending a battleship force through San Bernardino Strait, which was no small feat, navigating through those islands at night. I always admired them for their navigational feats in World War II. Halsey took the bait and headed north after the Japanese fleet. We launched an attack and did considerable damage.

Towards the end of the day, which happened to be 25 October 1944, I was launched to escort a photo plane. The Japanese fleet at this time was perhaps 150 miles away. It was just a little short of dusk when we were launched. We approached the Japanese fleet, which at this time was heading north, and some ships were burning, some ships were smoking. When we appeared on the horizon, they started shooting at us with everything they had. My photo pilot took pictures of the Japanese fleet as it was retreating to the north, in its beaten and battered condition. I stayed with him. When we got back to the *Essex,* an hour or so later, it was dark. I had never made a night carrier landing, nor had any night carrier landing practice. Just wasn't done. I followed the photo pilot around, and there was the landing signal officer in his lighted suit. He brought us aboard very nicely—my first night landing.

We were in the Western Pacific area until near the end of November 1944, and at this time the Japanese were very definitely on the run. Towards the end of our tour, we really didn't see many Japanese planes. VF-15 had shot down more than 300 airplanes. I had flown 71 flights and about 200 hours. About half those hours were training flights, combat air patrol over the force, and antisubmarine patrol. The flights where enemy planes were usually encountered were the fighter sweeps and the like. I did strafe a lot of planes on the ground but never any air-to-air combat. I never got a shot at a Japanese plane other than that Betty. I always flew what was called "tail-end Charlie," the last man in a flight, but I never personally got a shot at another plane, which was a big disappointment.

As a matter of tactics, the fighters were divided into four-plane divisions—two two-plane sections. And it was understood that the leader of the four-plane division led the fight. The second section and his wingman were there to protect him. They didn't normally shoot. So the people who became the aces were the division leaders, because presumably they were the most experienced. Our job was to protect them. You would follow them right through, whatever attack they were making.

I observed David McCampbell shoot down one or two airplanes. If we were in the air, it was understood that the group commander, Commander McCampbell, would get first crack at the enemy, and he usually brought them down. I thought David McCampbell was a very fine aviator, very aggressive. I think from that point of view, he was a great group commander, because that was his job, to be the leader. And if the leaders—namely, the group commander and the commanding officers of the squadrons—hold back, you're not going to have much of a combat group. So from the standpoint of being a combat leader and willing to go every day to meet the Japanese, David McCampbell didn't have a peer. In time of war, we need David McCampbells.

1945: The Defeat of Japan

Following the decisive victory over the Japanese fleet in the battles for Leyte Gulf, the U.S. Third and Seventh Fleets continued their support of General Douglas MacArthur's Southwest Pacific Forces during their invasion of Luzon in the Philippines. Escort carriers of the Seventh Fleet bore the brunt of continuing *kamikaze* attacks. To fight the increasing *kamikaze* threat, Marine Corsair squadrons were assigned to five *Essex*-class carriers from late December 1944 through June 1945. Marine squadrons also operated from escort carriers in support of the land campaign for the last four months of the war. From 9 to 20 January 1945, Adm. William F. ("Bull") Halsey's Third Fleet, with Vice Adm. John S. McCain as Commander, Task Force 38, entered the South China Sea and for 10 days pounded the Indochinese coast, Hong Kong, and the south coast of Formosa. On 25 January, the Third Fleet retired to the anchorage at Ulithi, where Admiral Halsey relinquished command to Adm. Raymond A. Spruance and the Third Fleet became the Fifth Fleet, with Vice Adm. Marc ("Pete") Mitscher commanding Task Force 58. Plans were to invade Iwo Jima in the Volcano-Bonin group, followed by an invasion of

Okinawa in six weeks. Planning was already under way for an invasion of Japan in the fall.

On 16 February, Spruance and Mitscher sent planes in for the first fleet attack on Tokyo since the "Doolittle raid" of April 1942. Following the raids on Tokyo, Task Force 58 joined in the assault on Iwo Jima, a prolonged, bloody fight that raged on for nearly a month with heavy casualties on both sides. About 19,000 Americans were wounded, and nearly 7,000 were killed. As Fleet Adm. Chester W. Nimitz observed, "Uncommon valor was a common virtue."

The invasion of Okinawa was the last and most violent of the major amphibious campaigns of the war for the Navy. For three months, the fast carriers were required to operate continuously in a 60-mile square area northeast of Okinawa, within 350 miles of Japan, supporting ground forces, maintaining control of the sea lines of communications, and neutralizing enemy airfields that could pose a threat to the battlefield. Large-scale *kamikaze* attacks were frequent. The carrier *Franklin* was grievously wounded, probably suffering more damage than any other ship in the war; she survived, despite losing more than 800 of her crew.

The British Pacific Fleet joined the fray with four carriers, operating south of Okinawa. All four ships were eventually hit by *kamikazes* but continued operating. On 6 April, the Japanese launched a massive attack involving some 400 aircraft. From this day until 28 May, the enemy expended some 1,500 aircraft, principally against naval forces supporting the invasion, with the result that 8 heavy, 1 light, and 3 escort carriers were damaged. On 7 April, the super battleship *Yamato* sortied on a one-way suicide mission to Okinawa but was sunk by carrier aircraft in the East China Sea.

By the end of May 1945, the strain on ships and men had exceeded acceptable limits. The Halsey-McCain team relieved the Spruance-Mitscher team, and the Fifth Fleet again became the Third Fleet. In the meantime, American defensive measures against the *kamikaze* threat were improving considerably. By 10 June, it was possible to unshackle the carriers and return them to an offensive posture. Nearly 13,000 Americans had been killed, including 3,400 Marines and 4,900 Navy men; in addition, 15 naval vessels were sunk, none larger than a destroyer, and more than 200 damaged.

From 10 July until the cease-fire on 15 August, the Third Fleet operated against the Japanese homeland, hitting airfields, shipping, naval bases, and other military installations from Kyushu in the south to Hokkaido in the north. The second carrier strike of the day against Tokyo was approaching the coastline of Japan when Admiral Halsey ordered the end of offensive actions.

The differences in operating styles of the great fleet commanders Halsey and Spruance and their fast carrier task force commanders, McCain and Mitscher, are the subject of Adm. John S. ("Jimmy") Thach's discourse. Thach was air operations officer for Admiral McCain and his loyalty, respect, and deep admiration for the man were genuine and lasting. Together they planned the system of blanketing enemy airfields with a continuous patrol of carrier-based fighters, and systematically destroying them. Together they planned and directed the final offensive blows against the Japanese homeland, and together they attended the surrender ceremony. A few days after returning home, McCain died of a heart attack; Jimmy Thach felt as if he had lost his father for the second time.

There were two occasions during the last nine months of the war when typhoons inflicted almost as much damage on the U.S. fleet as the enemy. In December 1944, Vice Adm. Gerald F. Bogan was a carrier task group commander aboard the *Lexington* when his group was caught in a typhoon "we never should have been caught in." Admiral Bogan's account of the ensuing events is critical of the poor judgment by his superiors that led to a tragic and needless loss of life and ships.

Then Comdr. Roy Johnson had the misfortune to be subjected to both the December 1944 and June 1945 typhoons while he was a member of the ship's company on the *Hornet*. In June 1945, the fleet was again taken through the eye of the storm, with predictable results. The *Hornet* emerged from a mountainous wave with the forward edges of her flight deck collapsed, a situation predicted by Lt. Comdr. James S. Russell some years before during the design phase of the *Essex*-class carriers. Under the close scrutiny and supervision of Rear Adm. J. J. ("Jocko") Clark, the *Hornet* succeeded in launching aircraft off the stern and recovering them over the bow, with the ship under way in reverse!

Stephen Jurika, Jr., briefed the Doolittle fliers before their historic flight in 1942 and three years later was navigator on the *Franklin* during its horrible disaster in March 1945. Enemy air attacks left the *Franklin* a burning derelict, without power, with little expectation of survival. Under the inspiring leadership of Capt. Leslie Gehres, Jurika and his shipmates performed untold deeds of heroism and sacrifice to save the ship and sail her back to the United States under her own power.

From the Marshall Islands action in early 1944 to the last day of the war, Ens. Arthur R. ("Ray") Hawkins was in combat with the fast carrier task forces. As he and his squadron mates patrolled the skies over the Philippines and the Japanese home islands, almost unopposed, Hawkins saw the gradual decline of Japanese combat pilots in terms of aggressiveness, airmanship, judgment, and leadership. He was in the air on the way to the Japanese mainland for a bombing mission when the cease-fire was broadcast to the fleet. Admiral Halsey's instructions to "Investigate and shoot down all snoopers—not vindictively but in a friendly sort of way" were followed to the letter and spirit in which they were intended.

In the carrier navy, the pilots and aircrew receive the major share of the awards, admiration, and adulation. Theirs is a glamorous, though dangerous, occupation, which is reflected to a fair degree in this volume's tales of the carrier wars. It is only fitting that we close the proceedings with Chief Ship's Clerk C. S. King's story of his years in the Pacific aboard the second *Hornet*. He had a special view of combat action from his perch high up on the ship's superstructure in secondary conn. He came into daily contact with the charismatic Jocko Clark and the martinet Miles Browning. He tells of shipboard life with a flair and obvious pride and of many memories—some good, some not so good: "bad actors" involved in extortion and gambling; a man who succumbs to heat prostration in the engine room while the aerial battles rage overhead the ship and who is later formally buried at sea, shrouded in canvas; Japanese prisoners who jump into the sea to die rather than live in disgrace as a prisoner; antiaircraft fire from a battleship at night that provides spectacular fireworks far exceeding any 4th of July celebration back home. C. S. King is an unabashed patriot and master storyteller. In the end, as the war is drawing to a close, King reflects on his life in the Navy and the Allied victory in the Pacific; he allows as how it was "just like Hollywood and the Marines coming up over the horizon in the last reel."

Halsey, McCain, and Thach

Admiral John S. Thach

I think it's interesting that Vice Adm. John S. McCain was a task group commander instead of immediately taking over from Mitscher as task force commander in August 1944. This was the way Admiral McCain wanted it. It was sort of a process of relieving, just going on a couple of campaigns and then having been a part of this with not quite so much responsibility, he would be better able to do the job when he took over as the Commander, Task Force 38. It was kind of unusual, because McCain was a vice admiral and senior to Mitscher. Usually a rear admiral was in command of a task group. But I think it was all right. Of course, working under Mitscher as Task Group 58.1, we broke our necks to be sure that we did everything exactly as it was planned. We didn't try to go off on our own in any way, and we got some particular "Well dones" from the task force commander, Mitscher, to Commander, Task Group 58.1, McCain. I know that Arleigh Burke wrote them, but nevertheless Mitscher did send them.

McCain was far easier than Mitscher to work with. He often said, "I like to talk to the people who are actually doing it. For instance, if I want to learn how to tie a bowline on a bite, I'll go to the bosun's mate, not my chief of staff." He liked to talk to the pilots who returned from strikes. I was delighted with this because I would pick the ones that had the most significant experiences and bring them up in droves to the flag bridge and go into the admiral's cabin. He'd sit around and give them a cup of coffee and listen to them say what they saw and what they did. Then he always said, "Do you think we're doing the right thing?" He'd ask them, young junior officers, and they loved it, terrific. It was something new to them, and this was good. He was a very human individual, very modest and thinking of his own experience and knowledge. He never quit learning. He didn't have complete and abiding faith in his own judgment, and didn't think anyone should.

Our standard operating procedure in the Pacific was for the fleet commander/task force commander teams to alternate so the "off-duty" team could get a little rest and begin planning future operations. The Halsey/McCain team would be relieved by the Spruance/Mitscher team and vice versa. During one of these periods ashore, Admiral McCain went back to Washington, D.C, and he took me with him. We went to see Adm. Ernest King, Commander in Chief, U.S. Fleet, and it was a very pleasant visit. I didn't think Admiral McCain would take me into Admiral King's office with him but he did, and I was very pleased that he would do that. I thought they'd probably want to talk about something that only they were cleared to discuss, but they had a good conversation. Admiral King had a great admiration for Admiral McCain. I knew— and, of course, Admiral McCain knew—that there were other officers who wanted very much to have that prize job of Commander, Fast Carrier Task Force. Mitscher and McCain were alternating, and there was a lot of talk started such as, "Wasn't it about time somebody else had a chance to do that?" But McCain had this experience, and he was a good fighter. This was where he wanted to be, and he felt that to give somebody else the job totally inexperienced in that sort of thing would be like changing to an inexperienced horse in the middle of a race, or in midstream, so to speak. Admiral King indicated, not directly but by what he said concerning the future plans, that he wasn't about to relieve Admiral McCain. It was a very cordial visit and pleasant and, at the same time, serious because they were talking about the job to be done from now on.

This might be a good time to mention some myths about McCain that were started in a book some time ago. It was stated that "Slew McCain was nothing more than a deputy to Halsey. He never enjoyed tactical command in any crucial situation and relied heavily on his operations officer, Jimmy Thach, for tactical innovations." This is not at all true. McCain had tactical command *all* the time. For instance, there was a time off Formosa, a critical tactical situation, when we had two damaged cruisers and Halsey left McCain, when he was a task group commander, up there between Formosa and Luzon, to protect them and get them out. We were just one task group where the enemy could hit us from all angles, and they did their best. Furthermore, all during the Philippines campaign McCain had tactical command.

It is important to understand the working relationship between fleet and task force commanders. The tactical commander, when he puts out a signal or a dispatch for an operation, includes the fleet commander as one of the information addressees. In other words, he informs the fleet commander what he's planning, which direction he's going to go, and so forth. There's a continual exchange all the time between them. Halsey was wonderful as a fleet commander—the best, as far as I'm concerned—and I experienced it under both Spruance and Halsey. As I related earlier, the business about having to turn on the lights during the battle of the Philippine Sea would never have happened if Halsey had been there, because Halsey had a better appreciation of the fact that you should run toward the enemy when you're going to have to run into the wind away from him the next day and you'd get too far away. Also, there were things that came from Halsey that you would prefer that he'd done it a little differently. If they were serious enough, McCain wrote out a long message describing why, and often Halsey would change, once he understood what was on our minds. Sometimes Halsey would want to change the target because he would get intelligence, maybe from CinCPac or maybe from somewhere else, to what looked like a better target. Maybe the night before we had planned to send 1,000 airplanes in to strike a certain target the next day. If you change a significant number of airplanes from one target to another, it affects everything else. You might uncover a field that you were going to cover.

Admiral McCain and I went over one time to Admiral Halsey's flagship to describe what had been happening, that if he wanted to redesignate the priority of targets, please do it early, don't wait until the last few hours because the pilots have to start getting briefed about where they're going in the morning, and if he changes it at midnight this just causes one heck of a problem. We went over to explain that to him. He understood and told his staff, "Now, look, we'll do no more of this last minute changing. We can handle a late change, for example, if there's something like the sudden appearance of a threat. Of course, we're flexible, but just because some intelligence tells you that there may be a better target than one of the many that you're hitting, don't do a change too late

Vice Adm. John S. McCain (left), Commander, Task Force 38, discusses operations against the Japanese with Adm. William F. Halsey, Commander, Third Fleet, 1944.

because it hurts the pilots. They have to stay up longer and get up sooner and so on." So he didn't do it any more. We had disagreements with him; this was one of them, but he changed.

Halsey and McCain had a marvelous rapport. I have photographs of them when they didn't know they were being taken, and they were just wonderful close friends. Halsey would kid McCain and McCain would come right back at him sometimes, and they'd laugh about it. They were very friendly and very cordial, and every time I went over, there was no inkling that there was not perfectly wonderful rapport between Halsey and McCain.

Kamikazes, Typhoons, and the China Sea

Vice Admiral Gerald F. Bogan

The first *kamikazes* were the ones that hit the *Franklin* and the *Belleau Wood* during the attacks off the Philippines, 28–30 October 1944. On 29 November 1944, the *Intrepid,* which was my flagship, took a *kamikaze* on the gun gallery which killed 10 men and a 20-mm gun crew but did little damage. Then, on 25 November, we got two *kamikazes* that were really bad. It happens that TG 38.2 was usually closest to the land targets and we were closest that day, and several Japanese groups had followed our own planes back towards the task force. Sherman's group was to the north of us, and they were engaging some, and then suddenly these 18 planes appeared from someplace and Sherman said, "I can handle them, too." The next thing we knew, about 10 minutes later, here were these 18 planes over our task group. One dived on the *New Jersey,* Halsey's flagship, and they had the best antiaircraft batteries in the fleet, in the world, at that time. They knocked it down, and two planes came in about 600 feet and passed over the *Iowa,* which was flagship of Rear Adm. Oscar C. Badger, Commander, Battleship Division 7. They shot one down, and it landed in the ocean, a mass of flames. This other one had a slight flame on one wing, but instead of shifting to that one, the *Iowa,* with all these antiaircraft guns, kept firing at this flaming mass in the water. The one that was on fire came on, and we were shooting at it with 40-millimeters and 20-millimeters, which was all we had at that range, and we didn't hit him. When he was about 400 feet off the starboard bow, he did a wingover and dived right into the center of the flight deck, just before the flag room. He had a big bomb that created a hell of a lot of damage in the area under the flight deck; and then, while this whole thing was obscured by smoke, just a few minutes later, this other one just came in as if he were making a carrier landing, and landed in the arresting gear, nose down, and his bomb exploded in the hangar deck. The body of the pilot and the engine rolled all the way forward and stopped near the bow. A few minutes later, I was down there, saw this Jap pilot, and I said to this kid who was standing there, "At Guadalcanal I understand the Marines used to knock out their teeth and get the gold." He reached in his pocket, and he said, "I heard about that, too. Here they are."

One thing happened that day for which I would like to give credit to my Air Combat Intelligence officer, a man named Ben Sturges, from Providence, Rhode Island. The reason the damage to the *Intrepid* was not greater was that one strike had been launched and had been out about two hours, and we had just finished launching the other strike, so there were only 17 planes aboard on the hangar deck. Admiral McCain, who was then commander of the force, said, "Well, when these planes come back, we'll land them on the *Hancock,* the flagship, take the pilots off, and throw the planes over the side." That was about $4 million worth of airplanes, and little Sturges said, "Well, they're over near the Philippines now. Don't you think they could land at Tacloban?", which was the new field there at Leyte. I said, "That's a hell of a good idea. Let's do it." So I called Rear Adm. Wilder D. Baker, McCain's chief of staff. My communications had been burned up so I couldn't talk to the planes, but I still had command of the task group. So I said to Baker, "Tell those planes to land at Tacloban instead of trying to return to the task group." He said, "The field isn't ready." I said, "There are over 100 Army airplanes on it right now. Tell them to land there, and don't give me any argument about it." Baker said, "This is your boss's chief of staff." So I said, "I'm commanding this task group. Tell them to land there." So they did, and four days later they flew from Tacloban to Palau, then to Yap, with a seaplane escort of Mariners, and then Ulithi. All the planes were there and able to be used again, and the pilots with the group. I got the kid a Bronze Star Medal for it, which I think he deserved. Four million bucks of planes just thrown over the side unnecessarily, even in wartime, I'd call tragic.

As an aside, Pete Mitscher, in my opinion, made over the years, was a consummate master of naval air power, and, when he ran Task Force 58 or 38, it was a professional outfit, doing a professional job, in a professional way. When McCain ran it, it was a goddamn circus. He'd come up with one screwy idea after another. One night we changed the bomb load on the planes three times for morning strikes. Now, those kids had been working 24 hours on the flight deck, and when you have to change a load of bombs on 47 planes three times during the night, because he thought that different bombs might be better on the targets we were going to hit, it was disgusting to me, but there was nothing you could do about it. But he went on in a big way and he came back here to Coronado and died of heart failure on 6 September 1945, four days after the Japanese surrender on board the *Missouri.*

Well, we had the fire under control in about two hours, went back to Ulithi, got the air group back, and then the *Intrepid* went back to the San Francisco Navy Yard, Hunters Point, for repairs, and came out again. We shifted to the *Lexington,* which had just completed repairs after being hit by a *kamikaze* on the starboard flag bridge about a month before. In the *Lexington,* we sortied from Ulithi 10 December and went back to the Philippines again. Then, on 18 December, we got caught in this typhoon, which we never should have been caught in. I asked Admiral Halsey not to take the course that he was taking. The weather station at Guam and my own meteorologists had said differently. But he had a date to support MacArthur two days later in the Philippines, and with the course the typhoon was taking, the weather would have been such that we couldn't have operated anyway. So I suggested he steer south, which he did for a few hours, and then came back and got on the same course he had been on. I'd left one of my destroyers, which McCain wouldn't let me finish fueling, with the oiler group, and the *Spence, Hull,* and *Monaghan* were lost with 805 men, which was just something. I couldn't live with that on my conscience. That was it. These destroyers that were low on fuel were just being capsized by the sea. The fueling group was several miles away from us, but they were in the general area, maybe 50 miles away, and they lost these three cans and 805 men. We spent the next few days in searching the area, but I don't think we picked up more than 10 people out of those ships. I felt that it was just plain goddamn stubbornness and stupidity. All the information was available that this area we went to was going to be the heart of the typhoon, and the further information was that the direction it was moving would prevent any strikes. Admiral Halsey felt he had to make the Philippines two days later. In other words, we would be over there with no ceiling and heavy storms. I thought it was a needless, tragic loss of life and material. At a court of inquiry later, they asked me, "Did you make any recommendations to Admiral Halsey about the course that he steered?" I had the copy of the message right with me, and I said, "There it is."

After Christmas at Ulithi, we went over to the Philippines and from the eastern side supported the landings in Lingayen Gulf; General MacArthur was landing in the north on the island of Luzon. After a few days there, we snaked through the Babuyan Island Straits north of Luzon, and went into the China Sea. We had quite a field day intercepting and sinking convoys, destroying a great many planes, and one French cruiser captured by the Japs at Saigon, driving several ships ashore in Cam Ranh Bay, and sinking two cruisers. The Japanese reinforced Saigon that evening with about 27 Betty aircraft, which a strike from our night group in the *Independence* completely destroyed on the ground at the airfield at Saigon. Then we swung north and, after two days of bombing Hong Kong and the islands nearby, came back through the strait between Taiwan and Luzon, and again attacked Formosa. Eventually we went back to Ulithi, and I went on leave on 25 January 1945.

The *Hornet,* Jocko, and Typhoons

Admiral Roy L. Johnson

Roy Lee Johnson was born in Big Bend, Louisiana, on 18 March 1906, son of John E. and Hettie Mae (Long) Johnson. He entered the U.S. Naval Academy on 15 June 1925, was graduated and commissioned ensign on 6 June 1929, and was designated a naval aviator on 25 January 1932. He had extensive command and staff duties afloat and ashore, and advanced in rank to that of admiral, effective 31 March 1965. Admiral Johnson was Commander in Chief, U.S. Pacific Fleet, from March 1965 until November 1967. He was transferred to the Retired List of the United States Navy, effective 1 December 1967.

Admiral Johnson was on duty in the Bureau of Aeronautics when the United States entered World War II. In May 1943, he was assigned duty as Commander, Carrier Air Group 2, and saw action against Japanese forces while aboard the Hornet *early in 1944. From May 1944 to September 1945, he served as air officer and then executive officer of the same ship.*

Admiral Johnson's awards include the Distinguished Service Medal with Gold Star, Legion of Merit with Gold Star and Combat "V," Bronze Star Medal with Combat "V," Air Medal, and other national and foreign medals and citations.

Adm. Roy L. Johnson, air officer and executive officer, USS Hornet, *1944–45.*

I was on the *Hornet* for almost 20 months, first as air group commander, then air officer, and finally as executive officer under Capt. Artie Doyle. Rear Adm. J. J. ("Jocko") Clark was Commander, Task Group 38.1, with his flag aboard the *Hornet*. We were involved in two typhoons in that ship. The first one was in December 1944, when the destroyers capsized, which was a needless thing. Jocko got criticized for the second one, not the first one, because, really, in both of them it was pretty much Halsey's fault. Nimitz as much as said so, but he wasn't going to be too critical of Halsey. Halsey was too much of a hero. In the first one, he took us right into the eye of the thing. The second one, McCain had relieved Mitscher as task force commander and Jocko was still on board, and we were due to make a strike on Kyushu, the mainland of Japan.

They knew this typhoon was coming up from the south, so in the early afternoon of 4 June 1945—I'll never forget it—they changed course to 110

The forward part of the flight deck of the Hornet *collapsed under the pounding of mountainous seas during a June 1945 typhoon in the Pacific.*

degrees, headed southeastward, and I said, "Well, we're heading away from this thing, that's good, not to worry." I turned in and pretty soon I felt the ship pitching and rolling. I mean it was rough. I thought I'd better get up and go see how the airplanes were doing. I got up on the bridge, and I mean we were in a storm. I looked in the radar, and you could see this typhoon. We were headed right for the center, and we were on course 330 degrees. We'd changed course, to go back up. McCain thought we could get across the eye and get on the other side of it, be in safe water over there, and be able to launch the next morning. Well, we didn't make it. There was all this water coming from the hangar deck, and Jocko, of course, still wanted us to keep going as much as we could and as fast as we could to close in with the other carriers. Well, actually, it was the responsibility of the commanding officer of the ship, and, if he thought we were being endangered, he should have slowed down himself.

Anyway, pretty soon, just about first daybreak, 5 June, we hit this mountain of water. Gad, it must have been 10 times as high as a house, and the impact of all of that, when it came down on the flight deck, carried away everything. The edges of the flight deck were bent down; all the antennae were gone; all the catwalks and some airplanes were over the side. We were in bad shape. Well, we slowed down about then. Luckily, we didn't lose any personnel, because we alerted people to stay away from the side. The next morning, of course, the question was could we operate airplanes, and Jocko said, "Yes." He wanted you to operate to kill Japs. He always wanted to operate, and there was no excuse for not being able to.

Well, you could see that, with the edges of the flight deck bent down, you were bound to get turbulence. So, we launched one F4U; we had F4U Corsairs out there then. The first one off hit that turbulence, and he just landed in the water upside down. Luckily, the pilot got out, but I said, "We can't launch with this; it's nonsense." So Jocko said, "OK, I agree. Now, what to do is to get those blow torches and cut those edges off." Well, it's protective armored steel on that flight deck, but the captain said, "OK, break them out." They were out there all the rest of that day and all night, and they only cut a small amount off. It was obvious you weren't going to cut that stuff off.

The guy never gave up. He said, "All right, try to find us a way of launching airplanes." So, for the first time in the war, and I think the only time in the war with an *Essex*-class carrier, we launched airplanes with the ship going full speed astern and the airplanes going off the stern, and, of course, we recovered them in the same way. Well, you can't do that for very long. The engineer was about to go nuts, using his power plant that way! We operated that way for two days, and finally we went into San Pedro Bay, Leyte. We went in there, and the *Bennington* was in the same shape that we were in. By that time, the *Hornet* had been west of Pearl for over a year. So, in view of that, they said, "All right, repair the *Bennington* here, but send the *Hornet* back to the States." So we went back to the States, arriving at Hunter's Point Naval Shipyard, San Francisco, 7 July 1945.

The *Franklin*—Tragedy and Triumph

Captain Stephen Jurika, Jr.

I reported aboard the *Franklin* as navigator in December 1944. The *Franklin* was a large carrier of the *Essex*-class, which had been damaged in the battle of the Philippine Sea and returned to the navy yard at Bremerton, Washington, for repairs. I reported aboard and called on Capt. Les Gehres. I had heard that he was a tough nut, that he was a mustang, that he made life very difficult, and he was very demanding of his officers. He had grown up in destroyers, was a magnificent shiphandler, never spared himself, and never demanded anything of his officers that he himself didn't produce. In this sense, I thought he was clearly a very remarkable man.

He and I got along famously, and I think I probably knew him better than any other officer I have met in the Navy. I was on the bridge all the time with him. Either he was on the bridge during the entire time the *Franklin* was at sea, or I was on or we were both on. But at no time during the 24 hours or during the months that followed were both of us off the bridge at the same time, ever, while at sea.

He invited me to join his mess, contrary to regulations, because he really loved good food and he brought from his last command a Filipino steward and a cook. I would say that our fare in the captain's mess was the finest in the entire fleet, bar none, including the Commander in Chief's at Pearl. We would have chicken livers sauteed in sherry. Of course, the sherry was illegal, and so were some of the other things. But I never knew him to take a drink on board ship, and I certainly didn't have any. The steward was given a day's ration from the various gallon jugs of sherry and things like that for cooking. So I know there were no shenanigans. Nevertheless, we did use wine for cooking with many meals.

Captain Gehres joined the Navy as an enlisted man in World War I. He became a warrant officer, then an ensign, and then on up the line. He was a straight man, absolutely no nonsense. He spoke his mind, said what he thought, never told an untruth. He had been a poor country boy from the Midwest, and he was a person who had literally educated himself by widespread reading and an inquisitive mind. He was a great captain to go to sea with, to go to war with.

He knew the ship backwards and forwards. He wanted every officer of the deck qualified for the conn; he let me have the conn time after time. We would make approaches to driftwood or debris out at sea. Later, when we were at San Diego, he let me navigate in through the Silver Gate and up to the dock at North Island to load our things. He was really magnificent. He demanded that every one of his watch officers be a competent seaman, be able to handle that ship, if he were killed, if I were killed, right down the line. The last lieutenant (junior grade) who was qualified as officer of the deck would be able to bring that ship in.

We ultimately had a flag on board, Rear Adm. R. E. Davison, and his carrier division staff, but Gehres told me: "When I ask you where we are, I want to know to a gnat's eyebrow, right down to the nitty-gritty. If we ever get a flag on board, I want you to say, 'Right here, Admiral,' and put the palm of your hand out here and cover 500 square miles and don't ever, unless he comes and peeks over your shoulder, tell him where you are. Just keep him in the dark." The reason for that was that, if you once let the admiral get in the navigating room and start nitpicking, he was afraid that he'd take up my time and his. "Well, have you reckoned with the current and have you had a sight lately, were the stars out this morning . . . ," and a thousand other nitpicking things. He didn't want me bothered, and he didn't want himself bothered. The admiral had a flag plot down below. It ran by machine, and, from our morning and noon and evening sights, we would fix our location. Of course, we also had Loran then. So we were able to fix our location even if we didn't get the sights. The admiral would come up every now and then and say, "Now, where are we?" and I'd say "Right here, Admiral," just the way the captain told me to do, put my whole palm on a chart.

The air group was exercised night and day. The ship just kept going all the time, and, as it was, either the captain or I were there. He'd go down and take a bath, eat a meal, come back up and relieve me, and I'd eat. He didn't want me eating off a tray in the navigating room. He said, "You've got competent navigators; I want you to eat a proper meal. I want you to go down and take your shower, change your clothes, and sit down and have a hot meal." It was really wonderful. Unless we were in the thick of things, when they did bring food up for all of us because everything was buttoned up below decks, when we were at general quarters, he went and ate in his mess and I went later and ate.

We had our Operational Readiness Inspection, and the air group came through with flying colors. The air group was really honed to a fare-thee-well. The first thing the admiral wanted was an air group that was coordinated. It was really remarkable that in coordinated attacks, the fighters would come down strafing in what they called flak suppression, to keep the gunners' heads down behind armor, and right after them in just seconds, would come the dive bombers. You'd be looking up at them, and torpedo planes would be sneaking in on the horizon. I thought the air group was extremely well trained. The air group commander was Comdr. E. B. Parker. His group commander plane, to control the entire group of four squadrons, almost 100 planes, was a torpedo plane equipped with multichannel radio so that he did have good control, and he could turn actual control over to a second pilot and give orders, instructions, and so on.

It was January 1945 when we left Hawaii. We sailed to Ulithi, headed for a rendezvous with the task force which was to pound the main islands of Japan as the final preliminary to the invasion of Okinawa. En route, the air group was not exercised a great deal, the ship's company took sun baths, and exercised only at morning and evening general quarters. Everybody was preparing for the long days ahead once we left Ulithi, because then we would be in the war zone, liable to submarine attack and air attack, and we would probably have many, many days when you would not get either a night's sleep or a chance to take a shower. So everybody was just relaxing.

The day before we pulled in to Ulithi, we saw signs that American naval ships were converging on Ulithi from, it seemed to us, all points of the compass. We were making about 20 knots, and most of these ships we passed were oilers, ammunition ships, amphibious ships—everybody headed for Ulithi Lagoon. By the time we arrived next morning, about 11 o'clock, we steamed through the principal entrance to the lagoon, and I was simply amazed at the vast armada.

There were at least 20 carriers there, lined up at the carrier anchorages. Then there were cruisers and battleships, flotillas of destroyers, ammunition ships, and tankers—just all kinds. Ulithi Lagoon looked to me as though it contained the entire U.S. fleet, let alone far more than there were prewar in the entire Pacific Fleet.

As we came in, the ships, knowing that the *Franklin* had been damaged at the battle of the Philippine Sea not too long before, had their crews up on deck. Even though it was a weekday and before lunch, everybody who was topside stood at attention, honors were rendered and messages flashed, "Welcome back to the fighting forces," and all sorts of words like that. We steamed in, past these carriers, all anchored facing into the wind. Captain Gehres was at the conn, and I was navigating with my two assistants and the chief quartermaster, and we had, of course, picked out all the points that we would use in the piloting part of it. The captain was just as cool and calm and collected as anything. He merely said, "Let me know before I have to change course and also to slow down."

We came in at 15 knots, which was the maximum speed in the lagoon, and he didn't slow at all until I said, "Slow to one-third, and 500 yards from now we make a turn to the starboard and go on this particular heading," and I gave him an exact heading to go to the anchorage. He said, "Great. That's all I want to know." So he cut the speed to five knots just before we got there and went into this turn still making pretty close to 15. He judged it just right for the 15 knots. He cut the speed, made the turn, and we were coming right up the line, really within 25 to 50 yards of the line, and he said: "Let me know because I'm going to keep my five knots until I drop anchor, then I'm going to back full," which he did. When we went in there, he was claiming we had a destroyer—that he could handle the ship that way.

We watched, and 100 yards from where the anchor goes, I said, "100 yards, Captain," and he ordered, "Back," and he knew we would carry forward. He had the chips thrown over the side, and he dropped that anchor. I don't think we were 25 yards out of position. One thing sure, he was not going to back off or make a second run. It's just the way he was. He was calm, he was confident, he had confidence in his crew on board, and that's the way it was.

Admiral Davison and his staff came on board. Strangely enough, having a staff aboard, it seemed like an alien entity, an incubus, had fastened itself on us. The ship was really a fighting unit; the exec ran everything, all the personnel down below decks. All the captain wanted to know was that things were going all right. If you needed any help, yes, but otherwise, "Joe, you're the executive

officer and you run that part of the ship. I don't have time to worry about that."
The engineer would come up at eight o'clock at night, the exec would come up,
the gun boss would come up, the air officer would come up, and we'd sit out on
the wing of the bridge there on little stools and hash over how the day had been.
The captain kept track of how everything was going on in his ship all the time.

Then the staff came aboard. They had a flag cabin for the admiral, and that
was OK because the ship was equipped that way, that's what the flag bridge
was for, and we tried to keep the flag personnel down on the flag bridge, not up
on our bridge for obvious reasons. The other thing is to keep them out of the
hair of the air group. The only staff function is to coordinate and provide
orders, and we carried them out. We didn't want them getting their fingers
down into the squadrons, getting people perplexed about who was their boss.
The captain was the boss. The captain not only commands the ship, but he's in
charge of that air group. The admiral has two, three, or four carriers under his
command. But his staff seemed to be involved. I guess they had been without a
ship for so long, on the beach, as it were, that they just wanted to get back into
the swing of things. It wasn't that they were being vindictive or deliberately
trying to upset us. It was just that they had not been aboard a flagship for some
time, and they were trying to get back into it.

The admiral was a shy, quiet person, unlike people like Mitscher and
others, who were the aggressive types. He seldom said anything. Very few of us
knew him at all, except by sight, and yet here he was on a bridge 10 feet below
us, no smiles, no cheerful greetings, or anything like this. All business, always
very pleasant, but no personal touch, no personal relationship at all with the
staff. I've been on many, many, many staffs, and this was the only one I can
think of that didn't have a really good working relationship with the ship,
which I think is a shame.

In the group of coral atolls that form the Ulithi Lagoon, there were a great
many palm trees and we found that on the major one an officers' club had been
set up on the beach. We did go over to see friends from the other carriers, and
it was just a hog-killing. Officers' motorboats were arriving and disgorging
thirsty officers of all ranks from ensign to admiral. The admirals had a section
of this beach hut reserved where they could sit down in peace and sort of talk.
It was captains and admirals in that particular place. I went over with Captain
Gehres and Joe Taylor, the executive officer of the ship. Joe knew a lot of
people, having been on the *Franklin* out at sea before. Gehres, of course, knew
most of the people, and I knew a goodly number of the younger captains who
were just getting command of these big ships and a few of the admirals. It was

sort of old home week, and as commanders they took Joe Taylor and me with them and we sat around, had a couple of drinks, and yakked, went surfing, sailing, on the inside of the lagoon, then went along the beaches, looking for seashells and swimming in the sea. At five o'clock or five-thirty, it was back to the ship for dinner, and that was the end of the drinking because a very short time later, five days later, the task group weighed anchor, with the *Franklin* as flagship.

The destroyers sortied first, followed by the *Santa Fe,* a cruiser, and another cruiser in the task group, and then the carriers. The destroyers fanned out in front of us and then fell in behind as they followed us out and surrounded us. We sailed in a circular formation, with the four carriers at the center and then cruisers at the cardinal points, and then destroyers all the way round the outside. It was one of the typical antiaircraft cruising formations. An attacking aircraft would be met, supposedly, by the combat air patrol directed by the carrier that had the duty, and should it escape the combat air patrol it would then run into the destroyers, the outer screen, then past the cruisers and, finally, come under the carrier guns. The distances had been arranged so that this little stuff like the 20-mm would not affect the ships next out from them. There were 2,500 yards between the circles in this screen.

We set sail on a course and the admiral had told me where he wanted to rendezvous and what time he wanted to get there, so we had figured out beforehand the necessary speed to be there and never less than 15 knots, which was standard procedure. The speed of advance would probably be about 12 because we were zigzagging. By this time, the Japanese submarines had been pretty well cleared from the area, but that did not keep the fleet from zig-zagging at night time.

I think that people were aware of the *kamikaze* threat, but they were not aware of the intensity or the length of time that it would continue. One of our principal strike goals was the elimination of as many as possible of the flyable aircraft of any kind that could be used as *kamikazes* in the Okinawa campaign, and, of course, Okinawa was a tremendously important Japanese bastion. It had tens of thousands of Japanese troops, an excellent harbor, all sorts of base facilities, and when Okinawa went the Japanese knew that their own hour for the principal main islands was really at hand. So they were committed to its defense in a great way, and that meant that they would use every available aircraft, major ship, and *kamikazes* as well. I don't think that we were aware of the fact that we would be up against people who would think nothing of hurling themselves as a human bomb against the carriers, which were the principal targets. If it happened to be a destroyer that was out on picket duty, they'd go after the destroyer, so there would be no warning.

I saw, in the early phases here, destroyers get hit, burst into flames, men jumping over the side to avoid flames, and the destroyers list and then taken in tow. Some of them were too damaged, some of them were sunk, some of them floated, just all kinds of major damage from these *kamikazes,* and they didn't come down after a picket destroyer just one at a time. The armament of a destroyer, in 1945, wasn't capable of coping with a coordinated attack. A picket destroyer was really bait, and I think that it did not take long for the crews of the picket destroyers to feel that they were being put out there as bait. They hoped that the carriers would provide enough of a combat air patrol overhead to get most of the *kamikazes* so that they might be able to cope with a few of the last ones that got through. But the carriers had so many other things to do, that to maintain a combat air patrol there would have kept two carriers busy right near Okinawa and subject to attack, and so it was felt that the principal course was to destroy the aircraft at their source, on main fields in Japan and Okinawa, but certainly in Kyushu, Shikoku, and along the Japanese coast west of Tokyo. There wasn't really any answer. Putting the destroyers out there on picket duty could not be avoided.

The mission of our task force was to raid Japanese airfields in Kyushu, Shikoku, and western Honshu, from which we expected all the Japanese aircraft would be launched against the Okinawa invasion, and, in truth, that's what happened. They were the only ones within range. Anything that was in the Tokyo area or north could not reach Okinawa, not even on a one-way trip. The launch point for our aircraft was 45 miles off the mainland of Honshu. It would take our fighters and bombers somewhere between 20 and 30 minutes from time of launch to arrive at the enemy airfields.

En route up there, we ran into an intertropical front which, as anyone who's been in the area knows, moves south toward the tropics in the summer and north toward the Japanese islands in the wintertime. This was spring, and the intertropical front, which provides almost 100 percent cloud cover, goes literally from 500 or 1,000 feet to 25,000 feet. There's no way to get through this. You could fly over the top in one of the modern jets, but in those days there was just no way to get through it. You were either on the Japan side of that intertropical front, where we ultimately launched our aircraft, or you were in it. Had we been in it and remained in it, we would have been safe from Japanese air attack. On the other hand, our own planes would have had difficulty finding their way back, unless we turned our low frequency radio beacon on, and that, of course, would draw the Japanese as well. So we were really perplexed and on the horns of a dilemma, and we maintained radio silence. We had to get out of that intertropical front.

It was the second day in that front that we began encountering enemy opposition, as far as we were concerned. The combat air patrols were engaged in shooting down Japanese aircraft in dribbles. They were apparently out looking for us. They'd find them 50, 75 miles from the force, and I doubt that these aircraft had really spotted the force. But you couldn't hide where our planes were coming from, the general direction, and there was no use playing cozy and telling them to go 100 miles down the coast and then sneak in because, after all, when they'd leave they wouldn't have gas enough to go back the same way. They'd still have to come back for the carrier direct. So it was no secret, obviously, to the Japanese that somewhere out there was a big task force.

I must mention our deck load. The *Franklin* carried a whole load of Tiny Tim rockets, which was an 11.75-inch rocket. We were the only carrier that had them, and our people had fired them in the ORI back in Hawaii. These were 10.5 feet long, with a 500-pound warhead. They packed a tremendous wallop. It would really be like a 12-inch shell going in, and they had armor-piercing and high-explosive heads, or other kinds of different heads to take out anything. In short, they'd penetrate the armor of any ship that the Japanese had. And they were tremendous in that you didn't have to come right down into the target. You could let them go a couple of miles away. They were carried ordinarily by the dive bombers and the torpedo planes. Our crews had to bring these Tiny Tims up from the magazines to the flight deck, run them on dollies under the aircraft, and load them on the aircraft.

Early in the morning of 19 March, our aircraft were taking off, all the elevators were up, and the flight deck officer was revving them up for takeoff. About five or six aircraft had gotten off when right out of the fairly low thin clouds a Japanese plane like a carrier attack bomber came right down the length of the *Franklin*'s deck.

I was on the wing of the captain's bridge, checking our bearings and keeping the ship in position while flight operations were going on. I saw this out of the corner of my eye, and I saw two bombs drop from the plane and hit just forward of the forward elevator, and within a fraction of a second, of course, an enormous explosion took place down below and the elevator lifted up, cockeyed, and then fell back down across the elevator opening. The planes just behind the elevator were spotted, ready for takeoff, engines going, fully loaded with Tiny Tims, loaded with 500- and 1,000-pound bombs; the entire flight deck aft of the island structure was loaded with aircraft ready to take off.

These two bombs exploded on the hangar deck, right under the no. 1 elevator, and they created havoc down there—fires were started, Tiny Tims caught up in the fire started going off and flying right up the deck. The explosions were really out of this world; one followed the other interminably. Sheets of flame came up, and then we really started to smoke. The smoke was acrid and thick, and it swung right over the bridge. Captain Gehres was caught with a choking lung-full of smoke and dropped to the deck. He was out of action for about 15 minutes.

The executive officer's battle station was up in the bow, under the flight deck, so he was isolated from the bridge. I was next in command and the only one who could get to the bridge. The air officer was down below in air control, and we didn't know whether he had survived or not. The intercom phone circuit was out. From what I could see out the side, and that quickly became obscured with smoke, the planes were exploding on deck. Mark XIII torpedoes were going off right on the deck.

There's a photograph of me taken from another ship with a telephoto lens showing an engine off one of the aircraft right under me on the flight deck going up past my head, about 30 feet in the air. I saw it go up and come down. It missed the bridge, so I wasn't worried about being hit by it. With everything else going on, there was simply no time to think about any personal safety. The thing was, first of all, to not interfere with the flight operations of the other ships. I knew that we weren't going to do any more fighting that day, if ever.

We could steer. The ship took a list very quickly of about 15 degrees to starboard. I had damage control on the phones and the damage control people said they were going to right the ship, and I remembered very quickly the story of my days on the *Hornet,* where they had over corrected, and I said: "I don't care if you carry a 5-degree list, don't overcorrect. Don't put too much water in. Don't flood too many compartments. Just take it easy, and get us fairly level." We started to turn to the right to get the smoke away from the bridge so that we could see what we were doing. All we had was the radar, a big radar screen, on the bridge, and with all the task force ships around, you just didn't know who was doing what to whom.

By this time, it was broad daylight. We steered to the right. Of course, our speed was cut. There was damage to the engine rooms and the boiler rooms because they were right under the hangar deck. The hangar deck was exploding, gasoline was catching fire down there. Men were jumping over the side, men were jumping off the flight deck, they were jumping off the little deck where the 20-mms were, under the overhang of the flight deck. As soon as the wind shifted from our change of course, we could see that two destroyers were picking people up out of the sea directly behind us, and they were throwing life jackets and life rings and hauling people aboard, a lot of them injured, people who were burned and needed immediate medical attention.

The explosions kept on going, smoke kept billowing, the entire after part of the ship was aflame. We finally made a left turn so that the wind came over the starboard side so that we could see as far down the deck as possible. We were listing to starboard. It was clear that the admiral was not on his feet, still choking from the acrid smoke. He had dropped to the deck. He was trying to get a breath of clean air down on the deck. The quartermaster, everybody, literally was choking. I had a handkerchief, wet, and I kept it over my nose and my mouth and was able to breathe. I'm sure I would have fallen just like all the rest of them, except for that handkerchief. I later recommended that there should be some sort of a gas mask, with small attachments, good for maybe 15 or 20 minutes, with big goggles so that you could see, that would give you total control in the event of fire and all of this smoke. I'm sure the war ended before anyone could take action on this, but certainly I wouldn't go back into battle on any kind of ship without a gas mask of some kind like that.

We were exploding and on fire until the middle of the next afternoon, but Admiral Davison, whom I could see down on the flag bridge, sent word up that he would have to move his staff out. That was a logical thing because, after all, here we were without power, and all we had was steering control by hand from steering aft. Fortunately, that phone was working, our guns were working, the hoists for 5-inch ammunition were working up forward, but that's all that was working. The engines were out, and the boilers were out. The first thing we had to find out was the extent of damage, how many men were available, how many men, roughly, had been killed, what sort of a crew we had left. Everything in the way of airplanes was gone.

The cruiser *Santa Fe* came alongside, and the name of the captain was H. C. Fitz. He handled that ship just like it was a destroyer. We were drifting slightly downwind. He didn't want the carrier coming down on him and so he did some nimble jockeying, but a couple of highlines were rigged. By this time, Captain Gehres was back in full command. We saw people being ferried across, first the admiral's staff. The admiral bid us, "Adios, good luck, and I hope you pull through," and all that kind of thing, and away he moved. After all, he had command of the group. We were just his vessel to carry him around.

The USS Franklin, *listing and apparently mortally wounded after Japanese air attacks 19 March 1945, survived to return to New York, where she was later decommissioned.*

He got on board the *Santa Fe,* and then came the business of who left the *Franklin.* The captain was determined that the officers on the ship, by God, were going to stay on that ship, they were going to save that ship, and we were going to get back home. It turned out that an officer whose name I will not mention but who has since made captain went over the highline. The captain saw him and yelled at him, "Get back here, get back aboard the ship." No way. He was over. So Captain Gehres, when he was writing up the fitness reports later, described him as a deserter and wanted him court-martialed. In truth, most of us who were on the ship felt that, although the ship was blowing up and on fire, the real danger was past. By this time, the only question in our minds was, well, when do the Japs come out and finish us because we were sure as hell caught here, we're not going anywhere until somebody takes us in tow, and there were no fleet tugs around.

The transfer went on. People were still jumping off the hangar deck, off the flight deck aft, because they couldn't come up toward us. There were flames between the after part of the ship and the forward part. There was no communication, no way to get back, so the captain didn't feel that these people were deserting the ship. That part was on fire and blowing up, and for the people back there it was every man for himself. You couldn't be heard on a bull horn. There was no way to communicate. Whoever went off aft, that was fine. Anybody the destroyer picked up was OK, but to get on the *Santa Fe* the captain had that under control and after the staff, the wounded went. He certainly didn't want any officers going over and no enlisted men. The air group, yes, because the air group we weren't going to use. We needed ship's company, so nobody from the ship's company was to go. The air group people would check off their men and get them off.

Anyway, we ended up with 772 people out of the 4,800 men that we had on board the *Franklin*. This is what our head count was the first evening, after they'd taken off all the people. I don't know how many people were blown up, how many died from burns. I looked over the side onto the flight deck, and I saw, for example, the executive officer up in the forward part leading fire-hose and damage control crews, giving orders up there, and I saw Father O'-Callaghan, the Catholic chaplain, giving extreme unction and the final blessing to people who were gravely injured and lying on the deck. As a matter of fact, at one particular time, a Tiny Tim went off from aft and flew over the chaplain's head. He looked up as the thing whistled by him and there was a trail of flame. He said he could feel the heat. He went on giving the final rites to the wounded on the deck. There were a couple of hundred people on the flight deck by that time, right opposite the island. I could look down and see. The flight deck from the forward elevator all the way back to the fantail was in shreds and tatters, with holes and massive beams and girders, the understructure, and the steel flight deck itself, all twisted metal, just a mass of twisted metal.

The only way to get from forward to the after part of the flight deck was to go down to the hangar deck and go aft and come back up, after we put the fires out. The metal was so twisted that all the way back to the New York Navy Yard we kept finding bodies in various stages of decomposition. The very last one we found while we were coming up Gravesend Bay in New York Harbor, just before we docked at the navy yard. The last body was, one might say, exhumed with a blow torch from the steel coffin in which it had been burned, burned to shreds.

So here we were with, by now, a 15-degree list to starboard again. The captain had started to count noses and we had 772, and it was imperative that we get the hell out of there, 45 miles from Honshu, and just drifting with the current. Meantime, the other ships were going ahead with air operations. We were taken in tow, a remarkable feat, by the cruiser *Pittsburgh*. The *Pittsburgh* floated a wire line down, a cable, to us, and the executive officer, who was in charge up on the forecastle, under the flight deck, and his group of people managed after two or three attempts to get it over some bits and hooked on to an anchor chain up there, and the *Pittsburgh* began taking us in tow very, very slowly. They were just taking the strain and letting out as much cable as they could so that part of it would dip in and take up the stress, because here we were a 40,000-ton carrier, and I would estimate that with the air group and all those things aboard we were probably 45,000 or 48,000 tons, and the *Pittsburgh* was nothing of that size. But the *Pittsburgh* took us in tow and I remember Jocko Clark, Admiral Clark, who was in command of another task group, was assigned to protect us by combat air patrol and air cover for the *Franklin* and the *Pittsburgh* until we got safely away from the Japanese islands.

We were under attack that afternoon; individual and sometimes small groups, never big groups, fortunately, of Japanese aircraft would come out to attack. The combat air patrol got almost all of them. Also, we did fire our own guns. I remember Captain Gehres congratulating a Marine who was running a 40-mm on top of one of our 5-inch turrets. That little Marine group there shot down a plane that was coming in at very close range. I tell you, everybody was at general quarters all the time, all day, all night, trying to receive reports, trying to get estimates of the damage in the boiler room, trying to get up steam. We did get a magnificent report that probably by the next morning we would be able to get up steam and probably by the next afternoon be able to get under way at five knots under our own power.

We ran on two of our eight boilers. We got six back before we got to Pearl Harbor, but we started out with only two. We lived on "C" rations; there was nothing that was warm or hot. In fact, the captain's mess was the only place where the food was any good. He and I were on the bridge the whole time. From early the morning we got hit until the following afternoon, neither of us left the bridge at all, taking reports from the exec. At nighttime, he'd come up and report in the wing of the bridge; we'd stand and talk, and the air officer— all he could report was that the air group was demolished, the flight deck was demolished, and the hangar deck was a shambles, and it was. We could see that. We were counting noses and trying to get up steam, and make sure that the people who were alive were getting hot food. There was no hot food, to begin with, just rations.

We had that list most of that afternoon and evening, but we got it back a degree at a time. The captain listened to me about my experience on the *Hornet,* and he countermanded the original order that I gave to come back very slowly and don't go over the other side. In other words, we didn't want any more water than we had to have. I think it's far better to do it that way than it is to go overboard and then have to pump out. The ship didn't take on water. But the fires, you see, were being put out with hoses and that's where a lot of the water came in. So we had pockets of water all over the ship, and its aggregate effect wasn't very nice to have, because it was still up high. It wasn't way down deep, and that's why we didn't want somebody counterbalancing, bringing in water forward and settling the ship further down and still having free water running around.

At the height of the explosions and because things looked so desperate in the early stages, in the first 15 minutes or so, the captain got up off the deck in the navigating cabin, took a look around, and came over to me and said, "Steve, what do you think we should do? Do you think we should abandon ship?" I said, "No, I don't think so. I wouldn't. I think we'll pull through, and there's no reason we really shouldn't if everybody gets to work." And he said: "I'm glad you said that." I really feel that was the key to his recommending me for a Navy Cross. I'm not sure that he would have said, "Abandon ship" later, had I said, "I really think it's desperate, it's hopeless." But I do know that ever after that he had just a tremendous affection for me, an affection that he had earlier and a respect, but I'm absolutely certain that little exchange was the key to his recommending me for the Navy Cross.

Jocko Clark and his task force protected us all during the night. We were subject to attacks during the night, and he had a night combat air patrol up. We could see him operating with his carrier not more than two or three miles away, between us and the Japs. By this time, of course, we had our TBS radio going and were starting to get equipment back, handy billies working here and there pumping out water, clearing wreckage, tossing things over the side, like aircraft engines that were lying around, pieces of wings and so on, defuzing bombs that had been red hot but somehow hadn't gone off—some of them hadn't—but people were very, very gingerly about those particular things.

During the night, we were on the bridge, drinking hot coffee and eating loaves of bread. At about 11 o'clock, the galley came back into operation. We had loaves of bread, and we were just tearing off huge chunks. There was no butter, no jam, nothing like that, just cans of sardines, cans of beans, while we watched the launching of the combat air patrol from Jocko Clark's carriers. By the next morning, we knew that we were going to make it at five knots; we were about 125 miles off the Japanese coast and getting harder and harder to find and obviously farther and farther away. Our chances of getting home were pretty good. We started getting messages, all kinds of messages from CinCPac,

Admiral Nimitz, the carrier division commander, everybody around, and especially we got some from Jocko Clark, who was covering us. We did get up steam on the 20th of March. In the afternoon, we had two boilers on the line and were able to make five knots, which was about one knot more than the *Pittsburgh* was towing us. The *Pittsburgh* was towing us at around four, sometimes, going downwind, five knots. Believe me, we were grateful for that towline and grateful for the guns that she had on board, which were used to assist our own guns, the combat air patrol, and the couple of destroyers that were our escort.

The last attack on us took place in the morning on the 20th, and this was the one that the Marines shot down. That was the last actual attack on us, and by that night the carrier with Admiral Clark and a combat air patrol were removed because now we were steaming. We started at five knots. By the 21st, we were able to do about 12. On the morning of the 21st, we had three boilers on. The principal thing was we wanted to work everything up very, very slowly. We didn't know whether our shafts had been damaged, whether our propellers had been damaged, just what had been done, and so we wouldn't undertake another action until we could check and make sure that things were balanced dynamically and so on.

We arrived in Ulithi to try to pull the pieces together and get assistance from repair ships that were there and do things like cutting away some of the overhang, unrolling some of the steel, and shoring up some bulkheads, work that we couldn't do with ship's force. We got a series of messages from Admiral Nimitz, Admiral Spruance, Vice Admiral Mitscher, commander of Task Force 58, and from Vice Admiral Murray, ComAirPac. The first of these was sent on the 21st of March from Admiral Mitscher to the *Franklin* and said: "You and your historic crew cannot be too highly applauded for your historic and successful battle to save your gallant ship in spite of the difficulty, the enormity of which is appreciated. Deep regrets for your losses which we feel as our own."

On the 25th, Admiral Spruance followed this, saying: "The courage, fortitude, and ability of you and your crew in saving and bringing back the *Franklin* for future use against the enemy cannot be too highly praised." Then on the 3rd of April, Admiral Nimitz: "It is evident that the return of the *Franklin* to port required skill and courage of the highest degree on the part of those who participated. The officers and men who returned on the *Franklin* and also the officers and men of the *Santa Fe* who rendered invaluable assistance have set a high standard of seamanship, courage, and devotion to duty which will always be an inspiration to the fleet. Well done to all hands."

I'd like to add my "Well done" to the *Santa Fe* because the captain handled that ship as though it were an officer's motorboat alongside. They had their firefighters out with hoses alongside us, and, mind you, our ship was still exploding. The *Santa Fe* was on our starboard bow, and so on the *Santa Fe*'s fantail, opposite our island and just abaft the island, there were still explosions. As a matter of fact, the explosions got so bad at one time that the *Santa Fe* had to pull away. Then they came back later when things quieted down, because after all he had not only his own ship's safety to take care of, he had our wounded on board, he had the admiral on board, and all this sort of thing. He simply couldn't sit there while we went on exploding. So, when those explosions died down, it was obvious that part of the ship was burned out, and he brought his ship back again and continued the evacuation of personnel.

He certainly was a tremendous shiphandler, handling that cruiser like a destroyer, and staying in there with his firefighters turning hoses on the ship. He was about 30 or 40 feet off from the side of our ship, with this big carrier burning and exploding, right up there, and dead in the water but drifting downwind. And there was a fair wind that morning.

I must say when we pulled into Ulithi there were ships, and, of course, everybody and his brother rendered honors again. Lord preserve, I hope I don't have very many more of those occasions, coming in and getting all these honors, but the word had gotten in about how beaten up we were and as we went down the line of carriers that were there, for some it was sort of a preview of what was going to come and, "Oh, dear God, look at what we're going to be up against." For others, it was a feeling of, "Well, great Scot, we've lost so many of these people because, remember the ready rooms—we lost pilots who were sitting in the aircraft ready to go, and we lost others in the ready rooms, which were directly under the flight deck where the explosions took place." We had a horrendous loss of life, especially officers and pilots, flight deck crews, arresting gear crews, ordnance handling crews, and hangar deck crews. Those were the people who really got clobbered there.

In Ulithi, we stayed only long enough to get some assistance from repair ships that came over and helped clear away some of the wreckage. By this time, we had six boilers on the line, and we took off then for Pearl Harbor at about 20 knots, no escort, single ship—no zigzagging or anything, 20 knots, for Pearl. One of the most heart-rending scenes, I think, of the entire war, even more pitiful to me than seeing all those wounded on the flight deck and the dead, pieces of bodies flying around during the explosions, was coming into Pearl Harbor. Admiral Nimitz was down there and a whole batch of brass, everybody and his brother, a band, no hula troupe. The welcome was a real solemn welcome. It was a real shock for those people. Nothing had come in blown up like this.

It was just a very short time in port, I would say 24 hours, and we were on our way again. The first time we'd had since we left Hawaii to get ashore to the officers' club to have a drink, go swimming, get out in the sun. So, from our arrival somewhere along about, I would say, 10 or 11 o'clock in the morning, until the following day, there was everybody and his brother off, just one-fourth of the ship, the duty section, on board, and we were down at that time to less than 200 men on board for one-fourth. We were 760, I think, by that time.

I have a card, it's called the Big Ben either 760 or 720 Club—the survivors, the people who brought the *Franklin* back. I think everybody called their wives. We were not permitted to say that we had been damaged but simply that we would be coming home within a few weeks. There were lots of transpacific phone calls at that time, and then there was a lot of just plain letting down. People who had been real lions broke down there and sort of started sobbing.

Watching people under action and under fire for two or three days at a time and under literally incessant attack, I was amazed at some of our big, good-looking officers whom you would expect to be towers of strength turned out to be little pipsqueak people who needed bucking up all the time, and some other little nondescript 135-pounders turned out be real tigers and real lions. And the same thing was true of the enlisted men. I made up my mind then that I'd never again judge a man, let alone a naval officer or a naval aviator, by whether he looked the go-go vigorous, hot-to-trot type. I found out a lot of things there. It was the little people who really came through. The ones whom you simply took for granted, and some of the ones I would have counted on to delegate responsibility and give orders to were literally down cowering, down under a deck or under furniture or under something when the next plane came over. Instead of standing up and shooting at them with everything we had, they'd dive for cover. It certainly separates the sheep from the goats. I was amazed, and I count it one of the blessings, one of the wonderful things I was able to do, in making out fitness reports for the people whom I saw, I was absolutely ruthless in putting out 100 percent fitness reports for the people who came through and making sure the ones whom I could see, actually saw with my own eyes, diving for cover and leaving their enlisted people to fight the ship got unsatisfactory ones. Seven officers left the *Franklin* over the highline to the *Santa Fe* in spite of orders to return to the ship, and Captain Gehres reported every one of them and recommended court-martial.

From Hawaii, we took off at 25 knots direct for Panama. Now the days were soft. We were back in the tropics again, watched the turtles drifting by in the current. We transited the canal in a fair hurry, and everywhere we excited tremendous curiosity and sadness on the part of the people who watched our passage. The commandant of the Fifteenth Naval District down there came aboard and transited the canal with us. We took off from the other end, Colón, direct for New York. We steamed up through the Caribbean, then through the Gulf of Mexico, and into New York Harbor. The last body was found as we were going through Gravesend Bay.

The ship was going into the Brooklyn Navy Yard for repair and overhaul. The end of the war was not yet in sight. That didn't come until August, and so the ship was going to be repaired. The captain had the conn and we were navigating the ship up the Narrows. There was a swift current coming down the East River. The captain handled the ship again just like a destroyer. We had a couple of fairly close calls on this very last trip because there was a lot of traffic in New York Harbor. Of course, we were light by now, very light, practically empty of fuel, all ammunition gone; we had unloaded ammunition at Pearl Harbor. We had all eight boilers back on the line by this time, so there was lots of power. He came in, and he wouldn't let the tugs touch us, the navy yard tugs or the pilot, until he was headed into the berth, the nose passing over the navy yard line, when he said, "It's all yours," and walked off the bridge.

If I had to go back to a war in the same kind of a position, I couldn't ask for a better skipper than somebody like Captain Gehres. He was a naval officer's naval officer, the kind of person you worship and you follow in wartime.

Two weeks later, I was on my way back to the war, ordered as chief of staff to Commander, Carrier Division 26, off the coast of Japan.

■
■
■

The Big Blue Blanket

Admiral John S. Thach

On 30 October 1944, Vice Adm. John S. McCain, who had been Commander, Task Group 38.1, relieved Vice Adm. Marc Mitscher as Commander, Task Force 38, just as the battles for Leyte Gulf drew to a close. Several days before that, the first *kamikaze* had hit an escort carrier on the 25th of October, and this was obviously an intended suicide attack. We were becoming quite concerned, of course, about this very effective method of hitting our carriers. It wouldn't have been worthwhile on any other target in the world. There's no use in diving into part of a factory, for example, or an antiaircraft installation. This was a weapon, for all practical purposes, far ahead of its time. It was actually a guided missile before we had any such things as guided missiles. It was guided by a human brain, human eyes and hands, and, even better than a guided missile, it could look, digest the information, change course, avoid damage, and get to the target. So we had to do something about this.

We devised some training practices as a defensive measure against Japanese suicide planes. We called it "Exercise Moose Trap," and the idea was to try to discover the disposition and size of our combat air patrols as they practiced enemy tactics. So we designated one or two squadrons to send planes out and come in as a *kamikaze* might approach, riding down the nulls of the radar and coming in at various altitudes. Some of the *kamikazes* came in pairs; one of them would come in high and draw a lot of fire, and the other would come low over the water and bust right into the side of the ship while the other one dove right straight down onto the flight deck. So we needed to have more than a good air defense; we had to have a completely airtight defense. Not one airplane must get through because usually the *kamikazes* would hit, not always, but often. This was one of the first orders that we put out, on 11 November 1944.

I don't think that Admiral Mitscher practiced this when he was the task force commander. He liked to depend on antiaircraft fire and the fighters, but I don't remember whether he ever adopted this or not later on. I know that he didn't adopt it right away because when he had command of the task force up around Okinawa quite a few carriers got hit by *kamikazes*. But this turned out to be successful. We also started putting combat air patrol over the picket destroyers. We put out a pair of destroyers quite a distance from the force in the direction that our own strikes would be returning and also in the direction from which enemy strikes might be made on us. We called them in one place Tom Cat and in the other one Watch Dog. The idea was to put a good fighter director in a destroyer and give him eight fighters, in addition to the combat air patrol that we'd have over the carriers, and put him way out 50 miles or so. We would require that our returning strikes make a turn over the Watch Dog picket, who would be offset a little bit to one side of the track of the returning strike. The returning strikes would go over the picket and check out so they could get "deloused." Pilots, after making a strike, would get tired on the way back, and they didn't look back under their tails to see whether there was a *kamikaze* tucked under there, and quite often there was. So we made them circle over the outlying picket before coming into the task group, so the fighters would look them over and "delouse" them of any enemy planes that were tucked in under there hiding. We also had a "fair game" area where enemy planes would normally come from their airfields toward the carrier. Any airplane out there was fair game, and we would send fighters out and shoot it down, no matter what it was, even if it was our own airplane. We told the pilots that they were just likely to get shot at if they didn't come back and "delouse" themselves over the picket. This left the area clear, and, if any attack was coming straight out, like they usually did, we'd pick him up very much quicker. So that worked.

Then we stacked the combat air patrol over each task group, and kept the task groups together close enough so that they would have mutual support, unlike the battle of Midway when we got too far away. Then, for the night attacks or dusk attacks where we had to have most of our fighters back, we sent out some flights called "Jack patrols." I wanted to call them Jack patrols because I had a son named Jack, and I just wanted one little thing named for him during this war! The Jack patrols would go out in a direction toward the enemy in a fan-shaped sector and search that sector down low to see if they could see any torpedo planes on the horizon. They had the habit of coming out and waiting to attack just at dusk. If we could catch them out there in formation, we could break them up or shoot them down before they got set to attack. This happened a few times. We got quite successful with these Jack patrols because the enemy figured that we would be taking everybody aboard before sunset, except night fighters, and they wouldn't expect us coming in low or below the radar. The night fighters at high altitude who were already up there wouldn't see the enemy down low, but the Jack patrols would pick them up visually and then alert everybody and go in and fight them. That way we reduced the dusk torpedo attacks almost to nothing.

We had developed another system against the *kamikaze*. In addition to Moose Trap training for the defense, we developed for the offense what we called the "three-strike system." Up until this time, strikes were sent in by deck loads; a carrier usually sent in half of the air group on a strike. It would go in and come back, and they would send in the other half. Inasmuch as *kamikazes* could come from any of scores of airfields in the Philippines, I figured out that we had to keep them covered a lot better. So I worked out a system of dividing the air group into three strikes and called it the three-strike system. I thought this would spoil *kamikaze* raids on the task force by providing a holey blanket over enemy known operational airfields—a holey blanket, but only small holes, I hoped. The reason I say "small holes" is that we couldn't keep airplanes over every field all day long. If we could, that would be great, but we came very close to doing it. By carefully scheduling our launch and recovery times throughout the day, we covered the targets with only a 10-minute gap between the departure of one strike and the arrival of the next one. We would split our strikes up and cover all the airfields and just watch them. Many times they'd see airplanes being towed out from under the trees just as they arrived. The field had been uncovered for 10 minutes, so the enemy would try to get this airplane out and get it on the field and here would come the next strike.

This was called the "blanket attack system." We were using around 15 and sometimes 16 or 17 carriers, so although we were using smaller strike groups, they were coming from all the different carriers, so by the time they got over their targets they made quite a force, almost a 1,000-plane air attack against enemy airfields in the Philippines. The Japanese were continuously feeding aircraft down from the homeland through Formosa and Luzon into the Leyte area. So for the rest of November and December 1944, we worked on Luzon and, using this blanket method of striking, we rolled up quite an impressive total of aircraft destroyed, some in the air but mostly on the ground. All of this was to get a big attrition against enemy land-based air power because enemy carriers were no longer a threat. There just weren't any operating on the high seas. In the last two months of the war when we were roaming up and down the Japanese coast, where there were many aircraft, and it wasn't because they didn't try, we shot down 130 airplanes attempting to get to the carriers. They did hit some destroyer pickets, but the last two months of the war not one carrier was hit by a *kamikaze* or anything else.

The three-strike blanket system, or the "big blue blanket," as someone called it, worked so that their fields weren't left alone except for a short gap between strikes and then another short gap between the late afternoon and before dark. On 5 January 1945, we were able to do something about closing that gap. The *Enterprise* and *Independence* joined with Rear Adm. M. B. Gardner, and we designated him Task Group 38.5, and they would operate at night, not in the daytime. They would handle all the night combat air patrols, the night hecklers who would go over the enemy airfields, and we formed a new little gimmick called "zippers" to help close that gap between the time the daylight strikes left the target and darkness. So, again, they couldn't have very much time to get organized, get their planes going, and come out and find out where we were. So it was a combination of those things, I think, that helped, although they were still trying to hit us and did have some success later.

On 26 January 1945, Admiral Halsey was relieved by Admiral Spruance, and McCain was relieved by Mitscher. Admiral McCain and I returned to Washington to see Admiral King for discussions. After some leave, we went back to Pearl Harbor to start planning the next series of events. Finally, on 27 May Admiral Halsey relieved Admiral Spruance as fleet commander, and, at the same time, Admiral McCain relieved Admiral Mitscher as task force commander and the staff shifted. Jimmy Flatley was the operations officer for Admiral Mitscher, just as I was operations officer for Admiral McCain. We had been very close all our navy lives, and this was a very fortunate thing. We knew how each other was thinking, we worked very well together, very closely, and, whenever he discovered something that he thought would be useful to us, he passed it to me immediately, wherever I was, and I did the same thing. When we actually made a change of command and McCain relieved Mitscher, we would take all of their reports and study them carefully and any changes that they had made in the task force instructions we would do likewise. There were some little differences in the task force operating instructions because of the differences between Mitscher and McCain. Mitscher wasn't very quick to pick up a new untried idea for a solution to a problem, such as the *kamikazes*.

The *kamikazes* were somewhat controlled by our strategy in the Philippines, and yet the toll from *kamikazes* was just overwhelming at Okinawa, in March–April 1945. Admiral Mitscher used the same strategy or tactics that had been developed by the Third Fleet, under Halsey, to a degree but not as much as we did. I don't remember hearing of his practicing this Moose Trap business, although I think that Jimmy Flatley did persuade him to go to the three-strike system when they were striking an area. But there he was in more of a defensive position at Okinawa, and the Moose Trap disposition would have helped him a lot, I think, but he didn't use it the way that we did. I know that Jimmy Flatley was all in favor of it, and little by little he would attempt to persuade Mitscher, but Mitscher was reluctant to take up new ideas, just as he was in the night fighter business. He was frankly dragging his feet on accepting night fighters. He was an old-time aviator, and in my opinion he figured that he had the experience within himself and he never took to new ideas or wasn't able to recognize them as well as McCain.

There were fewer fields in the Okinawa area. Furthermore, any place in the world is practical to use the blanket system, as far as you can reach and wherever you attack. You can use this and should if you want to keep the enemy from getting off the field and coming out and attacking you. Mitscher did put out the destroyer pickets to give him warning, but I think part of the reason he got hit pretty badly was because he was prevented from using mobility. He was pretty much attached to the beach by edict from Admiral Nimitz's headquarters in Guam.

Admiral McCain and I worked real hard on it to be sure that we got across just the things that we thought needed to be modified and the things that were unintentionally hurting the ability of the task force commander. We sent a message from Admiral McCain to the Commander in Chief, U.S. Fleet, via Commander, Third Fleet, and via the Commander in Chief, U.S. Pacific Fleet. This was prompted by discussions in various commands in the Pacific and in

Washington, D.C., about the number of fighter-type aircraft and the complement of aircraft for each carrier and the proportion of this number to fly on
combat air patrol. The implied criticisms that were appearing in various anal-
yses of air operations and outright criticism by those who had always opposed
aircraft carriers for political reasons made this exposition necessary.

In essence, we said that the terms "offensive" and "defensive" had been
loosely and, hence, confusingly used. A task force in enemy waters is strictly on
the offensive; every plane launched, whether to attack enemy targets at a
distance, to ambush enemy targets in the vicinity of the Watch Dog pickets and
the Tomcat combat air patrols, or to shoot down enemy targets over the task
force, is on a basically offensive mission. In any other interpretation, it might
as well be said that the creeping barrage ahead of an infantryman that advances
as the infantry advances is defensive in nature or that the infantryman firing as
he charges is committing a defensive act to save his life. The function of the
carrier is lost in this maze of loose thinking.

The carrier is a *base,* and carrier warfare is the warfare wherein a *base* is
moved and projected *into* the front lines. So protection of the task force, a
phrase too generally used, is rather an insurance, assurance, of the hitting
power of the task force. The phrases "protection of the task force" and "defense
of the task force" were interpreted by Admiral McCain as the destruction in the
most offensive practical manner of any enemy aircraft attacking, or in a
position to attack, or that may be brought to bear on the task force.

When we got word of the cease-fire on 15 August, I realized that Admiral
McCain wasn't feeling very well physically. He went to his sea cabin, and he
didn't pop out frequently into the flag plot and enter into things as much as he
had. I missed him, and I'd go in there and talk to him and tell him what I wanted
to do. One time, between the cease-fire and the surrender ceremony, I thought
we should get a photograph of all of our ships as close together as they could
get, so I went in to recommend to Admiral McCain that we do this. This was
one of the times when I realized he just wasn't feeling well at all, and he said,
"Okay, good idea. Just go ahead and do it; no problem. Do whatever you want
to." Then I said, "Admiral, you don't feel very well, do you?" He said, "Well,
this surrender has come as kind of a shock to all of us. I feel lost. I don't know
what to do. I know how to fight, but now I don't know whether I know how to
relax or not. I am in an awful letdown. I do feel bad." He didn't look too well,
either. But he went to the surrender ceremony, then we flew back and landed in
Coronado after stopping at Pearl Harbor for about a day, and Admiral McCain
didn't act too well then, either. In fact, he looked worse, but he invited me and

my wife to come by his house for a little while that afternoon, which we did. While we were there, he said, "I think I'll go in and get some rest." We weren't there very long, but we left and went over to San Diego. I got over there to my father-in-law's house, and got a telephone call that said that he [McCain] had died of a heart attack. I felt like I'd lost my father for the second time.

Admiral McCain was going to go to Washington, and he was going to take me with him. I'm not sure what he was going to do, but I felt that he would probably talk, among other things, about his recommendations for the future handling of fast carriers, and I knew that he was looking into the future. If we have another war, what kind of a thing will it be, and he pointed out that it would be fast carriers against land-based air and littorals, extended peninsulas, and so forth, and maybe deep into large continents, but working from the sea. It turned out that's just about what occurred.

He was buried in Arlington, so I went back to Washington with his family. We flew his body back. I did get to go in and see Admiral King and talk to him about some of the things I knew Admiral McCain wanted to emphasize. I don't know whether Admiral King ever saw our message on carrier warfare or not. I don't know whether anybody ever read it or not because the war was over and, you say in your mind, "Well, we've got other things to do now, forget this."

"Shoot Them Down in a Friendly Fashion"

Captain Arthur R. Hawkins

In the fall of 1944, after we had already hit Mindanao in the southern Philippines, TF 38 moved on up to strike the central islands, including the island of Negros; there were four enemy fields in that area. We went in as escort for the bombers, who were going in to bomb those four fields and try to put them out of commission while we were doing our business in there. We were flying low cover with the bombers. As we approached the fields with our large flight of bombers and fighters, two Zeros made a pass on the formation, and they came right through the formation, firing as they went through. They didn't hit any of our bombers. They were coming straight down, and they went right on through the force. We being on the low cover for the bombers, the air group commander called my flight leader, whose name was Stewart, and he released him, saying, "Go get them, Stew." So the four of us did a split-S and followed the two. We lost one in the dive. We didn't know where he went to, but the other one we followed down. I was able to get in position on him and came straight down on him and hit him with all six of the .50-calibers. It just thrust him into the ground.

As we pulled out, we were right over these four fields. They were right in line as we pulled out from our dives, and here the Japanese were taking off with the four of us down there. So we pulled straight up to get a little altitude, and then started picking these guys off as they were coming out. I had destroyed a couple, and the flight had picked up about three or four more, when they stopped coming off the field. So we pulled up, and we were sitting there waiting for them to get going again and not paying too much attention. You have to keep your six o'clock position covered, and we forgot about that, it was so much fun down below here. For some reason or other, I was sitting there looking down waiting for somebody to get brave enough to start off again, when I had a feeling there was something over here. "Look," and I looked. There sat a Zero in a perfect position to make his high side run on me. I will never forget that Zero. He had the markings of the Marine squadron, which was their famous group, and it was just a beautiful airplane. Boy, it was shining. I thought, "Well, here I am sitting here alone, and my partner is on the other side of the field." If he had seen him at the same time I did, we could have done the Thach weave and started protecting ourselves.

My first instinct was just to turn into him, even though I knew he could outmaneuver me. So I got the jump on him; when I turned, then here he came, but it was too late because I had already started my turn, which gave me the edge on him. As we pulled into each other, I was just shooting, and he flew into it. We did a turn to come back at each other, and he torched up and just went off. So, in that particular case, I'll always remember, I did outturn him in the F6F; if I had not have got the jump, I would never have been able to outturn him.

I had four kills up until then, and I picked up four that day. So I became an ace then, with a few to spare that day. Our first tour of 13 months out there was over soon after that. Our air group went back to the States for three months, and we missed the Okinawa campaign and the big *kamikaze* run. When we returned on the *Belleau Wood,* there just wasn't anything to shoot at, so to speak. They weren't in the air. We were on bombing sweeps, and we would go in, drop our bombs, and just sit around and shoot them on the ground. They just didn't get them in the air the latter part of the war, although the *kamikazes* were running over everybody. They were saving all their good stuff, because they knew we were coming.

Of course, you could never understand what the Japanese were thinking. They would send out one airplane to scout the fleet, and we would shoot him down. Then, they would do it again the next day. They sent him out; if he didn't come back, they knew the fleet was out there. That's basically the way it must have been, because you'd get that day after day after day. The Japanese never seemed to be able to adjust to situations and improve their tactics. For instance, we started hitting the southern Philippines at Mindanao. We hit that for three days. We'd pull off to replenish, then move up to the next island, hit that for three days. Pull out, go up, hit the next one. We would hit Mindanao, Negros, and then move up to Clark Field on Luzon.

By about the fourth set of raids, you would think they would be ready. They knew we were coming. I went in on a fighter sweep to hit Clark Field. We go in there, dive in, drop our bombs on the field, pull back up, getting ready to hassle with whoever is around. There is smoke and burning with all these bombs going off. Here comes a big old Emily flying boat from out to sea, coming straight in to Clark Field. We're in there just bombing the hell out of it, and here he comes, straight in. So we take care of him, and then we go back up, and we're circling over Clark Field, and here comes a flight of 12 Topsys, which is like our old DC-3. Here we are, we've just finished bombing the heck out of it, and we're over the field, and they come right under us, the 12 of them. Those things didn't last very long at all; they were just gone. Finally, they evidently got some fighters up from another field, and they came over and tangled with us over Clark. You think, "Well, don't they have any communications? Don't they know that we've hit here three days, been gone a day and come back, and hit here for three days and gone a day, and now they are going to be here tomorrow or the next day and be ready?" They didn't seem to. At least, that particular time they certainly didn't, because I wouldn't have been within 40 miles of that thing if you knew they were in there bombing and raising cane. Now, if you're a fighter, that's something else; you come in and tangle with them, but not 12 DC-3s coming right over the field or a big old P-boat coming back in over the field. That's just stupid. But you never understood them.

I was in the air on the last day of the war, after the bomb had been dropped at Hiroshima. We were going in on a strike. I had a 1,000-pound bomb on board. We were going in with our target assignment, and we got a call that the war was over. "Jettison your bombs in the water." So we did. We jettisoned our bombs, and the flight headed back in. Then Japanese airplanes started showing up all over the place, heading toward the fleet. So we reported that it looked like activity was picking up. Of course, we didn't know if it was sightseers coming out to see the fleet or if it was *kamikazes* coming out to get in their last match. So word came back from the admiral, "Shoot them down in a friendly fashion." That's what we did; there were about four or five airplanes shot down that day on that flight, because they headed for the fleet, and they wouldn't turn away. So we had to shoot them down.

We were in the big fiasco during the signing on the *Missouri*. We launched quite a few airplanes to fly over the *Missouri* at the time, and, man, you should have been there. It was something, I'll tell you. We put about 450 airplanes in the air. Then, from Iwo Jima they sent in the B-29s. It turned out the weather wasn't too good; it was down to about 1,500 or 2,000 feet. So everybody was trying to get down under it so you could be seen over the *Missouri*. Here comes the flight of 450 carrier airplanes going one way, and here are about 50 or 60 B-29s coming the other way, under this low overcast. It was impressive. Nobody got killed. It had to impress those on the *Missouri,* because planes were going in all directions everywhere.

![black bars icon]

Reflections of a Patriot

Chief Ship's Clerk (W-2) C. S. King

Cecil St. Clair King, Jr., was born in Alice, Texas, on 11 May 1917, son of Cecil S. and Ethel Jones King. He enlisted in the United States Navy in 1934 and advanced through the enlisted ranks to the grade of Commissioned Warrant Officer, Chief Ship's Clerk (W-2). Mr. King served four years as administrative assistant to the Chief of Naval Operations before becoming personnel officer on the USS Franklin D. Roosevelt *from February 1956 until his retirement in September 1957.*

Mr. King was based ashore in Manila at the outbreak of the war in the Pacific. He escaped from Corregidor aboard the destroyer Peary *in January 1942 and also from Java on the USS* Sturgeon *in February 1943 when it fell to the Japanese. Shore duty in Australia and a precommissioning detail on the USS* Carnegie *were followed by a year's service in the carrier* Hornet *during extensive combat operations in the Pacific. He served as the captain's writer on the carrier* Princeton *during the latter stages of the war.*

Mr. King was awarded the Good Conduct Medal with two Bronze Stars, Navy Presidential Unit Citation, Army Distinguished Unit Badge, and various theater ribbons for service in the Pacific.

CPO C. S. King, on duty in Batt II, ca. 1945. (Courtesy Cecil S. King)

In September 1943, I got a sudden set of orders to go to the *Hornet,* in Newport News, Virginia. I was a chief petty officer and was to be the chief yeoman in the ship's office. I went to Newport News and was in the fitting-out detail of the *Hornet,* which we put in commission 29 November 1943. There wasn't much time for extracurricular activities on the *Hornet.* It really was a high-velocity period. They were trying to get that thing to sea, because the first *Hornet* had been sunk. This *Hornet* had originally been named the *Kearsarge,* and they renamed it the *Hornet.*

I guess I worked almost as hard as I ever did in my naval career in that brief period of time, getting the *Hornet* ready to go to sea. I was chief in charge of personnel for the *Hornet,* so I had to check in every new man, account for them, and square away the service records. A lot of our people had been sunk on the old *Hornet*. There was a lot of work for a personnel person—a lot of work. I guess about half of the next four months were spent at general quarters, that is, battle stations, and the other half of it sorting out the personnel, getting things organized. One of the hardest jobs in those days, for me, was in going to sea when we had to get a list of everybody on board ship off the ship before we left. I cannot describe the tension when you've got the harbor pilot on board, you've got the air group on board, and you're trying to get to sea, and the captain wants to go, and the passenger list is not ready. By the time we were ready to dump the pilot, he would take the passenger list back in with him. If you're out there making circles and waiting for the passenger list, well, the poor guy in charge of the passenger list is not a very popular individual.

Capt. Miles R. Browning was the first commanding officer, and he was a hard driver. He had such a reputation from his days as chief of staff to Vice Adm. William F. Halsey when he was Commander, South Pacific Force. I think his reputation, generally, was of a martinet and hard driver. He was very strict and gave the impression that he was going to win the war himself with one airplane. He was really a dedicated guy. I would say fanatic comes pretty close to it. He was perceived by the crew more as a guy who was just so damn gung ho. I could understand why he felt that way because it was serious business, and I guess my sympathies were for him a little bit. I didn't have any negative feelings towards him, but he was harder on the officers than on the crew. He demanded an awful lot.

On the *Hornet,* my battle station was what we called Batt II or secondary conn. I guess that was one of the best battle stations on the whole ship because you saw everything up there. When the planes came in and landed, we were looking right at them from Batt II, which was in the after part of the superstructure, the island. The purpose of Batt II was to take over from the bridge in case the bridge was shot out. We had all the communications and that sort of thing duplicated in Batt II. As a matter of fact, when we would get under way, part of my job was to go on the circuit and pick up all of the stations and see if they were ready. I was a phone talker; yeomen have traditionally filled that role. I always enjoyed that, because I always felt on top of communications, knew what was going on. During my tour in 1943 and 1944, I spent every hour of every action back up there; it was a perfect picture. I mean, if I had said, "I want to be somewhere where I can see everything," I couldn't have picked a better spot. We didn't feel too vulnerable because we had a one-half-inch steel waist-high shield up there.

I recall a lot of incidents on the *Hornet* that were spectacular. One that I've seen 100 times, I guess, on *Victory at Sea,* and every wartime aviation movie I ever saw was where this one plane comes in, strikes the island superstructure, and breaks in two. I remember that incident very vividly. Another time, one of our planes came in and had been pretty badly damaged; the pilot was shot up. I believe it was a TBM. He hit the deck, one of his landing gear gave way, and he was swinging from side to side. He lost consciousness and hit the firing button. He sprayed Batt II; we tried to put our profiles in the steel deck.

Another time we were at flight operations, and I was walking up the ladder to the bridge, with my back to the after part of the ship. I heard these things flying past my ears—buzz, buzz, buzz—and an explosion at the same time. One of our planes had come in, and a 500-pound bomb broke loose from the rack. When it hit the deck, the bomb cartwheeled, and it kept hitting nose down, tail down, nose down. It armed itself about the first time it hit, and then it went off 20 or 30 yards farther up, and we had some severe casualties. It blew a hole in the deck and also blew the legs completely off one of the flight deck crew. I don't think we had any deaths from that particular incident.

Rear Adm. Joseph J. ("Jocko") Clark, Commander, Task Group 58.1, used the *Hornet* as his flagship in the Pacific. Captain Browning and Jocko Clark are viewed in that same aggressive vein, but somehow Clark's method seemed more colorful and Browning came across as a bit grim. Jocko Clark was as different from Browning as day is from night. I think he got similar results but in a different way. That brings on a lot of other things that I remember. Jocko Clark was part American Indian; his lower lip stuck way out, and was always sunburned. Finally, the doctor on the *Hornet* gave him no choice but to wear a gauze 4x4 with a string over his ears so the pad protected his lip. Jocko did it, but it made him madder than hell. I've seen him snatch three or four of those things off in the course of a couple of hours. He'd tear it off and throw it down. And here would come the doctor and make him a new one. Jocko was such a colorful guy. Whenever he came out on the bridge—GQ or any other time—he often wore the sick bay pajamas that he slept in. Sometimes his hairy stomach would be sticking out, but he was oblivious to his appearance. He was just universally loved, respected, and admired on the *Hornet*. He had a great feeling for the pilots. More than once, when a pilot landed aboard, shot up or whatever, the doctor, the emergency crew, and Jocko would get to him all about the same time. Jocko would bend over the stokes litter and pin a medal on the guy right there on the stretcher. You know pilots appreciated that. He was really and truly a great man. Another time on the *Hornet,* some Japanese ships were sunk off

Saipan. Survivors were collected out of the water by various ships and put on a tanker and then on the *Hornet.* So we wound up with a couple hundred POWs. I think they were a mixture of military and civilian. We had them for a couple of days, and Jocko didn't like that a damn bit because it interfered with the readiness of the ship. Of course, they had never seen American food before. They were struck by it, and what they really loved was bread. They saw our mess cooks making sandwiches, so the POWs would make sandwiches. They even made sandwiches out of hotcakes. They had the same breakfast we had, and, if the breakfast was hotcakes, they'd ask for bread and make a hotcake sandwich. They had one little guy on there who professed to be dead set against the Japanese. I think he said he was Korean, but he would write obscene phrases, Japanese, in chalk on bombs on the planes. He would write, "To hell with Tojo," and stuff like that. At least, I hope that's what he was writing. He was kind of a mascot. They thought a lot of him.

When the time came to get rid of the prisoners, Jocko was relieved. We were taking fuel from a tanker, and they put them off on this tanker by a highline. Taking on fuel under way is a split-second operation, so they rigged a canvas bag. They would put two or three Japs in the bag and send them over to the tanker. About the third bag, one of the early transfers hollered, "*Banzai*" or something and just dove over the bag and into the water. There was not that much distance between the tanker and a carrier refueling at sea. You just go backwards in these great big churning whitecaps, and when you get back there you got these screws—one or two screws on the tanker and four screws on the carrier—and it's just a meat grinder. This first guy that fell down there, that's all she wrote—just some pink foam. So the question was what to do. Jocko said, "Let's keep them going. If they want to dive over, we got to get going." I don't know how many jumped over. These tales grow in telling. I'm satisfied at least one of them did. Anyway, the transfer went on until they all got off the *Hornet.*

On the *Hornet,* we had a small group of real no-goodniks. I mean, these kids were not necessarily honest-to-God gangsters, but they were involved in anything that was seriously wrong on the ship—heavy gambling and extortion. One of them one night was thrown over the side. It was common knowledge around the ship that that's what had happened. He was officially listed as being lost at sea, but there's no doubt in my mind what happened. Those people he ran around with just threw him over the side. The executive officer was convinced of that too.

On occasion, damaged planes were just pushed right over the side. At the time, I thought, "Well, hell, that's the only way we can win this war. That's how we can win it, by being able to do that, because you can't take up valuable fighting space on the ship with duds." So they just pushed them right over the side. One time one of our pilots came back badly wounded and died. He was buried in his plane. They pushed the whole plane over the side. That was a very moving ceremony; they pushed him over the fantail with full honors. Then we had one other burial at sea, when one of our firemen—a big beefy guy—had heat prostration down in the fireroom. When he went berserk, he had this heat seizure. He was wearing earphones, and it is said that he took the lines from his phones and wrapped them around his hands, and pulled the heavy phone wire right in two. He had that much strength, and it took six or eight men to buckle him down to get him to sick bay. He was completely out of his mind and had the strength of 10 men. In the sick bay, his temperature got so high that they could not take his temperature with a medical thermometer. They had to use some kind of thermometer from the engineering department to take his temperature. He had some tremendous temperature. He died, and we had a formal burial at sea, where they wrapped him in canvas. That was my first experience seeing that kind of funeral at sea.

Once we got out into action we spent much time at Condition I-A. That was the condition immediately before GQ. At I-A, you're semi-GQ but not entirely buttoned up. When we first got out there, we spent more time at I-A, I guess, than an ordinary ship did because we were new. Our chiefs' quarters were back on the fantail about three decks down. We had a reserve ship's cook who was really great. I think he owned a restaurant or something in civilian life. About the second day, the word got around to all the chiefs through the grapevine that there were steak sandwiches in the chiefs' quarters. So, a few at a time, we would trickle down and break watertight integrity on I-A and get our steak sandwiches. So my time came, and I got relieved on watch and went down. This guy had made some hoagie rolls, and these steaks were just gorgeous. So I got in line and got my steak sandwich. Just as I put one end of it in my mouth, the alarm sounded for GQ. I don't like to be below decks at GQ. I do not like it at all. I feel claustrophobia and everything else. But we were under a pretty sustained attack for about five minutes. You could hear the bombs going off in the water. You could hear the noise against the hull. The ship was making sharp turns, and it was that sort of thing, antiaircraft firing, and just a lot of stuff going on. After about five or ten minutes, it was all over. I looked down, and my sandwich was gone. I had eaten that entire sandwich during that period, and I didn't remember taking one single bite of it. I remember I was mad. I thought, "Damn! I wasted a whole steak sandwich."

Before the full-fledged *kamikaze* days, I don't think being topside was an overriding fear during air attack. But I remember several occasions when we were under fairly heavy attack. It just seemed like the sky was full of planes and projectiles. Just as far as you could see, planes going in the water here, planes going in the water there, the tracers going through the air; just an intense moment of bright colors. During those moments, I seemed to get sort of a second sight. I could see farther and kind of sharper; it would go into slow motion kind of. These really were moments that I can close my eyes right now and see.

One time, it might have been the *New Jersey* was with us. We didn't operate with a battleship that much, but on this occasion we did. Along toward sunset, the *New Jersey* got in between us and the setting sun. We also had some tin cans and I think a couple of cruisers, and maybe a "jeep" carrier—a regular task force situation. I can remember the comforting feeling I had looking at that battleship against the setting sun. I thought, "You know, I'm just like I'm home in church." I thought that was such a great thing. I think that very same night we were under attack. In ordinary circumstances, the carriers were not supposed to open up our deck guns at night because the guns would silhouette the flight deck, and the Japs would know it was a carrier. On this one night, the *New Jersey* did open up, and it looked like a gigantic Christmas tree. I never saw so much fire and tracers coming from one place in my entire life. I don't know how much armament the *New Jersey* carried, but everything on that ship opened up. It just made a big cone up there, and the cone would move around. Then you'd see a plane light up at the tip of the cone and go down, and the cone would just keep on moving. It was a spectacular sight.

I remember one time when an aircraft engine got loose, out at sea. We had a hell of a time with it. It was in a crate on the hangar deck. It broke loose, and we were in pretty heavy weather. There was a famous book, or story, by Victor Hugo about a loose cannon. It was some ship way back in his time, and what a time they had getting this cannon pinned down. I thought of that at that time, because that damn aircraft engine was slipping across the deck and the sparks would fly, and on the hangar deck, you don't want sparks. Hell, there's napalm and everything else there. I wasn't up there, but I was close enough to it where you could hear some of the sound effects from guys yelling. And we'd go this way, and that damn engine would cross the deck, and whammo! But, finally, some honest-to-God hero somehow got a line on that engine and made it secure to the bulkhead and gradually pinned it down. That aircraft engine tore up a lot of planes. It caused a lot of damage.

Oh, one time Jocko Clark got some beer ordered officially for the *Hornet*. We worked out a system where one division at a time could have a beer party up on the forecastle; this is at sea in wartime. They could drink two beers a man, three beers a man—something like that—and that was it. I think the first time the first division had it; second time, second division, and so on. They had a couple hundred cases of beer stowed down in a storeroom up forward. The first night it was on board, all they had was a padlock on the hatch of this storeroom. I guess by 9:00 P.M. somebody had broken the padlock and stolen a few cases of beer. The supply officer was very upset, so the next day he had the shipfitter come around and put four hasps on that hatch, and put four padlocks on. Probably that took about five minutes the second night—all four padlocks off, and they got the beer. So the next day the shipfitters came up there and tack welded that whole damn hatch. And when the supply people took the beer out, they just took a jackhammer to the weld and took the tack off. That's how they kept that beer for our beer parties. That's the kind of thing that made Jocko so beloved.

We had movies at night on the hangar deck in port, and you don't smoke on the hangar deck. You don't smoke anywhere topside on a carrier at any time for any reason. That's worse than a magazine. Jocko would, I guess, have a couple of horns in his room, go up and go to the movies, and sit in the front row there. Jocko would put a cigarette in his mouth, reach over and strike a kitchen match on the deck, light up his cigarette, and sit there, smoking cigarettes at the movies. No one person ever said anything about that.

The battle that is bright in my mind is the "Turkey Shoot," on 19 June 1944. That's one that really stands out in my mind, because it was such a spectacular thing from the spectator's standpoint. I remember very vividly when our planes were out there, mixing it up with the Japs, and we'd get these fragmentary reports in: splashed two, splashed three, and so on. It seemed like this was what we went out there to do. We were shooting up the whole damn Japanese Navy. It seemed like that was the greatest thing in the world. The next day, there was much concern about the distance our planes had to go in trying to intercept the Jap fleet as it steamed away. I was just close enough that I could sense that this was a big damn decision, about whether to send them off or not. I remember all the suspense involved in that. That night, when they came back in, I was up topside, at my battle station. It was a memorable evening, because there were planes landing all over the place. It didn't matter what carrier they were from. The minute anybody flashed ready deck, somebody landed on it. Almost every landing was some kind of a deck crash. They were running on fumes. There were planes going in the water everywhere. That's when Mitscher lit up the fleet, searchlights, the whole damn thing. It was a spectacular, memorable occasion. I remember on the *Hornet* they passed the word to throw over anything that would float—wooden orange crates, anything. These guys were out in the water; there were just people everywhere. I couldn't believe what was happening. When it was all over, that's when we went down to chiefs' quarters and said, "Boy, this is it. We're going to break three or four regulations." Somebody had some booze of some kind, so we all had a drink of some kind. I remember that battle more than anything else that happened all the time I was on the *Hornet*.

I used to be very proud when they would put up our new stencils on the bridge structure for ships sunk, planes shot down. That kept growing, and growing, and growing. I got to know several of the pilots fairly well, especially when I was working with the combat intelligence officer in recording and debriefing the pilots. Then there was a lot of hero stories always passing around, like on every carrier, I guess. Some guy would do something spectacular, and by the time he got back to the ship, we'd have increased it by 10 planes and everything. There was a kind of gung-ho spirit, and I couldn't believe my good fortune at being on a carrier with all the things going on. This was a big change from when I'd spent the first three months of the war skulking around from island to island all over the place. Now I was on the winning team. That's the way it's supposed to be in the first place. That's the way it really should have been.

I've always been inclined to joke around. There was a young boy named Edwards from Hershey, Pennsylvania, who was a yeoman striker in my office. We were all pretty fond of him. He sort of enjoyed being kidded. He had a picture on his desk of his girlfriend in Hershey. Every time I came in the office, I would say, "Gosh, that's a nice looking picture of your mother, Eddie." He would say, "No, that's my girl." I guess she was a year older than he was, but I would always act like I really thought it was a picture of his mother. Later on he bugged me about getting a battle station. He said he wanted to be on a 40-mm gun. He wanted to shoot. I tried to talk him out of it, but he was adamant. He wanted to see and smell the smoke, and shoot down the Japs. Well, I finally gave in. I went to the gun boss and asked him about it. So we got him a battle station on the 40-mms. He hadn't been on it more than a couple of weeks or so until we had some kind of a fracas, and he came back after the session and told me all about it and how great it was. About a week and a half or two weeks later—he wasn't in the gun crew more than a month—a Jap plane strafed the flight deck, and a tiny piece of shrapnel hit this kid in one side of his stomach and went out the other. It just tore his insides up. He was the first combat casualty of any kind to the crew that we had on the *Hornet* directly at that time. It caused quite a stir, and, God, I felt bad about that. So I went down to see him in sick bay as soon as he could see people. He was lucid, felt good about it, and was proud of himself. I really felt bad. The kid died that very same night. I guess that's about the most negative thing in my mind about the *Hornet*. I felt a very deep sense of personal responsibility about that, even though that's the kind of thing I guess everybody runs into in a combat situation.

I never got ashore on any of the atolls for liberty. As a matter of fact, the *Hornet* was one of the first carriers to fuel at sea, take on ammunition at sea, completely replenish at sea, everything under way. I've forgotten the exact amount of time now, but at one time we set some kind of a record by being the longest operating carrier—eight months or some damn thing—just continually under way all that time. I had left the West Coast on the *Hornet,* and, except for Pearl Harbor, the next time I got off was when I was transferred. I don't think I got ashore anywhere else in the Pacific. I was aboard the *Hornet* for a year and a half, close to two years. I spent an ungodly amount of time out there in the Pacific without ever leaving the ship. I didn't really notice it. I mean, it wasn't that kind of a hardship.

I guess I had more time at sea than most other chief yeomen. That was really because I enjoyed every damn day that I was ever at sea—not enjoyed it in the sense that it was an obsession or anything. But I just felt comfortable on board a ship. I did when I went into the Navy. The first shore duty that I had was Naval Air Station Minneapolis, something like 10 years after I enlisted in the Navy in 1934. But I figured I was in the Navy to go to sea, and that's where I belonged. My personal feeling was that I loved sea duty.

I just felt at home at sea. I really did. I felt like that's what the Navy's all about. It's not that I didn't enjoy liberty or anything like that. On the contrary, I guess nobody ever hit the Navy that enjoyed liberty as much as I did. But I just felt like the Navy was sea duty, and that's where I belonged. On carriers, like the *Hornet,* the *Princeton,* all of them, many times I would wander around the ship at sea, particularly in late afternoon, just enjoying being there. I would go over to the deck edge elevator and stand there and watch the ocean going by. Also, I enjoyed very much going to different parts of the ship to see how they did things. I liked to go up on the bow and watch them drop anchor, or take it up, that sort of thing. That's impressive to lift the damn anchor—the size of that thing.

I feel like I'm probably one of the luckiest people in the entire world, first, for having been born in the year that I was, so I was at the proper age to be able to fight for my country in World War II; and secondly, this whole era that I've lived through is something that I feel real privileged for having gone through, and having been involved in it to the extent that I was. Also to some extent, World War II was a kind of a justification of my feelings. That is to say, I always felt that the United States Navy was the greatest outfit in the world. I really felt it deeply, and I don't ever recall a twinge of fear in the Asiatic Fleet as the war got closer or when it actually happened. So I felt after the war started like there was only one outcome possible: we were going to beat the living bejesus out of the Japs. I just knew that in my heart and soul. During all the ups and downs of the first days of the war, the main thing in my mind was, "We're going to get those bastards one of these days, and we're going to get them good." I accepted that like I accept Notre Dame and the New York Yankees and things like that. I mean, that's a given.

So later on, when I was on the *Hornet,* and we were doing exactly that, that didn't necessarily surprise me. I just felt good about it. I thought, "All right, I knew we were going to do it, and by God, we are doing it now; we're going to beat their tails off." A lot of people aren't that lucky to have this kind of a feeling come true. I mean, a lot of people have their worst fears confirmed some day. But for a person to feel as strongly as I did and do about the United States Navy, and have it come out this way, is just like Hollywood when the Marines come up over the horizon in the last reel. That's what I really feel good about.

APPENDIX A
The Leaders

United States Navy, 1943–1945
Naval Air Administration

A. Navy Department
1. Commander in Chief, United States Fleet—Chief of Naval Operations
   a. Fleet Adm. Ernest J. King, 1942–end of war
2. Deputy Chief of Naval Operations (Air)
   a. Vice Adm. John S. McCain, August 1943–August 1944
   b. Vice Adm. Aubrey W. Fitch, August 1944–August 1945
   c. Vice Adm. Marc A. Mitscher, August 1945–end of war
3. Assistant Chief of Staff (Operations), CominCh
   a. Rear Adm. Arthur C. Davis, March 1943–August 1944
   b. Rear Adm. Malcolm F. Schoeffel, August 1944–August 1945
   c. Rear Adm. A. R. McCann, August 1945–end of war
4. Assistant DCNO (Air)
   a. Rear Adm. Frank D. Wagner, August 1943–April 1944
   b. Rear Adm. Arthur W. Radford, April 1944–October 1944
   c. Rear Adm. John H. Cassady, October 1944–end of war

From *The Fast Carriers* by Clark G. Reynolds. Copyright © 1992, U.S. Naval Institute, Annapolis, Md.

5. Assistant Operations Officer (Air), CominCh
    a. Capt. Thomas P. Jeter, November 1942–December 1943
    b. Capt. Wallace M. Beakley, December 1943–May 1945
    c. Capt. Robert B. Pirie, May 1945–end of war
6. Assistant Secretary of the Navy (Air)
    a. Artemus L. Gates, 1941–July 1945
    b. John L. Sullivan, July 1945–end of war
7. Chief of the Bureau of Aeronautics
    a. Rear Adm. John S. McCain, 1942–August 1943
    b. Rear Adm. DeWitt C. Ramsey, August 1943–June 1945
    c. Rear Adm. Harold B. Sallada, June 1945–end of war

B. Pearl Harbor
    1. Commander in Chief, Pacific Fleet and Pacific Ocean Areas
        a. Fleet Adm. Chester W. Nimitz, 1941–end of war
    2. Deputy CincPac-CincPoa
        a. Vice Adm. John H. Towers, February 1944–July 1945
        b. Vice Adm. John H. Hoover, July 1945–August 1945
        c. Vice Adm. John H. Newton, August 1945–end of war
    3. Assistant (later Deputy) Chief of Staff (Plans), CincPac
        a. Rear Adm. Forrest P. Sherman, November 1943–end of war
    4. Commander, Air Force, Pacific Fleet (ComAirPac)
        a. Vice Adm. John H. Towers, 1942–February 1944
        b. Rear Adm. Charles A. Pownall, February 1944–August 1944
        c. Vice Adm. George D. Murray, August 1944–July 1945
        d. Rear Adm. Alfred E. Montgomery, July 1945–end of war
    5. Chief of Staff, ComAirPac (Deputy after December 1944)
        a. Capt. Forrest P. Sherman, 1942–November 1943
        b. Rear Adm. Arthur W. Radford, December 1943– February 1944
        c. Rear Adm. J. J. Ballentine, February 1944– September 1944
        d. Commodore Frederick W. McMahon, October 1944–end of war
        e. Rear Adm. Cato D. Clover, Jr., reporting August 1945

C. Combat Zone
    1. Commander, Third Fleet
        a. Adm. William F. Halsey, Jr., mid-1943–end of war
    2. Commander, Fifth Fleet (initially Central Pacific Force)
        a. Adm. Raymond A. Spruance, August 1943–end of war
    3. Commander, Fast Carrier Forces Pacific
        a. Rear Adm. Charles A. Pownall, November 1943– January 1944
        b. Vice Adm. Marc A. Mitscher, January 1944–August 1944
    4. Commander, First Fast Carrier Force Pacific
        a. Vice Adm. Marc A. Mitscher, August 1944–July 1945
        b. Vice Adm. Frederick C. Sherman, July 1945–end of war

5. Commander, Second Fast Carrier Force Pacific
   a. Vice Adm. John S. McCain, August 1944–September 1945
   b. Vice Adm. John H. Towers, September 1945–end of war
6. Commander, Carrier Division 1
   a. Rear Adm. DeWitt C. Ramsey, 1942–July 1943
   b. Rear Adm. Frederick C. Sherman, July 1943–March 1944
   c. Rear Adm. William K. Harrill, March 1944–August 1944
   d. Rear Adm. Frederick C. Sherman, August 1944–July 1945
7. Commander, Carrier Division 2
   a. Rear Adm. Ralph E. Davison, July 1944–April 1945
   b. Rear Adm. C. A. F. Sprague, April 1945–end of war
8. Commander, Carrier Division 3
   a. Rear Adm. Charles A. Pownall, August 1943–January 1944
   b. Rear Adm. Marc A. Mitscher, January 1944–March 1944
   c. Rear Adm. Alfred E. Montgomery, March 1944–December 1944
   d. Rear Adm. Thomas L. Sprague, March 1945–end of war
9. Commander, Carrier Division 4
   a. Rear Adm. John H. Hoover, August 1943–October 1943
   b. Rear Adm. John W. Reeves, Jr., October 1943–July 1944
   c. Rear Adm. Gerald F. Bogan, July 1944–end of war
   d. Rear Adm. Donald B. Duncan, reporting August 1945
10. Commander, Carrier Division 5
    a. Rear Adm. Frank D. Wagner, April 1944–June 1944
    b. Rear Adm. J. J. Clark, August 1944–July 1945
    c. Rear Adm. Arthur C. Davis, July 1945–end of war
11. Commander, Carrier Division 6
    a. Rear Adm. Harold B. Sallada, August 1944–November 1944
    b. Rear Adm. Arthur W. Radford, November 1944–end of war
12. Commander, Carrier Division 7
    a. Rear Adm. Matthias B. Gardner, December 1944–April 1945
    b. Rear Adm. J. J. Ballentine, June 1945–August 1945
13. Commander, Carrier Division 11
    a. Rear Adm. Arthur W. Radford, July 1943–December 1943
    b. Rear Adm. Samuel P. Ginder, December 1943–April 1944
14. Commander, Carrier Division 12
    a. Rear Adm. Alfred E. Montgomery, August 1943–March 1944
15. Commander, Carrier Division 13
    a. Rear Admiral J. J. Clark, March 1944–August 1944

D. Related Agencies
   1. Commander, Fleet Air West Coast
      a. Rear Adm. Charles A. Pownall, 1942–August 1943
      b. Rear Adm. Marc A. Mitscher, August 1943–January 1944
      c. Rear Adm. William K. Harrill, January 1944–March 1944
      d. Rear Adm. Frederick C. Sherman, March 1944–August 1944

  e. Rear Adm. William K. Harrill, August 1944–February 1945
  f. Rear Adm. Alfred E. Montgomery, February 1945–July 1945
  g. Rear Adm. Van H. Ragsdale, July 1945–August 1945
  h. Vice Adm. John H. Hoover, August 1945–end of war
2. Director of Marine Corps Aviation
  a. Major Gen. Field Harris, July 1944–end of war
3. Commander, Air Force Atlantic Fleet
  a. Vice Adm. Patrick N. L. Bellinger, March 1943–end of war

APPENDIX B
Glossary of Terms and Abbreviations

AA/AAA: antiaircraft fire

AAF: Army Air Forces

ACI: Air Combat Intelligence

air officer: ship's officer responsible for aviation matters in an aircraft carrier

air plot: air operations control center aboard a carrier

angels: altitude of an aircraft in thousands of feet (for example, "angels three five"—35,000 ft.)

arresting gear: arrangement of wires on a carrier flight deck that stops an airplane after airplane's tailhook has engaged it

ASW: antisubmarine warfare

bandit: enemy aircraft

barrier: collapsible fences on a carrier flight deck that stop those airplanes whose hooks have missed the arresting gear

blip: target indication on a radar scope

bogey: unidentified aircraft

BOQ: bachelor officers' quarters

BPF: British Pacific Fleet

BuAer: Bureau of Aeronautics

buster: fighter director term, to proceed at best sustained speed

CAP: Combat Air Patrol

carrier air group: aircraft of a carrier, made up of squadrons

carrier task force: force of aircraft carriers and supporting heavy ships and
     destroyers

cat: catapult

chief of staff: captain or admiral who assists an admiral, as his second in command,
     especially in supervising his staff

CIC: Combat Information Center; space in a ship containing radar, plotting, and com-
     munication gear

CinCPac: Commander in Chief, Pacific Fleet

CinCPoa: Commander in Chief, Pacific Ocean Area

CL: light cruiser

CNO: Chief of Naval Operations

CO: commanding officer

ComAirBatFor: Commander, Aircraft, Battle Force

ComAirPac: Commander, Air Force, Pacific Fleet

ComAirSol: Commander, Air, Solomons

ComBatPac: Commander, Battleships, Pacific Fleet

ComCarDiv: Commander, Carrier Division

ComDesRon: Commander, Destroyer Squadron

CominCh: Commander in Chief, U.S. Fleet

Condition I-A: relaxed general quarters condition

conn: control of ship's movements; to guide or pilot a ship

cut: mandatory signal from LSO for pilot to cut his power and land

CV: aircraft carrier

CVE: escort carrier

CVL: light carrier

CXAM: type of radar

DCNO (Air): Deputy Chief of Naval Operations for Air

division: with aircraft, a unit of four to nine planes

dud: disabled aircraft

FDO: fighter director officer

flag bridge: open bridge of a ship used by a flag officer and his staff

flag lieutenant: personal aide to a flag officer afloat

flag secretary: personal aide to a flag officer who handles the paper work of a staff *flag plot:* enclosed tactical and navigational center used by a flag officer and his staff in exercising tactical command of ships and aircraft

general quarters: condition of maximum readiness for combat with the crew at battle stations

handy billy: small portable water pump

IFF: Identification, Friend or Foe; an electronic, rapid recognition device
IJN: Imperial Japanese Navy

JCS: Joint Chiefs of Staff

kamikaze: an enemy suicide plane that attempts to crash into its target

Loran: system of electronic navigation that provides lines of position
LSO: landing signal officer; man stationed on a platform at the aft end of a carrier who assists pilots in carrier landings

Master-at-arms (MAA): ship's police, headed by a chief MAA

NAS: Naval Air Station

OOD: officer of the deck (*also known as* squadron duty officer); the officer who is responsible for handling the daily routine of the ship/squadron
ORI: Operational Readiness Inspection

RN: Royal Navy

sandblower: short person
SDO: squadron duty officer; staff duty officer (*see* OOD)
section: with aircraft, a unit of two to four planes
splash: enemy aircraft destroyed
squadron: with aircraft, a unit of 18 to 36 planes
strike: combat flight against ground or ship targets

tallyho: sight contact on his target by a fighter aircraft
TARCAP: Target Combat Air Patrol; fighter cover over target for strike group
TBS: talk between ships (radio)
TF: task force
TG: task group

tin can: slang for destroyer

VB/VF/VP/VS/VT/VO: designations for different types of squadrons: V refers to fixed
    wing; B is bombing; F is fighting; P is patrol; S is scouting; T is torpedo; O is ob-
    servation
VCN: night composite squadron
vector: aircraft's heading; to direct, to give a heading
VFN: night fighter squadron
VTN: night torpedo squadron

waveoff: mandatory signal from LSO to pilot not to land

XO: executive officer

YE: aircraft homing system

ZB: homing signal receiver

Ranks Used in Text

Adm.: admiral
Vice Adm.: vice admiral
Rear Adm.: rear admiral
Capt.: captain
Comdr.: commander
Lt. Comdr.: lieutenant commander
Lt.: lieutenant
Lt.(jg): lieutenant (junior grade)
Ens.: ensign
W.O.: warrant officer

Japanese Aircraft Mentioned in Text

Betty: Mitsubishi G4M1 Type 1 land attack bomber
Emily: Kawanishi H8K Type 2 flying boat
Judy: Yokosuka D4Y Type 2 carrier bomber
Kate: Nakajima B5N2 Type 97 carrier attack bomber
Topsy: Mitsubishi Ki-57 Type 100 transport
Val: Aichi D3A1 Type 99 carrier bomber
Zeke/Zero: Mitsubishi A6M2 Type 0 carrier fighter

APPENDIX C
Bibliography

Oral Histories

Unless otherwise indicated, all oral histories were conducted by John T. Mason, Jr., and are a part of the U.S. Naval Institute Oral History Collection.

Bogan, Vice Adm. Gerald F. 1969. Interviewed by Comdr. Etta-Belle Kitchen.
Bond, Roger. 1987. Interviewed by Paul Stillwell.
Burke, Adm. Arleigh. 1979.
Feightner, Rear Adm. Edward L. 1990. Interviewed by Paul Stillwell.
Foley, Rear Adm. Francis D. 1985. Interviewed by Paul Stillwell.
Hawkins, Capt. Arthur R. 1983. Interviewed by Paul Stillwell.
Hedding, Vice Adm. Truman. 1971. Interviewed by Comdr. Etta-Belle Kitchen.
Johnson, Adm. Roy L. 1980.
Jurika, Capt. Stephen, Jr. 1976. Interviewed by Capt. Paul B. Ryan, USN (Ret.).
King, Chief Ship's Clerk C. S. 1989. Interviewed by Paul Stillwell.
Lee, Vice Adm. Fitzhugh. 1970. Interviewed by Comdr. Etta-Belle Kitchen.
Lee, Vice Adm. Kent. 1987. Interviewed by Paul Stillwell.
Martin, Vice Adm. William I. 1979.

McCampbell, Capt. David. 1987. Interviewed by Paul Stillwell.

Miller, Rear Adm. Henry. 1971.

Ramage, Rear Adm. James D. 1985. Interviewed by Robert L. Lawson and Barrett Tillman.

Riley, Vice Adm. Herbert D. 1971.

Russell, Adm. James S. 1974.

Stroop, Vice Adm. Paul D. 1970. Interviewed by Comdr. Etta-Belle Kitchen.

Thach, Adm. John S. 1971. Interviewed by Comdr. Etta-Belle Kitchen.

Books

Baldwin, Hanson. "The Battle for Leyte Gulf." *Sea Fights and Shipwrecks*. Garden City, N.Y.: Doubleday, 1955.

Belote, James H., and William M. Belote. *Titans of the Seas*. New York: Harper & Row, 1975.

Bryan, Lt. J., III, USNR, and Philip G. Reed. *Mission Beyond Darkness*. New York: Duell, Sloan, and Pearce, 1945.

Buell, Thomas B. *Master of Sea Power: A Biography of Fleet Admiral Ernest J. King*. Boston: Little, Brown, 1980.

―――. *The Quiet Warrior: A Biography of Admiral Raymond A. Spruance*. Boston: Little, Brown, 1974.

Clark, Adm. J. J., USN (Ret.), with Clark G. Reynolds. *Carrier Admiral*. New York: David McKay, 1967.

Costello, John. *The Pacific War*. New York: Rawson, Wade, 1981.

Fahey, James C. *The Ships and Aircraft of the U.S. Fleet*. 8th ed. Annapolis, Md.: Naval Institute Press, 1965.

Falk, Stanley L. *Decision at Leyte*. New York: W. W. Norton, 1966.

Francillon, R. J. *Japanese Aircraft of the Pacific War*. London: Putnam, 1971.

Fuchida, Mitsuo, and Masatake Okumiya. *Midway: The Battle that Doomed Japan*. Annapolis, Md.: Naval Institute Press, 1955.

Gay, George H. *Sole Survivor*. Naples, Fla.: Naples Ad/Graphics Services, 1979.

Glines, Carroll V. *Doolittle's Tokyo Raiders*. Princeton, N.J.: D. Van Nostrand, 1964.

Green, William. *War Planes of the Second World War: Fighters*. Vol. 4. Garden City, N.Y.:Doubleday, 1961.

Halsey, Fleet Adm. William F., Jr., USN, and Lt. Comdr. J. Bryan III, USNR. *Admiral Halsey's Story*. New York: Whittlesey House, 1947.

Hoyt, Edwin P. *How They Won the War in the Pacific: Nimitz and His Admirals*. New York: Weybright and Talley, 1970.

Johnston, Stanley. *Queen of the Flat-tops*. New York: E. P. Dutton, 1942.

―――. *The Grim Reapers*. New York: E. P. Dutton, 1943.

Lord, Walter. *Day of Infamy.* New York: Henry Holt, 1957.

———. *Incredible Victory.* New York: Harper & Row, 1967.

Lundstrom, John B. *The First South Pacific Campaign: Pacific Fleet Strategy December 1941–June 1942.* Annapolis, Md.: Naval Institute Press, 1976.

———. *The First Team.* Annapolis, Md.: Naval Institute Press, 1984.

Miller, Thomas G., Jr. *The Cactus Air Force.* New York: Harper & Row, 1969.

Morison, Samuel Eliot. *History of United States Naval Operations in World War II.* 15 vols. Boston: Atlantic, Little, & Brown, 1947–1962.

———. *The Two-Ocean War: A Short History of the U.S. Navy in the Second World War.* Boston: Little, Brown, 1963.

Okumiya, Masatake, and Jiro Horikoshi. *Zero!* New York: E. P. Dutton, 1956.

Pawlowski, Gareth L. *Flat-tops and Fledglings.* New York: Castle, 1971.

Polmar, Norman. *Aircraft Carriers.* New York: Doubleday, 1969.

Potter, E. B. *Nimitz.* Annapolis, Md.: Naval Institute Press, 1976.

———. *Bull Halsey.* Annapolis, Md.: Naval Institute Press, 1985.

———, and Chester Nimitz. *The Great Sea War.* New York: Bramhall House, 1963.

———, and Chester Nimitz, eds. *Sea Power: A Naval History.* Englewood Cliffs, N.J.: Prentice-Hall, 1960.

Prange, Gordon W. *At Dawn We Slept: The Untold Story of Pearl Harbor.* New York: McGraw-Hill, 1981.

Reynolds, Clark G. *The Fast Carriers: The Forging of an Air Navy.* Huntington, N.Y.: Robert E. Krieger, 1978.

———. *Admiral John H. Towers: The Struggle for Naval Air Supremacy.* Annapolis, Md.: Naval Institute Press, 1991.

Sakai, Saburo, Martin Caiden, and Fred Saito. *Samurai!* New York: Bantam Books, 1978.

Sherrod, Robert. *History of Marine Corps Aviation in World War II.* Washington, D.C.: Combat Forces Press, 1952.

Stafford, Comdr. Edward P., USN. *The Big E.* New York: Random House, 1962.

Swanborough, Gordon, and Peter M. Bowers. *United States Naval Aircraft since 1911.* 2d ed. Annapolis, Md.: Naval Institute Press, 1976.

Taylor, Theodore. *The Magnificent Mitscher.* New York: W. W. Norton, 1954.

Tillman, Barrett. *The Dauntless Dive Bomber of WWII.* Annapolis, Md.: Naval Institute Press, 1976.

———. *The Wildcat in WW II.* Annapolis, Md.: The Nautical & Aviation Publishing Company of America, 1983.

———. *Hellcat: The F6F in WW II.* Annapolis, Md.: Naval Institute Press, 1979.

———. *Corsair: The F4U in WW II and Korea.* Annapolis, Md.: Naval Institute Press, 1979.

Ukagi, Matome. *Fading Victory: The Diary of Admiral Matome, 1941–1945.* Pittsburgh: University of Pittsburgh Press, 1991.

U.S. Navy, Deputy Chief of Naval Operations for Air. *United States Naval Aviation, 1910–1970*. Washington, D.C.: U.S. Government Printing Office, 1970.

————, Naval History Division. *Dictionary of American Naval Fighting Ships*. Vol. 2. Washington, D.C.: U.S. Government Printing Office, 1963.

U.S. Strategic Bombing Survey (Pacific). *Air Campaigns of the Pacific War*. Washington, D.C.: U.S. Government Printing Office, 1947.

Index